ADVENTURER'S NAME:

___

FROM:

___

DATE:

___

Walking with Jesus

PO Box 1599, Vereeniging, 1930, RSA

First edition 2017

Cover designed by Christian Art Publishers

Images used under license from Shutterstock.com

Set in 13 on 17 pt Palatino LT Std

Printed in China

ISBN 978-1-4321-1930-0

18 19 20 21 22 23 24 25 26 27 – 11 10 9 8 7 6 5 4 3 2

WALKING WITH JESUS

DAVE STREHLER

With grateful thanks
to my wife, Keryn, for her encouragement,
practical help and prayer support during
the writing of this devotional.

INTRODUCTION

You have probably heard the story of Jesus' birth many times. You have surely heard of the miracles He did, and that He died for us on a cross and rose again. Yet there is so much more to discover!

This 366-devotional will help you get to know Jesus better, as if you were one of His close followers. You will go with Jesus into private houses and overhear the things He said to His disciples, as if you were with them. You will find out how Jesus outsmarted the Pharisees; what Jesus said about the value of a child, and how to store up heavenly treasure.

Walking with Jesus joins up all the things Jesus said and did in the Gospels, making them flow into one complete story.

It is best to look up the daily readings in your Bible. Then pray that the seeds of Truth will grow in your heart as you think about what you've read.

May this book make you excited about God's Word and help you to love Jesus more and more.

"May the LORD smile on you and be gracious to you.
May the LORD show you His favor and give you His peace."
~ Numbers 6:25-26 ~

You will find these icons throughout the pages of this devotional. This is what you need to know about them:

SOMETHING TO PRAY ABOUT: An example prayer for you to pray.

SOMETHING TO DO: An activity which might require you to do something for someone, write it down in a journal, or make something creative.

SOMETHING TO THINK ABOUT: These prompts provide food for thought.

WARNING: The Bible sometimes gives serious warnings that we must listen to.

SCRIPTURE VERSE: An inspirational Scripture verse that links to the theme of the day. You can also memorize it.

Biblical principles that encourage and guide you on the right way.

FIND OUT

Things that you will need to look up in the Bible, on the Internet or in other resources.

A truth from the Bible to hold on to.

Interesting biblical facts.

A specific biblical instruction to help you strengthen your faith.

A challenge to help you grow in your walk with Jesus.

JANUARY

1 WAY
FOLLOW IT

1 TRUTH
BELIEVE IT

1 LIFE
LIVE IT

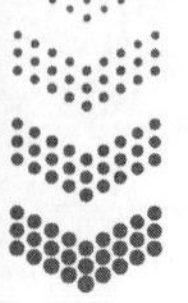

Matthew 1:1-2, 5-6, 16-17

FROM ABRAHAM TO JESUS

God had promised Abraham that, through his descendants (the children that would come after him), all the nations of the earth would be blessed (Gen. 22:18).

Matthew, a disciple of Jesus and the one who wrote the Gospel of Matthew, studied the Old Testament and joined up all the fathers and sons like a chain, linking Abraham to Jesus.

Why was this family line so important? It was a way to show God's faithfulness to His promise. It was also to make sure that when Jesus was born, there would be no doubt that He was the One whom God had promised to us.

In verse 6 of Matthew's list you will see King David's name. As a descendant of David, Jesus would rule on his throne (Isa. 9:6-7), but the kingdom of Jesus would not be an earthly kingdom, but a heavenly one. A kingdom that would last forever.

Jesus is the King of kings, and when we allow Jesus to rule in our lives we become part of His kingdom.

Add up the number of generations from Abraham to Jesus (see Matt. 1:17).

He will be great and will be called the Son of the Most High. The Lord God will give Him the throne of His father David.

~ Luke 1:32

The Lord is faithful to all His promises (Ps. 145:13, NLT).

Luke 1:5-17

A HEAVENLY VISITOR

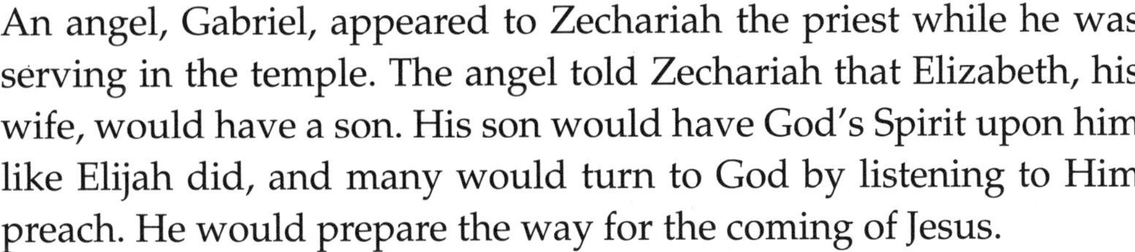

An angel, Gabriel, appeared to Zechariah the priest while he was serving in the temple. The angel told Zechariah that Elizabeth, his wife, would have a son. His son would have God's Spirit upon him like Elijah did, and many would turn to God by listening to Him preach. He would prepare the way for the coming of Jesus.

Usually, when an important person is about to make an appearance, someone first gets everyone's attention. Once he has introduced the person, he stands aside or walks off. That was John's job. His main goal in life was to introduce Jesus to the world.

Now that Jesus has come – and gone back to heaven – it is our job to introduce Him to people; or rather, introduce people to Him.

There are many people going about their daily business who don't know Jesus, or that He loves them very much. Jesus wants everyone to know about His love and forgiveness.

Tell someone today, "Jesus loves you!"

A voice of one calling: "In the desert prepare the way for the LORD; make straight in the wilderness a highway for our God."

~ Isaiah 40:3

Zechariah's name in Hebrew means "The Lord has remembered".

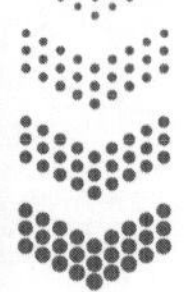

Luke 1:26-33

AN ANGEL APPEARS TO MARY

Six months after Elizabeth became pregnant, God sent the angel Gabriel again. This time he spoke to Mary – a virgin who was engaged to Joseph. Gabriel greeted her and told her that she would give birth to a Child – Jesus.

Then the angel told Mary, "You are highly favored." God had chosen her because He was pleased with her life. He saw that Mary was the right woman to raise Jesus in her home.

When God chooses someone for a special purpose, He looks at the person's heart. God didn't choose someone who was rich or popular or powerful; He chose someone who was humble.

When people choose someone, they usually look for things that impress them – things they can see, but when the Lord chooses someone, He looks at the kind of person they are on the inside (1 Sam. 16:7).

Lord, help me to live a life that pleases You so that when You want to use me, I will be ready and willing to do whatever You want. Amen.

You will conceive and give birth to a Son, and you are to call Him Jesus.

~ Luke 1:31

God uses angels as messengers and servants (Heb. 1:14).

Luke 1:34-38

THE ANGEL'S MESSAGE

Mary wondered how she could have a child, because she wasn't even married yet. Then Gabriel told her that the Holy Spirit would come on her and she would be pregnant.

Why was it important for Jesus to be born in this way?

- Since the first man, Adam, sinned, every person born on earth was also filled with sins. Although we read of good people in the Old Testament, and some who had great faith, only God could save people from their sin. Prophets could tell people about their sin, and priests could offer sacrifices for sin, but no ordinary man could take people's sins away.
- But, if Jesus came to earth only as God, He would not have been able to live among us and show us the right way to live. God is Spirit, and He is Holy! If Jesus had come as God, sinful people would not have been able to come near to Him, for no one can see God and live (Exod. 33:20).

Isn't it wonderful how Jesus, who was holy and perfect, could grow as a baby inside Mary, who was an imperfect human being?

The Holy Spirit will come on you … So the Holy One to be born will be called the Son of God.

~ Luke 1:35

When Jesus was on earth, He was completely God and completely human. He is awesome.

Luke 1:39-45

GOD OF THE IMPOSSIBLE

When the angel had left Mary, she hurried to go visit Elizabeth. As Mary greeted her, the baby inside Elizabeth jumped for joy, and she said to Mary, "You are blessed because you believed what the Lord said would happen."

When the angel told Elizabeth's husband, Zechariah, about the baby they were going to have, he wasn't so sure that this could happen because he and his wife were very old. They had never been able to have children before.

Because he doubted the angel's words, Zechariah was not able to speak until his baby was born (Luke 1:20).

Gabriel gave a similar message to Mary – that she would have a baby. She was young, and she too wondered how the Lord could make this happen (Luke 1:34). Maybe she wanted to know if there was something she needed to do. But when the angel told her that the Lord would do this, she said, "May it be to me as you have said."

Mary believed what the angel said; that is what it means to have faith. And because she believed, she was blessed (v. 45).

I believe with all my heart that nothing is impossible for You, Lord. Amen.

Jesus said, "Blessed are those who have not seen and yet have believed."

~ John 20:29

What is impossible for people is possible with God (Luke 18:27).

Luke 1:46-55

MARY'S SONG OF PRAISE

Mary started to worship the Lord through the beautiful words that flowed from her heart. Maybe she spoke the words; maybe she sang them. What's important is that the Holy Spirit who gave her those words helped her remember them, and that's why we can read about it in the Bible.

We worship the Lord by telling Him how great He is, and by talking (or singing) about the great things He has done. That's exactly what Mary did.

These are some of the things that she thought about the Lord:

- He takes notice of His lowly servant
- He has done great things for us
- He has lifted up the humble
- He has filled the hungry with good things
- His name is holy.

Write a short poem to the Lord, praising His name. Think about what God is like, and about what He has done. Then write down your thoughts.

Praise the Lord, my soul; all my inmost being, praise His holy name.

~ Psalm 103:1

The Lord is merciful to those who honor Him (Luke 1:50).

Matthew 23:12

WHAT DOES IT MEAN TO BE HUMBLE?

God chose Mary. She was a humble person with a simple home life and an ordinary family. Jesus, the Son of God, humbled Himself by leaving heaven to come to earth. But, what does it mean to be humble?

1. How we think about ourselves

Romans 12:3 tells us not to think more highly of ourselves than we should. In other words, we should not boast about who we **are** (our position in society), what we can **do** (our achievements), or what we **have** (our possessions). Everything we have comes from God. We should humbly thank Him for it.

2. Having the right attitude

Our attitude should be the same as Jesus Christ. Although He was God, He became human like us and came to earth as a humble servant (Phil. 2:5-7). With Jesus as our Example, we should not think of ourselves as being too cool to be friends with someone who is unpopular. We should give without expecting anything in return.

Fill in the missing letters "o" and "e" to complete the sentence.

G_d _pp_s_s th_ pr_ud but giv_s grac_ t_ th_ humbl_.

1 Peter 5:5, NLT

Be completely humble and gentle; be patient, bearing with one another in love.

~ Ephesians 4:2

Humility frees me to accept others in love (Ps. 25:9).

Luke 2:1-7

JESUS IS BORN

The emperor Caesar Augustus ordered that everyone in the Roman Empire should be registered in their own town. Joseph, who had now married Mary (Matt. 1:24), also went from Nazareth where he was a carpenter, to his family town Bethlehem. While Joseph and Mary were there, Jesus was born. There was no room for them to stay for the night, so Mary laid her Baby in a manger.

Have you ever wondered why the King of kings had no special place to be born? Does it seem right that Jesus should leave the glory of heaven and be placed as a helpless baby in a manger? Was this really the way things were meant to work out?

Yes, God had planned the birth of Jesus thousands of years before. This was the way God wanted it, and the way Jesus wanted it. Paul tells us that Jesus, although He was in the form of God and equal to Him, humbled Himself, took the position of a servant and was born as a human being (Phil. 2:7).

Jesus became like us so that we could become more like Him.

But when the right time came, God sent His Son, born of a woman, subject to the law.

~ Galatians 4:4, NLT

Your attitude should be the same as that of Jesus (Phil. 2:5).

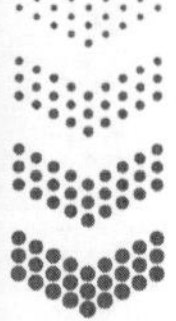

Luke 2:8-15

THE GOOD NEWS

When Jesus was born, Mary and Joseph laid Him in a manger. That night, there were shepherds looking after their sheep in a nearby field. All of a sudden an angel appeared to them and told them that Jesus had been born. Then many other angels came down and sang, "Glory to God in the highest …"

Why do you think the angel decided to tell this very important news to a small group of shepherds? Was it because it was late at night and they were the only ones still awake, or perhaps because they didn't want to disturb the peaceful town of Bethlehem?

Whatever the reason, the fact that the angel told some shepherds is meaningful because Jesus came to earth to be a Shepherd too. But He wasn't coming to help the other shepherds look after woolly sheep; He was coming to look for people (who were like lost sheep) and bring them back to God.

God loves to surprise us by doing unusual things in unexpected ways.

Lord, thank You that no one is too small for You to notice. Amen.

God chose things the world considers foolish in order to shame those who think they are wise. And He chose things that are powerless to shame those who are powerful.

~ 1 Corinthians 1:27

God promised that a Ruler would be born in Bethlehem who would shepherd His people (Matt. 2:6).

Luke 2:16-20

SHEPHERDS VISIT JESUS

When the angels had gone back to heaven, the shepherds set off to find the Miracle they had been told about. After they had found Mary and Joseph and the Baby, they went out and spread the news about what had happened, and they praised God.

A few things we can learn from the shepherds:

- **They decided to go see.** The Lord says that "if you look for Me (in other words, if you want to know Me with all your heart) you will find Me" (Jer. 29:13).
- **They spread the news.** They told everyone what God had done; and all who heard about it were amazed. Jesus said, "Wherever you go in the world, tell everyone the Good News" (Mark 16:15).
- **They glorified and praised God** for what they had seen and heard. They were amazed at seeing a part of God's awesome plan. Glorifying God is about being amazed at who He is; what He has done; and what He keeps on doing for His children (Neh. 9:6).

The shepherds didn't need to be told what to do. They knew their job. Their hearts overflowed with joyful praise because they believed.

They were all amazed at the greatness of God.

~ Luke 9:43

Seek the LORD while He may be found (Isa. 55:6).

Psalm 91:11

WHAT DO ANGELS DO?

Angels worship and praise God: This is something they do most of the time in heaven (Isa. 6:1-3, Rev. 5:11-12).

Angels are God's messengers: At times, they take important messages from God to people. Like when the angel appeared to Zechariah in the temple (Luke 1:11-20); or when an angel spoke to Joseph in a dream and told him what to do (Matt. 2:13).

Angels protect and rescue people: Angels kept the mouths of the lions shut so they would not harm Daniel when he was thrown into the lions' den (Daniel 6), and an angel broke the chains and released Peter from prison (Acts 12:1-10). Angels also take special care of God's little ones – His children (Matt. 18:10).

Angels strengthen and encourage people: At times, God has used angels to provide food for people like Hagar (Gen. 21:17-20) and Elijah (1 Kings 19:5-6), and to encourage people, like Paul, just before he was shipwrecked (Acts 27:23-25).

Angels fight against evil beings: Fighting with the strength of the Lord, holy angels win wars against the spiritual forces of darkness (evil). Revelation 12:7 tells how the angel Michael and his angels overpowered the devil and his angels.

It is important to know that we never pray to angels. We pray to God through Jesus (John 14:13, 1 John 5:14).

REMEMBER Angels are sent by God to protect us and help us inherit His full kingdom.

He will order His angels to protect you wherever you go.

~ Psalm 91:11, NLT

Whether you realize it or not, angels are watching over you this very moment.

John 1:1-5; Colossians 1:16

JESUS AT CREATION

We take a quick peep back in time – right back to the very beginning … before there was anything. We see that although Jesus was born on earth, He already existed before the earth was formed. In fact, Jesus has always been. God has no beginning and no end, and because Jesus is one with God He has always existed. "In the beginning was the Word, and the Word was with God, and the Word was God. He was with God in the beginning" (John 1:1-2).

Not only that; the world, and everything there is, was created through Jesus. John tells us that, "Through Him all things were made; without Him nothing was made that has been made" (John 1:3).

Knowing that may change the way you think about Jesus. Perhaps you've always thought about Jesus being born as a Baby and then doing miracles as a Man. Jesus, being the Creator of the whole universe, shows how powerful He really is. He is the One who chooses to love you and to be your Friend.

Lord Jesus, You are the awesome One who was there at creation, and You are the One who is with me now. Amen.

He [Jesus] is before all things, and in Him all things hold together.

~ Colossians 1:17

God was not alone when He created the world: He said, "Let us make human beings in Our image" (Gen. 1:26).

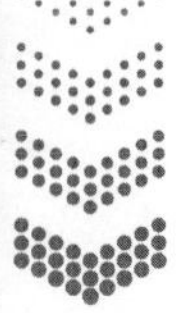

Matthew 2:1-6

WISE MEN START THEIR JOURNEY

At the time when Jesus was born, wise men (Magi) from a country in the east traveled to Judea in search of the newborn King. They had seen a bright, moving star in the east and followed it to the capital city of Jerusalem. They went to King Herod as that was the most likely place to find out about the newborn King.

But what made the wise men travel so far? When they set out, they didn't know how far the star would take them. They certainly didn't make the long trip for their enjoyment, or to get something for themselves. They set off on this trip in search of a newborn King, little knowing that they would find Jesus – the King of kings.

Jesus wants us to find Him as well. But it's so much easier for us. Jesus is just a prayer away. When we want to be close to Jesus, all we need to do is talk to Him and believe that He hears us. And when we ask Him to make us His child, His Spirit comes to live in us (Gal. 4:6).

Even though you cannot see the Lord, He is right there with you.

"You will seek Me and find Me when you seek Me with all your heart."

~ Jeremiah 29:13

Although some say there were only three wise men, the Bible doesn't actually tell us how many there were (Matt. 2:11).

Matthew 2:7-11

THE WISE MEN WORSHIP JESUS

King Herod called the wise men and wanted to know from them when the star had first appeared. Then he sent them to go look for the Child and report back to him when they had found Him. But Herod didn't want to worship Jesus, as the wise men did. He wanted to get rid of Him.

The star led the wise men to the house where Jesus was with His mother. When they saw Mary and her Child, they bowed down and worshiped Him.

For these men to bow down to a Child they didn't even know was quite unusual. But God had placed a faith in their hearts to believe that this Child was very, very special.

We should worship the Lord in the same way. We please the Lord when we have faith like the wise men had; when we are humble, and when we want to give Him what is precious to us.

Spend time at the beginning of each day to worship the Lord. Tell Him how awesome He is, how loving, powerful, faithful, holy, unchanging, patient and good He is.

He will be called Wonderful Counselor, Mighty God, Everlasting Father, Prince of Peace.

~ Isaiah 9:6

By the time the wise men arrived, Jesus and His parents were in a house (Matt. 2:11).

Matthew 2:11-12

WHY THE STRANGE GIFTS?

When the wise men bowed down to Jesus, they opened their treasures and gave Him gifts of gold, frankincense and myrrh.

After this, the Lord warned the men in a dream not to go back and tell Herod about the birth of Jesus. So they took a different way to return home.

You may wonder why the men would give such strange gifts to a young child. Although the gifts may seem strange, they had a special meaning.

- Gold is a gift that one would give to a king because it is precious, pure and beautiful.
- The frankincense was an expensive perfume used by priests as an offering of worship.
- Myrrh, a sweet smelling spice, was used to place with the body of someone who had died. This gift showed that Jesus came to earth to die for us.

What would you be willing to give to Jesus? Maybe a gift of your time, money or effort?

Each of you must bring a gift in proportion to the way the LORD your God has blessed you.

~ Deuteronomy 16:17

Whatever we do for others, we do for Jesus too (Matt. 25:40).

Luke 2:21-24

JESUS TAKEN TO THE TEMPLE

Jesus' parents Joseph and Mary took Him to Jerusalem to have Him circumcised and present Him to God. There at the temple, they brought an offering to God – a pair of doves or two small pigeons.

This was done in order to be obedient to a command in the Old Testament. The type of offering they brought showed that Joseph and Mary were rather poor (Lev. 12:8). One of the doves was used as a sin offering, a sign that God had forgiven the mother and made her clean.

Because Jesus came to earth to be the last and perfect sacrifice, parents no longer need to bring an offering for their sin. However, parents often take their children to church to dedicate them to the Lord. By doing that, they are showing that they want to bring their children up in the ways of the Lord.

God wants us to give our lives as a living sacrifice to Him. That means, we make Him first in our lives because we belong to Him.

Lord, I want my life to belong to You. Amen.

Therefore, I urge you, brothers, in view of God's mercy, to offer your bodies as living sacrifices, holy and pleasing to God – this is your spiritual act of worship.

~ Romans 12:1, NLT

We are made completely holy and perfect through the sacrifice of Jesus (Heb. 10:10).

Luke 2:25-40

SIMEON AND ANNA

While Joseph and Mary were at the temple with Jesus, a good, faithful servant of the Lord named Simeon came up to them. He took Jesus in his arms, and praised God for the Boy who would be a light to show sinners the way to God. He would bring glory to God among the people of Israel.

A prophetess called Anna also came up to them. Anna's husband had died many years before and she had lived at the temple since that time. She, too, gave thanks to God and spoke about the Child to all who were looking forward to the time when Jerusalem would be freed from the Romans.

Through the Holy Spirit, God had "whispered" in the hearts of these two faithful people that the Baby they were looking at was the Son of God. They had patiently waited many years, hoping and longing for God to send a Savior.

Now that Jesus has come and opened the way for us to have eternal life, our hope is that we know we'll be with Him in heaven one day.

Imagine if Simeon and Anna had given up hope of ever seeing God's miracle in their lifetime.

May the God of hope fill you with all joy and peace as you trust in Him, so that you may overflow with hope.

~ Romans 15:13

Because God has poured His love into our hearts we can put our hope in Him. We will never be disappointed (Rom. 5:5).

Matthew 2:13-18

ESCAPE TO EGYPT

King Herod, who had heard about Jesus, was worried that this Baby – the King of the Jews – would become a threat to him, so he decided to search for the Child to kill Him.

Meanwhile, an angel of the Lord appeared to Joseph in a dream and told him to escape to Egypt with Mary and Jesus. So that night, Joseph took the Child and His mother and left for Egypt.

Then Herod gave orders to kill all the boys, up to the age of two years, in and around Bethlehem.

What Herod did was wicked and cruel, and he did it because he was jealous. He was worried that one day he would no longer be number one. But God made sure that nothing would stop His plan to save the world through His Son.

Sometimes, pride and jealousy can cause us to be mean to others and hurt them. That's when we need to pray that the humility and love of Jesus will fill our hearts.

Lord, keep my heart pure and beautiful for You. Amen.

Pride leads to disgrace, but with humility comes wisdom.

~ Proverbs 11:2, NLT

The Lord hears the prayers of those who are helpless and hurt. He listens to their cry and He comforts them (Ps. 10:17-18).

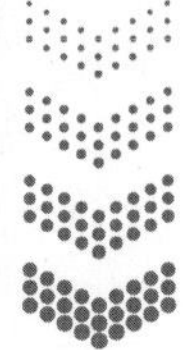

Matthew 2:19-23

RETURN TO NAZARETH

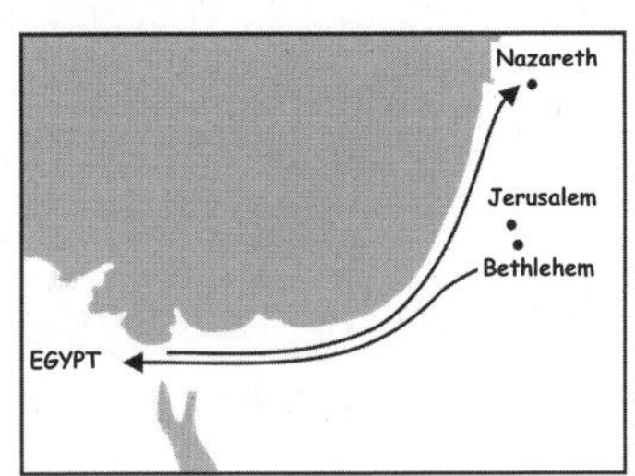

When Herod died, an angel appeared to Joseph in a dream and told him to go back to Israel.

But Herod's son Archelaus now reigned in Judea, so Joseph was afraid to go back to Bethlehem. Joseph rather went back to Nazareth in Galilee to live there.

Joseph and Mary might have wondered if God had carefully planned everything before He sent Jesus to this world. At first it may have seemed as though Herod and his son had upset God's plan. But God knew what He was doing (see Matt. 2:23).

We know that although life isn't always perfect, and the plans we make don't always work out, God is in control. He knows what obstacles lie before you. He knows that people will sometimes make life difficult for you, and perhaps they will even hurt you. But remember this: Jesus did not have an easy life, and He didn't promise us an easy life. But He did promise never to leave us.

Even when things don't make sense, remember that the Lord is with you and He will help you.

He [God] controls the course of world events; He removes kings and sets up other kings.

~ Daniel 2:21, NLT

God makes everything that happens in our lives work out for our good (Rom. 8:28).

Luke 2:41-50

JESUS GOES MISSING

When Jesus was twelve years old, He went with His parents to celebrate the Passover in Jerusalem, as they did every year.

After the feast was over, Jesus stayed behind in the temple courts while His parents – thinking He was with the other children – joined a group traveling back home. When they realized that Jesus was not with them, they went back and searched for Him all over. After searching for three days, they found Him, sitting with the teachers in the temple, listening to them and asking questions.

While Jesus was on earth, He was still God; but, because He was willing to become a man too, He had to learn things the way we do. He even had to learn Scripture (the Old Testament), and He asked many questions.

If Jesus wanted and needed to learn all He could and learned Bible passages off by heart, we should follow His example by going to church, reading the Bible and learning all we can about God.

Set aside time each day to read the Bible and pray.

I rejoiced with those who said to me, "Let us go to the house of the Lord."

~ Psalm 122:1

When we learn about the ways of the Lord from an early age, we are not likely to choose any other way when we get older (Prov. 22:6).

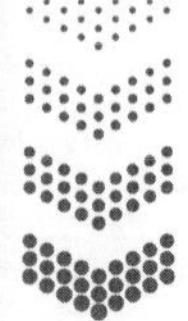

Luke 2:51

LEARNING OBEDIENCE

Jesus was God, yet because He was also human, He needed to learn right from wrong at an early age. However, even as a Child, Jesus never sinned – He never disobeyed His father and mother.

Being obedient wasn't any easier for Jesus than for us. Every time He was faced with a choice to disobey, He had to decide to do what was right. It didn't matter whether His parents were fair or that He as the oldest brother was probably expected to do extra chores. He never questioned His parents' instructions, but humbly did what He was asked to do.

Obeying may be hard at times, but it is always best. We first learn obedience to our parents, then our teachers, then the leaders of our country. And so, when we are obedient to our parents, we will find it easier to obey others later in life. More importantly, we will find it easier to obey God.

The Bible tells us that if children are taught the right way early on in life, they will stick to that way when they are older.

Lord, help me to remember to obey at all times, just as You did when You were a Child. Amen.

Children, obey your parents in everything, for this pleases the Lord.

~ Colossians 3:20

When we love God, it is far easier to obey His commands and keep all the rules (1 John 5:3).

Luke 2:40; Luke 2:40, 52

JESUS GROWS UP

The Bible doesn't tell us about the everyday life of Jesus from the time He was twelve to the age of about thirty. What Luke does tell us, though, is that Jesus grew in all the important areas of His life.

Jesus grew in ...

Wisdom. He learned to *say* the right thing, and *do* the right thing in every situation.

Stature. He became a man – tough and strong.

Favor with God. He started having a deep relationship (a close friendship) with God His Father.

Favor with man. People liked Jesus and were drawn to Him because of His friendliness and love.

God wants us to grow in this way too; for example, by being eager to learn, getting enough exercise, reading the Bible and sharing with others.

Growing in these areas will help you to make good decisions, have a healthy body, and develop a strong character.

We are happiest when we put God first in our lives, and when we get on well with those around us.

Grow in the grace and knowledge of our Lord and Savior Jesus Christ. To Him be glory both now and forever!

~ 2 Peter 3:18

Jesus' earthly father Joseph was a carpenter. Jesus probably helped His father, that's why people called Him a carpenter too (Mark 6:3).

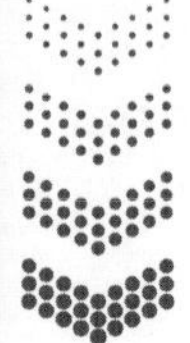

Luke 3:7-14

PREPARING HEARTS

Before Jesus was well-known among the people, God spoke to John the Baptist while he was in the Desert of Judea. John started preaching all along the Jordan River, telling people to repent. Those who were sorry for the wrong things they had done were baptized to show how God had washed their sins away.

Hundreds of years before, God had planned that John would be His messenger and prepare the way for Jesus the Messiah. Now, John was doing just that. He was making people aware of God's standard of holiness so that they would want to stop their sinful ways and get to know God. John was like a farmer plowing a field and preparing it for the seed that would be planted. Jesus would come and sow the seed of Truth into the hearts of people.

You may think that you could never do what John did, but remember that it is the *message* that is important. The message of Jesus is powerful because it is about God's love and His forgiveness (John 3:16). Let your friends know that God loves them and wants to save them from sin.

Tell others what you know about Jesus.

"I will send My messenger, who will prepare the way before Me."

~ Malachi 3:1

The Lord used prophets to tell people what would happen in the future. They were right about John (Isa. 40:3), and about every other thing they said.

Luke 3:15-18; Matthew 3:11-12

NOT WORTHY

While John was baptizing people in the Jordan River, some wondered whether he was, perhaps, the Messiah – the One who would save them. But John said, "No! One more powerful than I will come – so powerful that I am not even good enough to untie His sandal straps. He will baptize you with the Holy Spirit" (Luke 3:16-17).

John could have become proud of the fact that so many people were coming to hear him, and that some important people were asking him what they should do.

But we learn from John's actions that he remained humble and spoke about the coming Messiah. He told people the truth, even if it upset those who weren't interested in repenting.

When you do well at something and people notice you, do you give the glory to God by saying that He helped you? The next time you are tempted to be popular with your friends, rather be humble and say what you know is right and true instead of trying to impress them.

John said, "He must become greater; I must become less" (John 3:30). How can you follow John's example?

So you also, when you have done everything you were told to do, should say, "We are unworthy servants; we have only done our duty."

~ Luke 17:10

John told those who came to be baptized, that they should do what is good and right, or God would judge and punish them (Luke 3:7-9).

Matthew 3:13-15; Luke 3:21-22

JESUS IS BAPTIZED

Jesus had traveled from Galilee to the Jordan River in Judea. There at the river, Jesus asked John to baptize Him. John wasn't sure that he should, because Jesus was sinless; but Jesus told him that it was the right thing to do. And so, John baptized Jesus.

Why did Jesus ask to be baptized?

- Jesus said that He must be baptized in order to fulfill all righteousness; in other words, to show that – although He was God – He would do everything we are meant to do to obey God's law perfectly.
- Jesus showed that He was willing to become human like us. He came to live with us and to die for our sins, and although He never sinned He became sin for us (2 Cor. 5:21).
- Jesus' baptism was the start of His ministry among the people – His preaching, teaching and healing.

Jesus, thank You for becoming human and for being willing to be baptized even though You were sinless. Amen.

"Don't ever think that I came to set aside Moses' teachings or the Prophets. I didn't come to set them aside but to make them come true."

~ Matthew 5:17

Jesus was about thirty years old when He started His earthly ministry (Luke 3:23).

Matthew 3:16-17; Mark 1:10-11

GOD SPEAKS FROM HEAVEN

As soon as Jesus was baptized and came up out of the water, He saw heaven being torn open and the Spirit coming down on Him like a dove. Then a voice from heaven said, "You are My Son, whom I love. I am very pleased with You."

What a sure sign that Jesus is the Son of God! The "curtain" of heaven opened and God Himself said that Jesus is His Son. Then the Holy Spirit, in the form of a dove, came down on Jesus. That means that God the Father, Jesus the Son, and the Holy Spirit were there at the baptism.

The Holy Spirit poured God's power on Jesus so that He would be able to do far more than any human could ever do (Acts 10:38).

God was pleased with Jesus because He was obedient to Him in every way (Phil. 2:5-8). We should follow Christ's example of humility and obedience.

Up till now, God had spoken from heaven at different times. But after Jesus had gone back to heaven and Saul was hurting the believers, it was Jesus who spoke from heaven (Acts 9:5).

The Father loves the Son and has placed everything in His hands.

~ John 3:35

Although God, Jesus and the Holy Spirit are three persons, they are One, and they are equal (John 10:30; 2 Cor. 3:17).

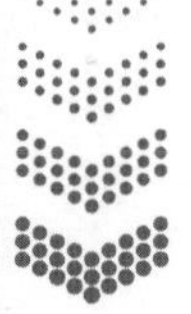

Luke 4:1-4; Matthew 4:1-4

BREAD ISN'T EVERYTHING

After Jesus was baptized, the Holy Spirit led Him to the desert of Judea. There in the desert, Jesus chose not to eat anything for forty days and became very hungry. Then the devil came to Him and said, "If you are the Son of God, tell this stone to become bread." But Jesus replied, "God's Word says that a person cannot live only on bread – he needs to feed [his heart] on the words from God" (Luke 4:1-4).

Jesus had the power to feed 5,000 people with five small loaves of bread (Luke 9:16-17), and He miraculously changed water into wine. Surely He could have turned the stones into bread. But Jesus didn't choose the easy way out by using His power for Himself.

Many people work hard so that they will have enough food to eat. Yes, food is important. Yet, what Jesus showed us is that even the most simple food, bread, is not more important than spending time with God.

Find a smooth stone that looks a bit like a bread roll. Put it in a place where it will remind you that reading the Bible is very important because it feeds your heart.

"My food," said Jesus, "is to do the will of Him who sent Me and to finish His work."

~ John 4:34

God used hunger to teach people that food isn't the most important thing in life (Deut. 8:3).

Matthew 4:5-7; Luke 4:9-12

FOOLISHNESS ISN'T FAITH

When Jesus was tempted, He used the Word of God to speak the truth. But the devil did not give up. He took Jesus to the temple in Jerusalem and had Him stand on the highest point. Then he said to Jesus, "Jump down, and God's angels will make sure you don't get hurt" (Ps. 91:11-12). But Jesus said to him, "It is also written: 'Do not test the Lord your God'" (Deut. 6:16).

This time, the devil tried to use Scripture to trap Jesus. But instead of using Bible verses to speak the truth, he twisted the meaning of what was written. He used a verse that speaks of God's protection and told Jesus to do something that was unnecessary and foolish.

We should never take foolish risks and expect God to protect us from harm. That's why God wants us to obey the rules at home, at school, and on the road – to keep us safe and to keep others from getting hurt.

Learn Scripture like Jesus did. Read the Bible and memorize verses by writing them out. That way you will know the truth and not get tricked by the devil's lies.

I have hidden Your word in my heart that I might not sin against You.

~ Psalm 119:11

The devil also knows the Bible. He tries to make us misunderstand or doubt what it says; that's how he tempted Eve (Gen. 3:1, 4-5).

Matthew 4:8-11; Luke 4:5-8

WORSHIP GOD ONLY

The devil took Jesus to a high mountain to tempt Him again. He showed Jesus all the kingdoms of the world and said, "If you bow down and worship me, I will give you all this that you see." But Jesus said, "Get away from me Satan! For it is written, 'Worship the Lord your God, and serve only Him'" (Deut. 6:13).

If the devil could tempt Jesus to take a shortcut and not take the difficult road ahead, he would have stopped the reason Jesus came to earth – to *show* us the way to God and *become* the way to God.

In order to have all the earthly kingdoms handed to him, the devil wanted Jesus to submit to him. It seemed such a simple plan out here in the desert where no one would see or know about it. But Jesus knew why He had come to earth – to die on the cross and so defeat the devil and crush his power over people.

Jesus resisted the devil by using the most important commandment; to worship and serve God only.

How should we love God? Read Deuteronomy 6:5, NLT.

Love the LORD your God with all your __________ , all your __________ , and all your __________ .

When tempted, no one should say, "God is tempting me." For God cannot be tempted by evil, nor does He tempt anyone.

~ James 1:13

Jesus was tempted in every way we are tempted, yet He never sinned once (Heb. 4:15).

1 Corinthians 10:13

WHEN YOU ARE TEMPTED

As humans, we are all tempted. Our temptation comes in different ways and at different times, but temptation itself is NOT sin! We only sin when we *do* what we are tempted to do. It is reassuring to know that the Lord will never allow us to face a temptation that is greater than we can handle, and He will always help us to find a way out.

Avoid temptation by:

- staying away from places where you are more likely to be tempted.
- not going around with those who do wrong things and want you to do the same.

When you are tempted:

- Resist the devil and he will flee from you (James 4:7).
- Use Bible verses, like Jesus did, to speak the truth and squash the devil's lies.
- Pray that the Lord will help you to be strong so that you will win over temptation (Matt. 6:13).

If you have done wrong:

- Ask for forgiveness from God. Tell Him that you are sorry. God is faithful and will forgive you (1 John 1:9).
- If you have wronged someone, say sorry for what you did.

Lord, You know the temptation I am facing today. I need Your help in this battle. Amen.

"Keep watch and pray, so that you will not give in to temptation. For the spirit is willing, but the body is weak!"

~ Matthew 26:41, NLT

What you're willing to walk away from determines what God will bring to you.

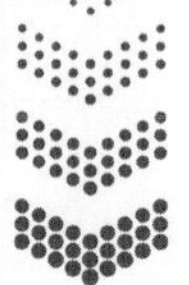

John 1:35-36

JESUS, THE LAMB OF GOD

The Gospel of John wasn't written by John the Baptist but by Jesus' disciple, John. Here we read that when John the Baptist saw Jesus, he said to his two followers, "Look, the Lamb of God!"

In Old Testament times, the lamb offered for a person's sin had to be perfect in every way. The lamb had to be killed for the forgiveness of sin (Lev. 4:32-33), because the payment for sin is death (Rom. 6:23).

The sacrifice of a lamb showed what Jesus would be when God sent Him to this world. Jesus was perfect (He never sinned), and so He could take our sin on Him and die in our place. Jesus became the Lamb that God sacrificed for our sin. But unlike the lambs sacrificed in the Old Testament, Jesus only needed to do this once because He died for the sins of the whole world (1 Pet. 3:18).

Ask God to forgive you; and if you haven't done so already, ask the Lord to make you His child.

For you know that God paid a ransom to save you from the empty life you inherited from your ancestors. And the ransom He paid was not mere gold or silver. It was the precious blood of Christ, the sinless, spotless Lamb of God.

~ 1 Peter 1:18-19, NLT

Jesus will always be called the Lamb, even at the end of time, because He became God's sacrifice for our sin (Rev. 5:12).

FEBRUARY

1 WAY
FOLLOW IT

1 TRUTH
BELIEVE IT

1 LIFE
LIVE IT

John 1:37-42

JESUS' FIRST DISCIPLES

The first two disciples of Jesus were Andrew and his brother Simon.

They had been searching for the truth, wanting to find out all they could about God. They were fishermen from Galilee, yet they had come all the way to Judea and were following John the Baptist. He told them about Jesus. After he had found Jesus, Andrew immediately went to find his brother Simon. He told him, "We have found the Messiah [the Savior sent by God]." And Jesus said to Simon, "You are Simon but, from now on, you will be called Peter, which means a rock."

Do you long to find out all you can about God too? The Bible tells us everything we need to know about the Lord, and about having a close relationship with Him.

Once we have decided to follow Jesus Christ, our names also change. We are called by His name (2 Chron. 7:14); we are called Christians (Acts 11:26).

"I love those who love Me, and those who seek Me diligently find Me."

~ Proverbs 8:17

God sometimes changed the name of someone He chose for a special purpose, like Abram and Jacob (Gen. 17:5, 32:28).

John 1:43-51

PHILIP AND NATHANAEL

The next day Jesus decided to leave Judea and head down to Galilee. There He found Philip and said to him, "Follow Me." Philip went to find Nathanael and said to him, "We have found the One Moses wrote about. It is Jesus of Nazareth!" But Nathanael wasn't so sure, yet he still followed Philip. When Jesus saw Nathanael coming towards Him, He said, "Here is someone who is good and honest."

"How do You know me?" Nathanael asked.

"I saw you under the fig tree," Jesus replied.

Then Nathanael said, "You are the Son of God; You are the King of Israel."

It didn't take much for Nathanael to change his mind about Jesus because, in his heart, he believed in God and always tried to do what was right. Those who seek God will find Him because God sees their hearts and will make Himself known to them.

Thank You, Lord, for the Holy Spirit in our hearts who makes You real to us. Amen.

O Lord, You have examined my heart and know everything about me. You know when I sit down or stand up. You know my thoughts even when I'm far away.

~ Psalm 139:1-2, NLT

Just as Jesus saw Nathanael, God sees you wherever you are. He has His eyes on everyone all the time (Prov. 15:3).

John 2:1-11

JESUS' FIRST MIRACLE

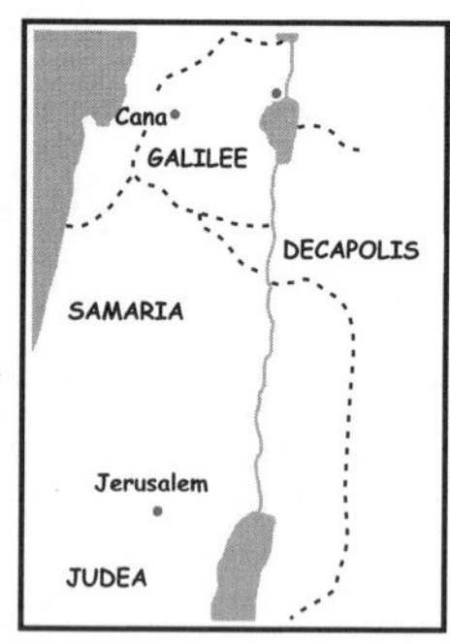

Jesus and His mother, together with the disciples, were invited to a wedding in Cana. During the wedding feast, the wine supply ran out. Nearby were six large stone jars. Jesus told the servants to fill the jars with water. When the jars had been filled right to the top, Jesus told the servants to scoop some out and take it to the master of the banquet. When the master tasted the water that had been turned into wine, he was surprised that they hadn't served this wine first, because it was the best wine he had ever tasted.

This was the first miracle Jesus did and the first time He showed His glory to people. This made His disciples believe in Him even more.

Jesus' first miracle was to help someone out of a tight spot – to save the bridegroom from being very embarrassed. Like the water in the jars, Jesus wants to turn the ordinary things in your life into something special and meaningful. Trust Him and obey Him.

The servants did what they were told without question. Can you obey Jesus without question too?

So the Word became human and made His home among us. He was full of unfailing love and faithfulness. And we have seen His glory, the glory of the Father's one and only Son.

~ John 1:140, NLT

Water jars often stood at the entrance of a house so that people could wash their hands before eating (Mark 7:3-4).

John 2:12-17

JESUS CLEARS THE TEMPLE

From Cana, Jesus went down to Capernaum with His mother and brothers, and His disciples. He stayed there a few days then went up to Jerusalem for the Passover feast. When Jesus arrived at the temple, He found people selling cattle, sheep and doves on the temple grounds.

So He made a whip from ropes and chased them all away. He drove out the animals and tipped over the tables of traders who exchanged money for people from other countries. "How dare you turn My Father's house into a market!" He said.

You may wonder why Jesus was so angry with the traders at the temple. It wasn't about what they were doing, but about where they were doing it. Instead of a beautiful place of praise and prayer, they had turned the temple into a noisy market where making money was more important than worship.

When you go to church, are you excited about worshiping God? Do you pray and think about God or are your thoughts on other things?

Lord, remind me of Your holiness and help me to focus my thoughts on You. Amen.

Guard your steps when you go to the house of God. Go near to listen rather than to offer the sacrifice of fools.

~ Ecclesiastes 5:1

Those who disrespected God's sanctuary (place of worship) in the Old Testament faced God's judgment (Lev. 26:2, 14-17).

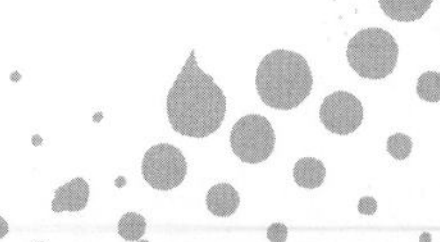

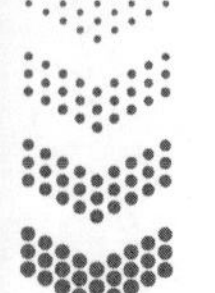

John 2:18-22

IN THREE DAYS

The Jews wanted Jesus to give them a sign to prove that He had the right to chase the traders out of the temple. So Jesus answered, "Destroy this temple, and I will raise it again in three days." But they didn't understand what Jesus meant – He was talking about His body and not the temple building.

When God chose a nation for Himself (the Israelites), He got them to make a "Tent of Meeting" where He could come down and be with them. This was the first time since Adam and Eve sinned in the garden that God came down to be with His people. Later, when the Israelites were in the Promised Land, a temple was built where people could go and worship God.

Now that Jesus had come to Earth, *He* became God's presence among us – God with us in a human body, as a *living* temple.

When Jesus talked about the temple being destroyed and raised within three days, He was talking about Himself – about His death and the Resurrection.

How long had it taken to build the temple in this story? ____ years (John 2:20)

I did not see a temple in the city, because the Lord God Almighty and the Lamb are its temple.

~ Revelation 21:22

King Solomon built the first temple, which was destroyed by the Babylonians. A second temple was built 70 years later (Ezra 6:15; Dan. 9:1-2).

John 2:23-25

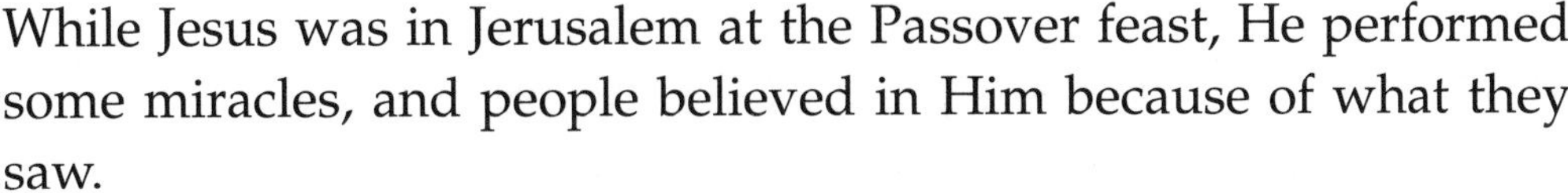

MIRACULOUS SIGNS

While Jesus was in Jerusalem at the Passover feast, He performed some miracles, and people believed in Him because of what they saw.

However, Jesus didn't rely on these people to help Him in His work of building the kingdom of God. He knew that, although the people may have been impressed by what they saw, it didn't mean that they were willing to change their way of life and follow Him with all their hearts.

Jesus didn't need people to make Him look good or to let everyone know about Him. John the Baptist had already prepared the way for Him and now He was doing the will of His Father. Jesus didn't trust the motives of people whose hearts were not committed to Him.

Jesus sees our hearts and knows what's really important to us. He wants followers who have a pure heart.

Lord, even though I haven't seen You, or perhaps haven't seen any miracles, I want to follow You and tell others about You because I love You. Amen.

[Jesus said] "I am One who testifies for Myself; My other witness is the Father, who sent Me."

~ John 8:18

When the Lord comes again, He will bring to light everyone's motives - their good motives and their bad motives (1 Cor. 4:5).

John 3:1-15

YOU MUST BE BORN AGAIN

One night, Nicodemus came to speak to Jesus, and Jesus said to him, "No one can become part of God's kingdom unless he is born into God's family. You must be born again!"

Nicodemus didn't understand what Jesus meant by born again. So he asked Jesus, "How can an old man become a baby again?"

Only the Holy Spirit can make a person new on the inside, Jesus explained. That's the part that needs to be "born again" and made right with God. Then Jesus added, "I must die for the sins of the world so that all who believe in Me will have eternal life."

When we ask God to make us new, He takes away all our sins and gives us a new heart – a heart that wants to do what is right and good (Ezek. 36:26-27).

Even though God makes us new on the inside, we are not altogether perfect, but by being obedient to God we allow Him to make us more like Jesus.

He saved us, not because of the righteous things we had done, but because of His mercy. He washed away our sins, giving us a new birth and new life through the Holy Spirit.

~ Titus 3:5, NLT

We can be born twice: the first time when we are born into our earthly family; the second time when we are born into God's family (John 1:13).

John 3:1-5

HOW CAN I BE BORN AGAIN?

Jesus spoke to Nicodemus about being born again, and about being made new by the Spirit of God.

Nicodemus knew about the need to be sorry for one's sin, but he didn't understand what Jesus meant when He said that in order to have eternal life, you must be born into God's family.

Perhaps *you* have been wondering whether you are truly born again. Follow the steps below and know for sure that you are a child of God.

- **Believe** that you have sinned against God and that Jesus can save you (Rom. 3:22-24).
- **Ask** Jesus to forgive you and make your heart clean (Ps. 51:2; Rom. 10:9-10).
- **Trust** Jesus to free you from your sinful habits and give you a new life that goes on forever (Rom. 6:22-23).
- **Tell** Jesus that you want to follow Him and that you want Him to be Lord of your life (John 12:26).

Dear Lord Jesus, I believe that You came to earth to die for my sins. Please forgive me and make my heart new. Change me on the inside and help me to follow You. From this day on I want You to be Lord of my life. I love You, Lord! Amen.

All praise to God, the Father of our Lord Jesus Christ. It is by His great mercy that we have been born again, because God raised Jesus Christ from the dead.

~ 1 Peter 1:3, NLT

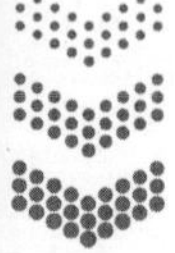

GOD LOVED THE WORLD

Jesus told Nicodemus that God loved the people He created so much, that He sent His only Son to earth to die for our sins. This way, whoever believes in Him will not be separated from God, but live with Him forever.

God did not send His Son to judge people, but to save them by taking the punishment for their sins on Himself. But those who do not believe that He can save them, and do not put their trust in Him, will be judged for their sins.

There are many things we don't know about God, and things we cannot fully understand, but one thing is certain: God loves us more than we will ever know. John tells us in the Bible that we can rely on God's love for us because God *is* love (1 John 4:16).

God's love can never be measured, and although it is for the whole world, it is also personal. God loves you! And remember this: nothing can come between you, and God's love for you (Rom. 8:39).

Thank You, God, that You sent Jesus to die for my sins so that I can live forever with You in heaven. Amen.

This is real love – not that we loved God, but that He loved us and sent His Son as a sacrifice to take away our sins.

~ 1 John 4:10, NLT

Nothing in all creation can separate us from the love God has for us (Rom. 8:39).

John 3:19-21

GOD'S LIGHT HAS COME

Jesus said to Nicodemus, "Light came into the world, but men loved darkness more than the light because their actions were evil. Those who do evil hate the light and don't want to go near it because they don't want their bad deeds to show up in the light. But those who believe in Me do what is right and good. They come to the light so that everyone can see that they are doing what God wants."

God is light, and Jesus came to the world to bring us this light. This light is not like the light of the sun; it is the beautiful light of God's holiness.

Because of our sinfulness, we cannot fill our dark hearts with light. The light has to come from God, who is light. That's why God sent Jesus to bring this light into our world, and He shines it into the hearts of all those who follow Him (2 Cor. 4:6). Sin brings darkness and death to the world; Jesus brings light and life to those who come to Him.

Walk in the light of God's truth by reading the Bible every day (Ps. 119:105).

This is the message we have heard from Him [Jesus] and declare to you: God is light; in Him there is no darkness at all.

~ 1 John 1:5

Light is always more powerful than darkness. Where light shines, darkness disappears.

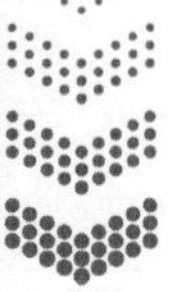

John 3:22-36

LET JESUS TAKE OVER

Jesus and the disciples went to the countryside of Judea, where Jesus spent time with them. Meanwhile, as John the Baptist was baptizing those who were sorry for their sins, some of his followers came to him and said, "Teacher, the Man you spoke about at the Jordan River – the Lamb of God – He is baptizing too, and everyone is following Him."

John the Baptist replied, "Remember how I told you that I am not the Messiah – the One sent from God. I am only here to make the hearts of people ready for Him. Jesus must become greater and greater, and I must become less and less."

John knew from the start that this was not about him. He could not save people; he could only point them to Jesus. Those who had followed him needed to follow Jesus now. John needed to step back and let Jesus take over.

Sometimes we forget that this life is not all about us, about being the greatest or the most popular; it's about loving and serving the God who made us.

He has come from above and is greater than anyone else. We are of the earth, and we speak of earthly things, but He has come from heaven and is greater than anyone else.

~ John 3:31, NLT

Although we can, and should, tell others about the Lord, only He can truly change a person's heart (1 Cor. 3:7).

Luke 3:19-20; Matthew 4:12

HEROD PUTS JOHN IN PRISON

Soon after this, John the Baptist spoke out against King Herod because of the many evil things he had done. So Herod locked John up in prison to keep him quiet. When Jesus heard that John had been put in prison, He left for Galilee with His disciples.

John wasn't afraid or ashamed to speak out for Jesus. He spoke boldly to all those who came to hear him. He couldn't ignore what was going on in the palace where Herod was living in sin.

People often follow a ruler's example, and John wanted them to know that the way Herod was living was wrong and that he would be judged like everyone else.

As children of God we know what is wrong, but that does not mean that we always do the right things. When someone keeps doing something wrong, talk to them about it without being mean or judging them. We take a stand for what is right, not because we think we are better than others, but because of what God says in His Word.

REMEMBER God always wants us to do the right thing, even when everyone else is doing wrong things.

Preach the word; be prepared in season and out of season; correct, rebuke and encourage – with great patience and careful instruction.

~ 2 Timothy 4:2

Kings and kingdoms come and go, but God's Word never changes from one generation to the next (1 Pet. 1:24-25).

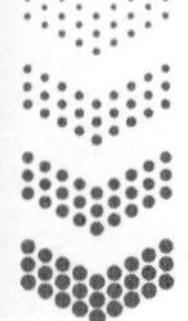

John 4:1-8

THE WOMAN AT THE WELL

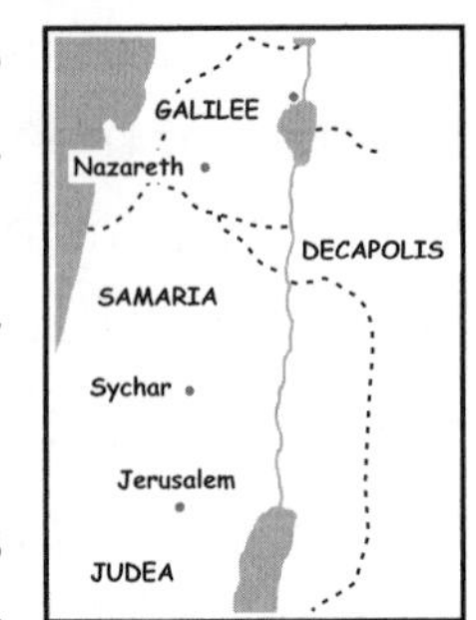

The Pharisees heard that Jesus and the disciples were baptizing more followers than John. This, too, was a reason why Jesus decided to head for Galilee. So, to get from Judea to Galilee, He and the disciples traveled through Samaria.

At midday, they came to a town called Sychar. Jesus was tired from the journey and rested at a water pit outside the town while the disciples went into the town to buy food. It wasn't long before a woman came to draw water, so Jesus asked her to give Him a drink of the water from the well.

We often forget how human Jesus was; that He could become tired, hungry and thirsty. We think of Jesus as someone who was almost superhuman, who could go without food and sleep and feel perfectly okay. But Jesus chose to feel what it feels like to be human so that He could understand our weaknesses. Tired as He was, Jesus never became irritable or impatient with people because He loved them with the love of God.

Thank You, Jesus, that You were willing to become human so You could feel what it feels like to be me. Amen.

This High Priest of ours understands our weaknesses, for He faced all of the same testings we do, yet He did not sin.

~ Hebrews 4:15, NLT

God gives extra strength to those who spend time with Him and who put their hope in Him (Isa. 40:30-31).

John 4:9-14

LIVING WATER

On His journey, Jesus stopped to rest at a well. A Samaritan woman came to get water and Jesus asked her to give Him some water too. The woman noticed that Jesus was a Jew, and Jews didn't like the people from Samaria. Also, in those days it was unusual for a man to talk to a woman he'd never met; so the woman was surprised and asked, "Why are You asking me for a drink?"

Jesus said to her, "If only you knew the gift God has for you and who you are speaking to. Then you would ask Me, and I would give you living water."

The woman didn't understand so Jesus said, "Anyone who drinks this water will get thirsty again, but those who drink from the water I give them will never be thirsty again."

What was this living water that Jesus was offering the woman? Jesus was saying, "I can make you new on the inside so that the Holy Spirit can come and live in your heart" (Gal. 4:6). The Holy Spirit is the living water inside a person. This fountain of life never dries up!

Thank God for His gift of eternal life that is like a spring of water in our hearts.

"Come!" Whoever is thirsty, let him come; and whoever wishes, let him take the free gift of the water of life.

~ Revelation 22:17

God has made us to long for something that only He can give. It is a spiritual thirst for God's living water of Life (Ps. 42:1-2).

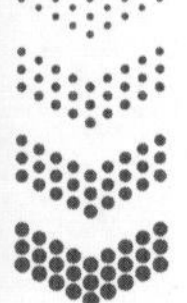

John 4:15-19

JESUS KNOWS ...

The woman at the well said to Jesus, "Sir, give me this water so that I won't get thirsty and have to keep coming here to draw water."

Jesus replied, "Go call your husband and come back."

"I have no husband," the woman answered.

Jesus said to her, "What you are saying is right because even though you have had five husbands, the man you are living with now is not your husband."

"Sir," the woman said, "I can see that You are a Prophet."

It didn't take long for the woman to realize that there was something very special about Jesus. Only He could have known the details of her past – all those things that had happened in her life and the things she had done.

Jesus knows us in the same way because He made us and He watches over us. He loves us so much that He cares about the smallest detail of our lives.

Jesus, thank You that You know me and care about me. Amen.

Nothing in all creation is hidden from God's sight. Everything is uncovered and laid bare before the eyes of Him to whom we must give account.

~ Hebrews 4:13

Did you know that God is watching you every minute of the day? (Ps. 139:1-3).

John 4:20-26

WHERE AND HOW SHOULD WE WORSHIP?

The woman told Jesus that the Samaritans worshiped on a nearby mountain while the Jews worshiped God at the temple in Jerusalem.

Jesus said to her, "Soon, those who worship God with a pure heart will be led by the Spirit to worship Him in truth. For God is Spirit, and those who worship Him must worship in spirit and in truth."

What is worship?

To worship God is to enjoy Him and to tell Him all the things you love about Him.

Where should we worship God?

You can worship God anywhere! You don't have to be in a church. You can pray or sing to Him wherever you are!

How should we worship God?

Jesus said that we should worship in spirit and in truth: in spirit means that we should worship God with our hearts – the inner part of us that connects with God. Our hearts should be filled with love for God and be amazed at His greatness.

To worship in truth means that we should worship God with honest hearts that love His Truth – the Bible.

Come, let us bow down in worship, let us kneel before the LORD our Maker.

~ Psalm 95:6

True worship is not something that has to happen at a specific time or in a specific place. You can worship God anywhere and at any time.

John 4:27-34

FOOD OF A DIFFERENT KIND

When the disciples returned from the nearby village with the supplies they had bought, Jesus was busy telling the woman that He is the Messiah. The woman hurried back to the village to tell the people about Jesus.

The disciples offered Jesus some food, but He said to them, "I have a kind of food you know nothing about." The disciples wondered whether someone had brought Him food while they were away.

Jesus said, "My food is to do the will of God who sent Me, and to finish His work."

Do you ever get so busy with something that you don't even feel like taking the time to eat? Although Jesus should have been hungry because it was lunchtime, doing what His Father wanted satisfied Jesus more than any food could. Working for His Father and helping this woman receive eternal life was far, far better!

Lord, may I love You so much that I will never lose my appetite to learn about You. Amen.

How sweet are Your words to my taste, sweeter than honey to my mouth!

~ Psalm 119:103

The Bible encourages us to fill ourselves with that which is good, and not waste money on things that spoil our spiritual appetite (Isa. 55:2).

John 4:35-38

PLANT SEEDS OF FAITH IN OTHERS

Jesus told His disciples, "You know the saying, 'Four months between planting and harvest.' But I say, open your eyes and look around you. The fields are already ripe for harvest."

The harvest Jesus was talking about is people who are ready to receive eternal life. There is great joy for those who plant the seeds of God's message in the hearts of people, and for those who help them receive the eternal life that God gives.

There are many ways God uses us to spread the message of His love and forgiveness. Sometimes you may be a sower as you tell others about Jesus. Be patient when you don't see a change in that person straight away. The Holy Spirit will remind that person of your words.

At other times you may be a harvester. This means you pray with someone who has heard about God's love and forgiveness, and wants to become His child.

Tell a friend about Jesus and use what you learned so far to help them give their hearts to Jesus.

The man who plants and the man who waters have one purpose, and each will be rewarded according to his own labor.

~ 1 Corinthians 3:8, NLT

If you don't sow good seed in God's Kingdom, you can't expect to reap a great reward (2 Cor. 9:6).

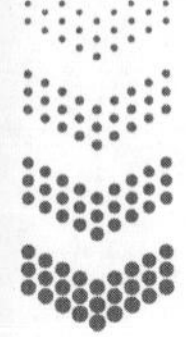

John 4:39-42

SAMARITANS COME TO JESUS

The woman from Samaria, whom Jesus had spoken to at the well, told the people in her village that Jesus knew about everything she had ever done. The people were amazed and went to meet Jesus at the well outside the village.

At first, many of the villagers only believed because of what the woman had told them, but when they heard the words of Jesus, they truly believed that He really is the Savior of the world. The people asked Jesus to stay with them in the village, so He and the disciples stayed there for two days before they went on their way.

God often changes the heart of someone who seems unlikely to believe in Jesus. Like the Samaritans who did not follow the Old Testament laws as most of the Jews did.

It would have been more understandable if the religious Jews who obeyed God's laws believed in Jesus, but they were stubborn and their hearts were hard. Often, people who think they are good are less likely to change than those who realize that they need Jesus to save them.

Does obeying God's laws save us from sin?

Today, if you hear His voice, do not harden your hearts.

~ Hebrews 4:7

Jesus came to the world to save those who know they are sinners, not those who think they don't need to change (Luke 5:31-32).

John 4:43; Luke 4:16-20

JESUS BRINGS GOOD NEWS

From Samaria, Jesus and the disciples traveled to Galilee where news about Him spread quickly. Jesus taught the Jewish people in the synagogues – their place of worship – and everyone praised Him.

When Jesus arrived in Nazareth where He had grown up, He went to the synagogue on the Sabbath day – the day of worship. There in the synagogue, Jesus stood up to read the Scriptures. He was handed the scroll (book) of Isaiah and started reading the part where it says; "The Spirit of the LORD is upon Me, for He has chosen Me to bring Good News to the poor."

Does that verse mean that the Good News is only for those who have little or no money? Not at all. The Good News is for everyone, but the poor (those with needy hearts) are more likely to want what God has to offer. They are glad to accept God's forgiveness because they know that money cannot buy eternal life. God gives this free gift to all who believe in Him.

Lord, thank You for the Good News of Your free gift of salvation and eternal life. Amen.

"To him who is thirsty I will give to drink without cost from the spring of the water of life."

~ Revelation 21:6

You don't have to be rich or important to become a child of God. We are saved by believing in Him (Eph. 2:8).

Luke 4:18-21

JESUS, GOD'S MESSENGER

At the synagogue in Nazareth, Jesus read aloud, saying, "He has sent Me to announce that those who are captured will be set free, that the blind will see, that there is hope and freedom for those who have it hard, and that the time of the LORD's favor has come." Then Jesus said, "What I have just read has come true today."

The book of Isaiah was written hundreds of years before Jesus came to earth. God had told the prophet Isaiah the exact words to write about His plan to send a special messenger. But Isaiah didn't know that the messenger would be Jesus, God's own Son.

No one living in Nazareth had made the connection either, until Jesus told them that the words He had just read had come true before their eyes – in other words, that He (Jesus) is God's messenger of Good News.

Jesus came to set us free from the sin that keeps us trapped. He came to open the eyes of our hearts, and He came to say to the world that the time for God's plan to save us has come.

Find the book of Isaiah in your Bible and look up the passage in Isaiah 61:1-2.

When the right time came, God sent His Son, born of a woman, subject to the law.

~ Galatians 4:4, NLT

Jesus is the last messenger from God because He brought us the Good News of forgiveness and made forgiveness possible (Eph. 1:7-10).

Luke 4:22-30

NO MIRACLES HERE

All the people in Nazareth were amazed when they heard the powerful words Jesus spoke, and they asked each other, "Isn't this the son of Joseph?"

People in Nazareth knew Jesus as a Son of an ordinary family. He was a carpenter like His father (Mark 6:3). No one realized that His real Father wasn't Joseph but God, the Creator of heaven and earth. Yet, the people had heard about the miracles Jesus had done in other places and were hoping that He'd do miracles for them to see. But Jesus saw their hard hearts and told them that God doesn't do miracles among people whose hearts are unbelieving.

When the people heard this, they became angry and took Jesus outside the town to throw Him over the cliff. But Jesus walked right through the crowd and went on His way.

Jesus had the power to do any miracle, but sadly, because the people of His hometown did not welcome Him and even wanted to kill Him, the only miracle He did was to disappear from them.

Lord, I believe in You and You are welcome in my heart. Amen.

Make sure that your own hearts are not evil and unbelieving, turning you away from the living God.

~ Hebrews 3:12, NLT

Although many tried, no one had the power to take Jesus' life. When the right time came, Jesus gave His life for us (John 7:30, 19:11).

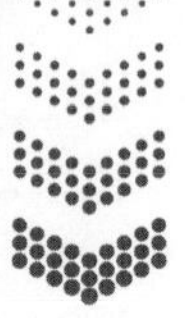

John 4:46-54

AN OFFICIAL'S SON HEALED IN CANA

Jesus went back to the town of Cana where He had turned the water into wine. A royal official from Capernaum, who heard that Jesus was in Galilee, came to Jesus and begged Him to heal his son. His son was lying at home with a fever and was close to death. "Sir, come to my home before my child dies," the man pleaded.

Jesus answered, "Go back home. Your son will live."

The man believed Jesus and went on his way. Before he arrived home, his servants met him with the news that his son was alive and well. When they told him the time the boy was better, the man realized that it was the exact time Jesus had said to him, "Your son will live." So the official and all those in his home believed in Jesus.

It can be hard, sometimes, to believe that God has heard and answered our prayers when we cannot see any proof. When you pray for others far away, and they have no way of telling you what has happened in their lives, just keep believing that prayer can change things, and that God is faithful.

Pray for a friend who needs Jesus in a special way.

The prayer offered in faith will make the sick person well; the Lord will raise him up.

~ James 5:15

God has the power to heal every sickness (Ps. 103:3).

Luke 4:31-32

JESUS HEADS TO CAPERNAUM

From Cana, Jesus made His way to the town of Capernaum, located on the shore of the Sea of Galilee.

Many years before, Isaiah the prophet had said to the people living in that area that they would see a great Light. This Light would shine on them like the sun when it comes up in the morning (Matt. 4:14-16).

The people there were living in darkness, not because the sun didn't shine, but because they didn't know God, the One who created light and who is light. God's purity makes Him shine, and it is this light that He shines into our hearts.

When Jesus started speaking to the people, they were amazed because He spoke like someone who had authority. He had the right to say what He did and the power from His heavenly Father to back His words.

When we read the powerful words of Jesus, God's light shines on us too. His words of light help us see the right way to go in this world that is dark with sin.

Where light shines, darkness disappears.

The people walking in darkness have seen a great light; on those living in the land of the shadow of death a light has dawned.

~ Isaiah 9:2, NLT

God's Word, the Bible, is a light that guides us and shows us the way to live (Ps. 119:105).

Matthew 4:18-22; Mark 1:16-20

FOLLOW ME

Jesus went to walk along the Sea of Galilee where He saw Simon and his brother Andrew. Both were fishermen. They were busy fishing with a large net when Jesus called to them, "Come, follow Me, and I will make you fishers of men."

At once, Simon and Andrew followed Jesus. This was not the first time they had seen Jesus. They had met Him just after He was baptized, and first started telling people to turn away from sin and live for God.

So Jesus, Simon and Andrew carried on walking along the shore. A little way farther, Jesus saw James and John, two brothers who were also fishermen. Jesus called them too. So James and John left their boat and followed Him.

Although Jesus is in heaven now, He still calls people to follow Him. Yet, we don't follow Jesus from place to place as His disciples did when Jesus walked on earth. We follow His ways by living the way He lived and by doing the things He did.

Do your friends know that you follow Jesus?

To this you were called, because Christ suffered for you, leaving you an example, that you should follow in His steps.

~ 1 Peter 2:21

Disciple and discipline come from the same Latin word. It means to give up certain things while giving ourselves completely to something or someone.

Luke 4:38-39; Matthew 8:14

SIMON'S MOTHER-IN-LAW IS SICK

It so happened that while Jesus was in Capernaum, the mother of Simon's wife became sick and had a high fever. When Jesus arrived at Simon's home, they asked Him to help the sick woman. So Jesus spoke healing on Simon's mother-in-law, and she got up and began serving them.

When Adam was disobedient and did what God had told him not to do, sin came into the world. Sin brought sickness, sadness, pain and death.

The sin, and all that went with it, was passed down from the parents to the children that were born to them. That means that everyone is a sinner, that we all get sick, and that we will all die someday.

Adam, the first man, brought sin into the world. Jesus, the Son of God, came to take our sin away. He makes our spirits perfect when we ask Him to save us. But our bodies are not yet perfect. While we live in this world, we will, at times, still get sick and feel pain. But one day we will get a new and perfect body when we go to live with the Lord in heaven.

REMEMBER Jesus is the same yesterday and today and forever (Heb. 13:8).

Just as we are now like the earthly man [Adam], we will someday be like the heavenly Man [Jesus].

~ 1 Corinthians 15:49, NLT

TRUTH Jesus was whipped so we could be healed. Our sorrows weighed Him down. He was punished so that we could enjoy peace with God (Isa. 53:4-5).

Luke 5:1-11

WHAT A CATCH!

One day, as Jesus was preaching on the shore of the Sea of Galilee, people crowded around Him to hear the Word of God. Simon's boat was at the water's edge, so Jesus went to sit in the boat and carried on teaching the people from there.

When Jesus had finished speaking, He said to Simon, "Take your boat out to where it is deeper and let down your nets to catch some fish."

Simon answered, "Master, we worked hard all last night and didn't catch a thing. But because You say so, I'll let down my nets again."

To Simon's astonishment, the net filled up with so many fish that it began to tear. He shouted for James and John in the other boat to come and help, and soon both boats were so full that they almost sank. Peter was afraid because he was so sinful and Jesus was so holy and powerful. But Jesus said to him, "Don't be afraid, from now on you will be fishing for people."

Simon obeyed Jesus' command to let down the nets again, and he saw a miracle. Jesus wants to use us in a special way too. All we need to do is be obedient.

Lord, help me to do whatever You tell me to. Amen.

I will hurry, without delay, to obey Your commands.

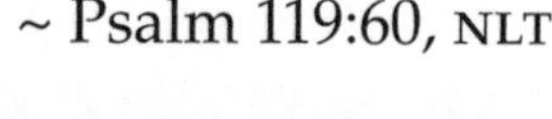

~ Psalm 119:60, NLT

When you listen to the Lord and do what He says, you are wise (Matt. 7:24).

Luke 5:12-16; Matthew 8:2-4

BE CLEAN!

In one of the villages, Jesus met a man with a terrible skin disease called leprosy. When the man saw Jesus he begged to be healed. "Lord, if You are willing, You can heal me and make me clean."

Jesus reached out His hand and touched the man. "I am willing," He said. "Be clean!" Straight away the leprosy left the man and his skin was clean and smooth.

Leprosy was a very bad skin disease that could spread to anyone touching the person. Everyone knew that by touching those sores on the skin one could get leprosy too, and die. It is likely that no one had touched this man for a long time. Maybe the man longed for someone to care enough to touch him. Jesus did.

In a way, our hearts have a terrible disease too – a disease called sin. Jesus, who is sinless and pure, came to earth to walk alongside us sinners to show how much He loves us. He was willing to take all our terrible sin and put it on Himself. He died so that we could be healed and live.

Jesus, please forgive my sins and make my heart clean. Amen.

God showed His great love for us by sending Christ to die for us while we were still sinners.

~ Romans 5:8, NLT

In Bible times, anyone who had leprosy would not be allowed to go near other people and would have to shout out, "Unclean!" (Lev. 13:45-46).

Luke 5:17-26; Matthew 9:2-8

THROUGH THE ROOF

People had come from all over Galilee and Judea to see Jesus. While Jesus was teaching them, the room where they had gathered became so full that there was no way to get in. Some men brought their paralyzed friend to Jesus to be healed.

When they couldn't get inside because of the crowd, they decided to go up onto the flat roof. They lifted off some roof tiles and lowered their friend into the room on his mat.

When Jesus saw the faith and determination of the friends, He said to the lame man, "Your sins are forgiven." However, some thought that it was wrong of Jesus to forgive someone's sins.

But Jesus knew what they were thinking and said, "So that you know that I have the right to forgive someone, I will say to this man, 'Get up, take your mat and go home.'" The man was healed right there and went home praising God.

There are people around us who are weak and needy, and some are alone and cannot help themselves. You could be a friend to someone like that. Show others the love of Jesus by helping them in some way.

Help and encourage someone in a practical way.

Encourage those who are timid. Take tender care of those who are weak.

~ 1 Thessalonians 5:14, NLT

We need others to get through life. To have a friend you must be a friend, and to be a good friend you should be kind and loyal (Eccles. 4:10).

MARCH

1 WAY
FOLLOW IT

1 TRUTH
BELIEVE IT

1 LIFE
LIVE IT

Luke 5:27-32; Matthew 9:9

THE TAX COLLECTOR

After healing the lame man, Jesus went out and saw a tax collector sitting in his small office. "Follow Me!" Jesus said to him. So Levi, better known as Matthew, got up and followed Him.

Then Levi had a big party at his house for Jesus. Some temple officials, who were also at the party, criticized Jesus for being friends with such a bad person. But Jesus said to them, "It is the sick who need a doctor, not those who are well. I have come to change the hearts of sinners."

Tax collectors were usually dishonest. They charged people too much tax and kept some of the money for themselves. But that didn't worry Jesus. He wanted Levi to be part of His team of disciples.

To Jesus, people are never so bad that His love cannot change them. The temple leaders – who thought they were almost perfect – didn't impress Him. Jesus has no favorites! He accepts all those who are willing to follow Him and live for Him.

Thank You, Jesus, that You called me and accepted me the way I am. Amen.

God shows no favoritism. In every nation He accepts those who fear Him and do what is right.

~ Acts 10:34-35, NLT

Tax collectors made people pay an amount of money depending on the value of what they carried on the roads or brought in through the city gates.

Luke 5:33-39; Matthew 9:14-17

JESUS WILL MAKE US NEW

The Pharisees and teachers of the law, who were leaders in the temple, said to Jesus, "The followers of John the Baptist fast and pray often. Why are Your disciples always eating and drinking?"

Jesus answered, "Do the wedding guests fast while they are celebrating with the groom? Of course not! "

Jesus was talking about Himself and added, "Someday the groom will be taken away from them. That's when they will fast."

"No one pours new wine into old wineskins, for the new wine would burst the wineskins and spill out," Jesus said. (Old wineskins become cracked and can burst as the wine slowly bubbles and builds up pressure.)

What Jesus was saying is that the Pharisees were so worried about their old traditions and rules that their hearts couldn't be filled with the new truths that He was teaching. Like the disciples, they needed a new heart – a heart of humility and faith.

Do I have some stubborn ideas that keep me from hearing and believing the truth?

Therefore, if anyone is in Christ, he is a new creation; the old has gone, the new has come!

~ 2 Corinthians 5:17, NLT

Holders for wine were usually made of goat and sheep skins that were sewn together in the shape of a pouch.

John 5:1-15

AT THE POOL OF BETHESDA

Some time later, Jesus went back to Jerusalem in time for the Passover feast. There, in the city, was a pool called the pool of Bethesda. Many sick, blind and lame people lay around the sides of the pool; one of them, a man who had been paralyzed for thirty-eight years. When Jesus saw him, He asked the man, "Do you want to get well?"

"Sir," the man replied, "I have no one to help me into the water when it bubbles up." They believed that if they could be the first one in the water when it moved, they would be healed.

Jesus said to him, "Get up! Pick up your mat and walk." At once he got up, rolled up his sleeping mat and started to walk. Later, when Jesus found him at the temple, He said to him, "Now you are well; stop sinning, or something worse may happen to you."

Jesus had compassion on this man even though he was sinning in some way. Jesus loves and cares for the people He has made, whether they are good or bad.

REMEMBER A good heart is better than a perfect body.

The Lord is good to all; He has compassion on all He has made.

~ Psalm 145:9

Jesus showed God's love to everyone. God is good to the righteous and the unrighteous – those who are good and those who are bad (Matt. 5:44-45).

John 5:16-23

JESUS IS GOD'S SONS

The Jews, especially those who were leaders in the temple, challenged Jesus because He was healing people on the Sabbath day and teaching the people things they didn't agree with. In fact, they became so jealous because of the crowds that followed Him that they wanted to kill Him.

But Jesus wasn't going to stop what He was doing. He said to them, "My Father is always working, and so am I; but I do nothing on My own. Whatever the Father does, the Son also does. For the Father loves the Son and shows Him everything He is doing. Whoever does not honor the Son does not honor the Father, who sent Him."

Although Jesus had the power to do any miracle He wanted to, He only did the things He saw His heavenly Father doing. Jesus had passed the test of obedience when He chose to follow His Father's will and resist the devil in the desert (see Luke 4:1-13).

Even Jesus needed to be completely obedient to His heavenly Father.

Although He was a Son, He learned obedience from what He suffered and, once made perfect, He became the source of eternal salvation for all who obey Him.

~ Hebrews 5:8-9, NLT

The first sin wasn't cheating or swearing or stealing or murder. It was disobedience (Gen. 2:16-17, 3:1-6).

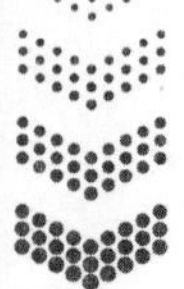

Matthew 12:1-8; Luke 6:1-5

WALKING ON THE SABBATH DAY

One day Jesus and His disciples were walking through the grain fields. It was the Sabbath day – a day of rest. The disciples were hungry so they began picking some heads of grain to eat.

When the Pharisees saw this they said to Jesus, "Look! Your disciples are breaking the law by harvesting grain on the Sabbath."

Then Jesus reminded them how David went to the House of God and broke the law by eating bread meant for the priests (1 Sam. 21:6). "I tell you, someone far greater than the temple is here now. For the Son of Man is Lord, even over the Sabbath!"

God gave us a command not to work (for an income) on the day of rest so that we can spend time with Him (Exod. 20:8-11). But the Pharisees made their own petty rules about what one could and couldn't do on the Sabbath. They didn't get the idea that our bodies should rest so that our spirits (hearts) could worship God.

Where do we find our rest? (Ps. 62:1, 5)

We have been released from the law, for we died to it and are no longer captive to its power. Now we can serve God, not in the old way of obeying the letter of the law, but in the new way of living in the Spirit.

~ Romans 7:6, NLT

Picking kernels of grain by hand while walking in someone's field was quite okay in Bible times (Deut. 23:25).

Matthew 12:9-13; Luke 6:6-10

THE VALUE OF A MAN

Jesus, and His small group of followers, carried on from the fields and went to the synagogue in the city.

There they met a man with a shriveled hand. The Pharisees tried to trick Jesus by asking Him, "Does the law allow a man to work by healing on the Sabbath?"

Jesus answered, "Of course one is allowed to do good on the day of rest! If one of you has a sheep that falls into a pit on the Sabbath, wouldn't you pull it out? How much more valuable is this man than a sheep?" Then Jesus told the man to stretch out his hand, and as he did, his hand became normal like the other one.

Hands are important. We use our hands to make things, to work, to help others. We hold, we touch, we feel with our hands. But hands can also be used for the wrong purpose: to hurt others, to break things and to steal.

Eve took the forbidden fruit with her hand and disobeyed God. David played his harp and lifted his hands in worship to God.

How are you using your hands?

Lord, I lift up my hands to You. Use my hands for good today. Amen.

Whatever your hand finds to do, do it with all your might.

~ Ecclesiastes 9:10

With our hands we do things. When we say that something is in the Lord's hands, we are saying that we trust Him to help us (Isa. 49:4).

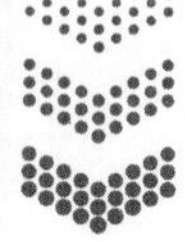

Matthew 12:14-21; Mark 3:6-7

MEN PLOT TO KILL JESUS

The Pharisees were so angry that Jesus was openly challenging their rules about the Sabbath that they started planning to kill Him.

But Jesus knew what they were up to, so He left that place. Many people followed Him, but Jesus warned them not to say who He was.

Once before, when Jesus was in Nazareth, the people there tried to throw Jesus over a cliff to kill Him. But He simply walked away and left the people (Luke 4:28-30).

Jesus is God's Son and no one could take His life. Yet Jesus came to give His life for us, but this was to happen at the right time and in God's way (John 19:11).

In the same way, God has every day of your life planned (Ps. 139:15-16). Only He knows when your time on earth is done. You are completely safe with Him!

Lord, help me to use the days of my life to honor You. Amen.

"The reason My Father loves Me is that I lay down My life – only to take it up again. No one takes it from Me, but I lay it down of My own accord. I have authority to lay it down and authority to take it up again."

~ John 10:17-18

Life on earth may seem as though it will never end, but compared to eternity it is like the width of one's hand (Ps. 39:4-5).

Matthew 12:33-37

THE STORE ROOM

Jesus had left the Pharisees and headed for another town. But soon enough the Pharisees found Him, and although the crowds were amazed at what Jesus was doing, the Pharisees tried to make Him seem like a bad person.

So Jesus said to them, "How can you who are evil say anything good? A good person brings good things out of the good stored in his heart. An evil man brings evil things out of the evil stored in his heart."

The heart is like a store room. Whatever you see and hear gets stored in your heart (where you think about things).

The devil uses the bad thoughts stored there to get you to say and do the wrong things, while the Holy Spirit will use the good things you have stored up in your heart. That's why the Bible says, "Fix your thoughts on what is true, and honorable, and right, and pure, and lovely, and admirable. Think about things that are excellent and worthy of praise" (Phil. 4:8, NLT).

Do I watch bad programs or movies or spend time with friends who want me to do wrong things?

So rejoice in the LORD and be glad, all you who obey Him! Shout for joy, all you whose hearts are pure!

~ Psalm 32:11, NLT

When the Bible talks about the heart, it is talking about the part that feels and thinks, determines our attitude, and makes decisions (Heb. 4:12).

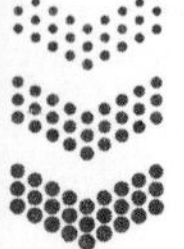

Luke 6:12

JESUS PRAYS ON THE MOUNTAIN

So many people were following Jesus every day that He had little time to be alone. At times, He would get away with His disciples for a short while. But when He needed to spend time on His own, He would go and pray in a quiet place, usually at night.

On one particular evening, Jesus went up a mountain alone and spent the whole night talking to His Father.

Jesus didn't make important decisions by Himself. He always wanted to make sure what God's plan was. Jesus was about to choose a small team who would understand and accept all that He taught. This team of men would have the important task of spreading the Gospel once Jesus returned to heaven.

Whenever we need to make an important decision, we should ask God to show us what to do. Although God has given us a mind that is good at making decisions, we cannot see into the future, and we don't always know what's best. Like Jesus, we should spend time alone with God talking to Him about His plans for us.

Lord, You know all things; help me to choose Your way. Amen.

Listen to my voice in the morning, Lord. Each morning I bring my requests to You and wait expectantly.

~ Psalm 5:3

When we trust the Lord to lead us, and we don't rely on our own ability to make the right choice, He will help us to take the right path (Prov. 3:5-6).

Luke 6:13-16; Mark 3:13-19

JESUS CHOOSES 12 DISCIPLES

When morning came, Jesus called all the disciples together. Up till now, quite a number of people followed Jesus and, from here on, He needed a smaller team who would be committed to Him for life – through thick and thin. Many hardships lay ahead, but Jesus assured them that He had overcome the world and that they were on the winning side (John 16:33). These are the twelve men Jesus chose to be His close disciples:

- Simon (Peter)
- Andrew (Peter's brother)
- James (John's brother)
- John (a fisherman)
- Philip
- Bartholomew
- Matthew (a tax collector)
- Thomas
- James
- Simon (the Zealot)
- Judas (son of James)
- Judas Iscariot

These were very ordinary men who were far from perfect. Perhaps you have been in a situation where a team gets chosen and you wonder whether you will make it onto the team or not. Be assured, Jesus has already chosen you for His team. He isn't looking for the strongest or cleverest or best looking. He wants those who believe in Him, who love Him, and are obedient and loyal.

Lord, help me to be the best person I can be for You. Amen.

Remember that few of you were wise in the world's eyes or powerful or wealthy when God called you.

~ 1 Corinthians 1:26

God knew you and chose you before He created the world (Eph. 1:4).

Luke 6:17-19; Matthew 4:23-25

NEWS ABOUT JESUS SPREADS

As Jesus spread the news of God's love, the people spread the news of Jesus' power. Some came from faraway places to be healed, others came to see miracles. The time had now fully come for this Old Testament prophecy about Jesus to come true:

The Spirit of the Sovereign LORD is on Me,
because the LORD has anointed Me to
preach good news to the poor.
He has sent Me to bind up
the brokenhearted, to proclaim
freedom for the captives and
release from darkness for the prisoners.
~ Isaiah 61:1

Jesus healed people because He had compassion on them, but He wanted to do a more lasting work – to change their hearts. So He taught them. He taught them about God's love, about how they should live, and about having a new and different heart. He wants to free people from the darkness of sin and release those who are trapped by the devil's hold on them.

The news spread as people spoke about Jesus.

This is the message of Good News for the people of Israel – that there is peace with God through Jesus Christ, who is Lord of all.

~ Acts 10:36, NLT

The main way in which people get to know about Jesus is by those who already know Him, telling others what they have seen and heard (1 John 1:3).

Matthew 5:1-3

BLESSED ARE THE POOR IN SPIRIT

Jesus went up on a mountainside and started teaching His disciples. Others also gathered around to listen as He explained some important truths. He began by telling them why they, as His followers, would be blessed:

"Blessed are the poor in spirit,
for theirs is the kingdom of heaven."

What does it mean to be poor in spirit? Unlike the snobbish and proud, those who are poor in spirit are humble and need God. They have nothing to offer to God in order to earn their way into His kingdom.

Jesus paid the price for sin and became poor so that we might be rich. "Though He was rich, yet for your sakes He became poor, so that you through His poverty might become rich" (2 Cor. 8:9, NLT). Jesus was willing to pay for us with His life, and that's what makes us so valuable to God.

Although our hearts are poor and weak, we are very precious in God's eyes, and He has planned for us to live with Him in heaven one day.

Thank You, Lord, that You have made me precious! Amen.

Has not God chosen those who are poor in the eyes of the world to be rich in faith and to inherit the kingdom He promised those who love Him?

~ James 2:5

A person who is proud and bossy (and thinks he or she is better than others) will stumble and fall (Prov. 16:18).

Matthew 5:4

BLESSED ARE THOSE WHO MOURN

Jesus knew that life on earth could be tough. He saw the misery that sin has brought to the world. He had seen people lonely, hurt, sad and discouraged. And so He said to them,

"Blessed are those who mourn,
for they will be comforted."

Sadness comes from relationships that aren't right – either because we cannot be with someone we love, or because something has spoilt the closeness.

Jesus came to heal our broken relationship with God and with each other. Because sin separates us from God, we would never be able to see Him, and He would never be able to enjoy us in His kingdom.

But because Jesus came to take away our sin, we can have a closeness with God, and with each other – something we could never have experienced without Jesus.

Because things are not perfect here on earth, and people aren't perfect, we will get hurt. Yet, when we are sad, Jesus comforts us through the Holy Spirit in our hearts and brings us hope that joy is on its way.

God can use our sadness to draw us close to Him.

"I will turn their mourning into gladness; I will give them comfort and joy instead of sorrow."

~ Jeremiah 31:13

There will be no more sadness or crying or pain in heaven (Rev. 21:4).

Matthew 5:5

BLESSED ARE THE MEEK

Jesus had come across many people who were proud and uncaring. The Pharisees challenged Him as though they knew everything about God's law, and treated Him as an ordinary man who knew nothing.

Then there were the Roman soldiers and officials, who abused their power by ordering people around like slaves. But that's not the way things work in God's kingdom! Jesus taught us to see things differently, and said,

"Blessed are the meek,
for they will inherit the earth."

What does it mean to be meek? It means to be humble in our attitude and gentle in the way we act and speak. Being meek doesn't mean that we are weak, or that we cannot think for ourselves. It means that we have the self-control to react in a way that honors God. In fact, the meek are stronger in character than those who lash out at others, argue, and demand things.

We should allow the Holy Spirit to control our hearts like an operator controls a powerful machine.

Lord, help me to be sensitive to the Holy Spirit's work in my heart so that You can use me the way You want. Amen.

He guides the humble in what is right and teaches them His way.

~ Psalm 25:9

God has the power to bring down rulers and kings from their thrones, and the power to lift the humble up (Luke 1:52).

Matthew 5:6

HUNGER FOR RIGHTEOUSNESS

Jesus knew what it was to be hungry. He had gone without food in the desert for forty days. When one is starving, all one thinks of is food. Nothing else matters. Let's face it, our stomachs need food.

When God created us, He put something else inside us that needs to be fed – our spirit that connects with God. Jesus spoke about that part of us when He said,

"Blessed are those who hunger
and thirst for righteousness,
for they will be filled."

Just as your body becomes weak when you don't eat, your spirit becomes weak when you don't fill it with God's Word. Often we spend our time and energy on things that are not of God and we don't satisfy the deep longing inside. The Lord said, "Why spend money on what is not bread, and your labor on what does not satisfy? Listen, listen to Me, and eat what is good" (Isa. 55:2). In other words, don't waste all you've got on the "junk food" that the world offers. Fill yourself with the things of God.

Worldly "junk food" spoils our appetite for God's Word.

You satisfy me more than the richest feast. I will praise You with songs of joy.

~ Psalm 63:5

Moses went without food or water for forty days when he spent time with God on the mountain (Exod. 34:28).

Matthew 5:7

BLESSED ARE THE MERCIFUL

God is a God of mercy. "The LORD is compassionate and gracious, slow to anger, abounding in love" (Ps. 103:8). Jesus came to show us God's mercy, and He wants us to be merciful too. He said,

"Blessed are the merciful,
for they will be shown mercy."

To show mercy means to forgive someone who has wronged us or owes us something (e.g. Matt. 18:23-27). Showing mercy also means to take pity on someone (e.g. Luke 10:30, 33-35).

Being merciful, either by forgiving someone or having the compassion to help someone, shows that we are wanting to be like Jesus, and that pleases God. The Lord loves people, and we are the ones who can do something to make this world a better place.

By forgiving, we empty our hearts of bad feelings and allow God's peace to flow in. By being kind, we empty our hearts of selfishness and allow His joy to flow in.

Lord, help me to show mercy and be more like You. Amen.

The LORD has told you what is good, and this is what He requires of you: to do what is right, to love mercy, and to walk humbly with your God.

~ Micah 6:8, NLT

Jesus told us to be merciful to others just as our heavenly Father is merciful to us (Luke 6:36).

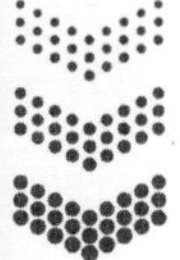

Matthew 5:8

BLESSED ARE THE PURE

In the Old Testament, God instructed priests to wash and be clean before they entered into His presence in the tabernacle (Exod. 30:17-21).

One would not go into the throne room of a king all dirty and smelly. In the same way, when we come into God's presence, we need to prepare ourselves. In Hebrews 9:10, we read that the ceremonial washing was the old way of doing things. The old way helped us to realize how unworthy we are. But Jesus came to make us pure by taking away the sin that makes our hearts unclean. Now we have the assurance from Jesus that we can come into the presence of God. He said,

> "Blessed are the pure in heart,
> for they will see God."

Even though we have asked Jesus to save us and make us pure, we still sin. We will only be perfect when we get to heaven. So, when we do sin, we should ask for forgiveness by saying something like this: "Purify me from my sins, and I will be clean; wash me, and I will be whiter than snow" (Ps. 51:7, NLT).

Thank You, Lord, that I will see You one day! Amen.

Create in me a pure heart, O God, and renew a steadfast spirit within me.

~ Psalm 51:10

We can keep ourselves pure by obeying God's Word (Ps. 119:9).

Matthew 5:9

BLESSED ARE THE PEACEMAKERS

For many years, Israel had been at war with the heathen countries surrounding them. However, in the time of Jesus, the Romans who had conquered Judea were in charge, and there was peace.

But Jesus wasn't talking about that kind of peace when He said,

"Blessed are the peacemakers,
for they will be called children of God."

Peace isn't just a time when there is no war going on around us. People also have trouble in their hearts and the bad feelings that come between them cause them to become enemies. "What causes fights and quarrels among you? Don't they come from your desires that battle within you?" (James 4:1).

But by our wise words and kind actions we can bring the peace of God into a situation. "The wisdom from above is first of all pure. It is also peace loving, gentle at all times, and willing to yield to others. It is full of mercy and the fruit of good deeds. It shows no favoritism and is always sincere" (James 3:17).

Our actions are an example to others.

If it is possible, as far as it depends on you, live at peace with everyone.

~ Romans 12:18

Peace is listed in the first three fruit of the Spirit, the other two being love and joy. *Love* brings *peace*, and they both result in *joy* (Gal. 5:22).

Matthew 5:10-12

BLESSED ARE THE PERSECUTED

In the Old Testament, we read about the many prophets God sent to warn His people not to turn away from Him. But instead of listening to the prophets, the people hardened their hearts.

They didn't want someone telling them what to do, so they killed the prophets. They didn't listen to Jesus either and started persecuting Him. Jesus knew that those who followed Him would also be treated badly, so He encouraged them by saying,

"Blessed are those who are persecuted
because of righteousness,
for theirs is the kingdom of heaven."

When others tease you, when they lie about you, when they call you names and insult you for doing what is right, be glad because you have a great reward waiting for you in heaven.

Jesus said, "Remember the words I spoke to you: 'No servant is greater than his master.' If they persecuted Me, they will persecute you also" (John 15:20).

Lord, please help me to be bold and brave for You. Amen.

But even if you should suffer for what is right, you are blessed. "Do not fear what they fear; do not be frightened."
~ 1 Peter 3:14

Paul suffered more than most other Christians, yet to him it was worth it (2 Cor. 11:23-27).

Matthew 5:13

BE THE SALT OF THE EARTH

Jesus told His disciples that they are the salt of the earth. Then He said, "If salt doesn't taste like salt anymore, it becomes useless and may as well be thrown out on the street."

What did Jesus mean when He said that we are salt? Salt is useful because it flavors food and makes it tasty. Just as salt is sprinkled on food, we who believe have been sprinkled around the world in schools and offices and factories so that we can let others enjoy "tasting" God's Word, and want more of it.

Salt is also used to keep food from going bad. Through prayer and by their witness, Christians keep the world from becoming completely rotten.

Long ago there was a city called Sodom where the people were very wicked (Gen. 13:13). Nothing could make the place good again. So, in order to keep the rot of sin from spreading, God wiped out the city completely. But now God uses us as salt to spread His goodness and keep the world from becoming altogether bad.

Lord, help me never to lose my saltiness by losing my appetite for Your Word. Amen.

Let your conversation be always full of grace, seasoned with salt, so that you may know how to answer everyone.

~ Colossians 4:6

Every cell in the body contains salt – an adult has about 250g of salt in his or her body. Too little or too much salt is harmful to the body.

Matthew 5:14

LET YOUR LIGHT SHINE

"You are the light of the world," Jesus said. A city on a hill cannot be hidden at night because the little lights from all the houses make a big light that can be seen from far away.

"God is light; in Him there is no darkness at all" (1 John 1:5). The Holy Spirit brings the light of God's goodness into our hearts. So when we shine for Jesus, it is His goodness that people will see.

A candle doesn't *try* to shine. All it does is continue burning when it is lit with a flame. As it lights up a dark room, it quietly shines without a big fuss. It doesn't matter whether it is a big, fat candle or an old, stubby one. It does what it is supposed to do – shine!

So how does one shine? The Bible says, "Do everything without complaining and arguing, so that no one can criticize you. Live clean, innocent lives as children of God, shining like bright lights in a world full of crooked and perverse people" (Phil. 2:14-15).

Are there bad habits in my life that keep me from burning as brightly as I should?

For God, who said, "Let there be light in the darkness," has made this light shine in our hearts so we could know the glory of God that is seen in the face of Jesus Christ.

~ 2 Corinthians 4:6, NLT

In heaven there will be no sun, yet it will never be dark because God will be the light (Rev. 21:23; Isa. 60:19).

Matthew 5:17-20

KEEPING THE LAW

Jesus brought a new way of living that focuses on the importance of loving God and others. The laws and commandments of the Old Testament focused on showing up our sinfulness (because we are unable to keep those commandments).

There is nothing wrong with the commandments, but they cannot save us. In fact, by not keeping the commandments we sin, and sin brings death and separation from God.

However, Jesus didn't come to do away with the law, but to obey every one perfectly and remain sinless. That is the reason only He can save us!

Does Jesus' new way mean we don't have to keep the law? God's standard doesn't change, and we should always obey God's commands.

However, what makes us right with God is not our attempt to keep the rules, but the perfect goodness of Jesus in us, and it is that goodness that helps us to love and obey God.

REMEMBER As a child of God, even when you do wrong you are perfect in His eyes because of Jesus.

Loving God means keeping His commandments, and His commandments are not burdensome.

~ 1 John 5:3

We are to obey all those in charge – like the teachers in our schools and the officials in our country (Titus 3:1).

Matthew 5:21-22

ANGER AND FORGIVENESS

Jesus used an example to explain what He meant about keeping the law while following the new way of love and respect. He said, "You have heard what was told to those who lived long ago. Do not murder, for you will be judged. But I tell you, even if you are angry with someone you will be judged."

Although we must still keep the law that says, "You must not murder" (Deut. 5:17, NLT), Jesus gave us a new law that says we are to love one another (John 13:34). When we are angry with someone, there is a good chance that we don't act lovingly toward that person and so, break Jesus' command to love others.

Angry feelings usually come when we are treated unfairly, feel hurt, embarrassed or disappointed. This anger is like a small flame inside. Our angry thoughts can feed the flame until it grows into a roaring fire that harms us and others. We need to snuff the flame out by forgiving, by trusting God to work things out for the best, and by caring more about people than things.

REMEMBER If you are angry with someone, pray for that person, then go and talk to him or her.

"In your anger do not sin": Do not let the sun go down while you are still angry, and do not give the devil a foothold.

~ Ephesians 4:26-27

A calm, gentle answer turns away anger, but harsh words stir up anger and only make matters worse (Prov. 15:1).

Psalm 37:7-8

FORGIVING OTHERS

Jesus told us not to be angry. The best way to get rid of those angry feelings is to forgive the person you are angry with. Here are a few thoughts that may help:

- By forgiving someone, you are not saying that what the other person did is okay, but rather, that you have decided not to hold it against him or her.
- Forgiveness is not a feeling; it is a decision – a choice you need to make.
- God will help you to forgive others. Ask Him to fill your heart with His love.
- Let the person who hurt you know what made you feel the way you do, then tell the person that you have forgiven him or her.
- Forgiving someone doesn't take away the bad memory or the hurt immediately, but filling your mind with other things does help.

When it is hard to forgive:

- Write on a piece of paper what happened and how that made you feel. Then destroy the paper.
- Ask the Lord to help you get over the feelings of hurt.
- Any act of kindness done for the person who hurt you will show your love in action and will help you get over your hurt more easily.

Forgiveness enables your faith to work (Ps. 51).

For if you forgive men when they sin against you, your heavenly Father will also forgive you.

~ Matthew 6:14

Mercy is like money – your deposits determine your withdrawals (Matt. 6:15).

Matthew 5:33-37

MAKING AN OATH OR PROMISE

"You have heard it said that one must not break an oath made to the Lord. But I say, do not swear an oath at all," Jesus said.

Jesus was talking about the command of God in the Old Testament (Num. 30:2). Taking an oath or making a promise is a serious thing, especially when one brings the name of the Lord into it.

Jesus meant that we should rather tell the truth at all times so that people believe what we say, then it won't be necessary to convince them by taking an oath. In other words, simply say "yes" or "no." Also, we should never promise something in the Lord's name if we don't intend to keep our promise (Lev. 19:12).

In the same way, we should be careful of the promises we make to the Lord or anyone else, because we don't know whether circumstances may change in a way that keeps us from doing what we promised. It is far better to say, "If I am able, I will do this or that."

Am I the kind of person others can trust?

If you make a vow to the LORD your God, do not be slow to pay, for the LORD your God will certainly demand it of you and you will be guilty of a sin.

~ Deuteronomy 23:21-22

To keep a vow he made to the Lord, Jephthah had to take the life of his only child (Judg. 11:30-39). Never make a vow without thinking!

Matthew 5:38-42

AN EYE FOR AN EYE

Jesus spoke to those who were proud of themselves for keeping the law, explaining that there is so much more to living a life that pleases God.

He said, "You have heard the law that says the punishment must match the injury: 'An eye for an eye, and a tooth for a tooth.' But I say, do not resist an evil person! If someone slaps you on the right cheek, offer the other cheek also."

In other words, don't take revenge. Instead, let God's anger take care of it. "I will take revenge; I will pay them back," says the Lord (Rom. 12:19).

When people are mean to us, we want to lash out at them and do to them what they did to us so that they'll know what it feels like. Or if they tease us, our natural reaction is to think of something nasty to say to them. Bullies often tease because they enjoy the reaction they get. But imagine their surprise if you are kind and generous towards them.

Lord, please help me to be patient and kind with those who are mean to me. Amen.

Don't say, "I will get even for this wrong." Wait for the Lord to handle the matter.

~ Proverbs 20:22, NLT

Don't try to get even or bear grudges; instead, love those around you as much as you love yourself (Lev. 19:18).

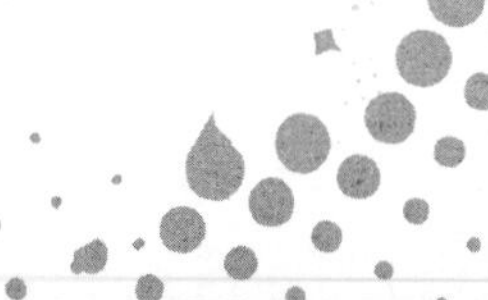

Matthew 5:43-48

LOVING YOUR ENEMIES

Continuing with the teaching about revenge, Jesus said, "You know what is said about loving your friends and hating your enemies. But now I tell you: love your enemies and pray for those who give you a hard time. This shows that you are children of your heavenly Father. For He makes the sun shine on the good people, and the bad people; and sends rain on those who do what is right and those who do wrong. If you love only those who love you, what reward can you expect for that?"

This is a tough one. It's hard enough trying to be patient and understanding with our enemies and not to say the wrong thing to them, but actually love them?

Yes! That's what Jesus said we should do, and when He tells us to do something, He helps us to do it.

God has poured His love into our hearts by the Holy Spirit (Rom. 5:5). When we allow the Holy Spirit to take control of our lives His love flows into our hearts and helps us to love others.

Think of a practical way you can show kindness to someone who is unkind to you.

If your enemies are hungry, feed them. If they are thirsty, give them something to drink. In doing this, you will heap burning coals of shame on their heads.

~ Romans 12:20, NLT

The only one we should always treat as an enemy is the devil (1 Pet. 5:8).

DEALING WITH BULLIES

Everyone knows them – the few who make life miserable for others. Here are a few thoughts to help you deal with bullies:

- Whenever possible, stick with a friend. Also, go out of your way to make new friends! This will help you be more confident around others.
- If you are afraid or upset, try not to show your feelings. A bully feels powerful when he can make others afraid of him; but when he gets little or no reaction, he often becomes bored.
- In a firm, confident way ask the bully to stop being mean.
- Be kind to your enemies (Rom. 12:17-21). You might get a surprising reaction from them!
- Be aware of what others find amusing or odd about you. Try to avoid doing those things that irritate or amuse them.
- If you are being hurt or you feel scared, tell a teacher and let your parents know too. You have nothing to be ashamed of!
- Always remember what makes you special: the abilities and dreams you have that the others don't. Your private thoughts and positive attitude are things that no one can take away from you.
- Lastly, think about this: Jesus, your best Friend, was mocked too. People laughed at Him, spat on Him, cursed Him and beat Him. Jesus knows what you are going through, and He is taking note.

Lord, soften the hardened hearts of bullies. Amen.

"I will take revenge; I will pay them back. In due time their feet will slip. Their day of disaster will arrive, and their destiny will overtake them."

~ Deuteronomy 32:35, NLT

People who love the way God has made them, don't hurt other people (Matt. 7:20).

Matthew 6:1-4

GIVING FOR THE RIGHT REASON

Speaking to the people who had gathered to listen, Jesus said, "Be careful not to do good deeds to impress others. If you do, you have no further reward from your Father in heaven. When you give to the poor don't make a big show of it. Don't even let your left hand know what your right hand is doing. By giving your gifts in private, your Father, who sees what is done, will reward you."

The Pharisees loved being admired by people and so they would make sure everyone around would see them giving some money to a beggar. The problem wasn't who saw and who didn't, but their motive (reason) for giving. Was it to be noticed or was it to help someone in need and please God?

There are a number of ways we can meet the needs of people. We can give them food, money or clothing; we can say something kind to them, and we can pray for them. Whatever kindness we do, the Lord sees our heart and will reward us.

Think of something practical you can do or something you can give to help a person in need.

God is not unjust; He will not forget your work and the love you have shown Him as you have helped His people and continue to help them.

~ Hebrews 6:10

When you give freely - without expecting anything in return - the Lord will make it up to you in some way or another (Prov. 3:9-10).

Matthew 6:5-8

HOW AND WHERE TO PRAY

There were some who loved to pray on street corners so that the people passing by would admire them for their godliness. But Jesus said, "They have their reward already." Those who hope to be noticed and praised by men have got what they want.

Prayer is talking to God. It actually doesn't matter whether we stand, sit or kneel; whether we are in bed, at school or in a car. God is far more interested in *what* we say than how or where we say it.

God is everywhere, so when we talk to Him, it's as though He is right there next to us. We don't need to go to a church for God to hear us, although He is there just as He is in your bedroom and in your classroom. You can talk to Him any time, day or night.

You can talk to God as you would talk to your friend; you can whisper a prayer, or even just think the words you want to say to Him because He can even read your thoughts (Ps. 139:2).

Thank You, God, that I can talk to the One who made the universe, and who made me. Amen.

Evening, morning and noon I cry out in distress, and He hears my voice.

~ Psalm 55:17

Daniel prayed three times a day after being told not to pray. Then some bad people threw him into a den of lions. But God kept him safe (Dan. 6:1-23).

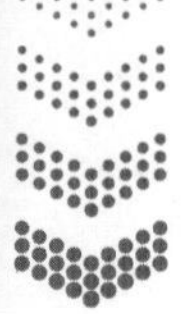

Matthew 6:9

OUR FATHER IN HEAVEN

Jesus had told His followers *how* they should pray. Now He wanted to give His disciples an example of *what* they should pray. This is how Jesus began His prayer:

"Our Father in heaven."

Jesus was the first to talk about God as our "Father in heaven." The thought of God the Creator being so personal that we can call Him "Father" was something the religious people would never have done up till then. Although God is the actual Father of Jesus, when He prays with His followers, Jesus says *our* Father, which includes us. At other times, Jesus talked to the disciples about *your* Father in heaven (Matt. 5:45).

When we pray, it is as though we come as children into God's throne room to talk to Him, and we can only do so because Jesus has made us pure. "We can boldly enter heaven's Most Holy Place because of the blood of Jesus" (Heb.10:19).

My Father in heaven, I praise You for allowing me to talk to You, and that my prayer is important to You. Amen.

"I live in the high and holy place those whose spirits are contrite and humble."

~ Isaiah 57:15

The Bible talks about a third heaven. The first is the atmosphere above, the second is the universe, and the third is the place where God is (2 Cor. 12:2).

APRIL

1 WAY
FOLLOW IT

1 TRUTH
BELIEVE IT

1 LIFE
LIVE IT

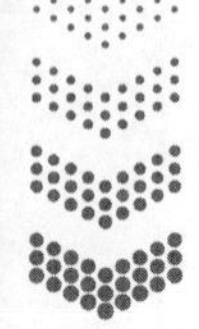

Matthew 6:9

HALLOWED BE YOUR NAME

Jesus spoke directly to His Father (and *our* heavenly Father), and said,

"Hallowed be Your Name."

By saying this, Jesus taught us how to begin our prayers, and that is by worshiping God. Worshiping God is declaring (telling Him) *who* He is and *what* He is like. There is so much we can say to God, and in this prayer, Jesus focused on the name of God. He was saying, let Your name be kept holy and honored.

When God spoke to Moses, He told him to take off his shoes because the ground around him was holy. God then told Moses that His name is "I AM" (Exod. 3:14). God has many other names and each of those names tells us something more about His character – what He is like. And so, when we say, "Your name is holy," we are declaring that the Lord is holy.

His name is also powerful, so we are protected by His power when we pray in His name (John 17:11).

When we say the words, "For Your name's sake," we are praying that the Lord's name would be honored and glorified by our prayer.

Praise the Lord, O my soul; all my inmost being, praise His holy name.

~ Psalm 103:1

The name of the Lord is a strong tower. When we're in trouble and call on the name of the Lord it is like running into the tower for safety (Prov. 18:10).

Matthew 6:10

YOUR KINGDOM COME

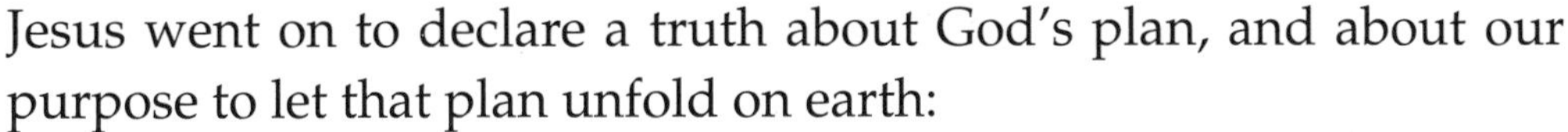

Jesus went on to declare a truth about God's plan, and about our purpose to let that plan unfold on earth:

"Your kingdom come,
Your will be done,
on earth as it is in heaven."

Another way of saying this is: "May Your total reign come on earth, and may Your perfect will be done [through us] on earth just as Your will is done in heaven." Or simply, "May things on earth be as they are in heaven."

Wherever Jesus went, He spread God's Kingdom on earth by changing the hearts of people. And so, in a way, God's Kingdom had come. Yet, because God gave man a free choice, many chose to let the devil rule in their hearts. That means God was not King in their lives and they were not part of His kingdom.

God's Kingdom is in every place He reigns in heaven and on earth. If you let God rule in your heart, His kingdom is right inside you (Luke 17:20-21).

Lord, thank You that You rule as King in my heart and that I am part of Your kingdom. Amen.

For He [God] has rescued us from the dominion of darkness and brought us into the kingdom of the Son He loves.

~ Colossians 1:13

Those who want to be part of God's Kingdom must have a humble and believing heart like that of a child (Mark 10:15).

Matthew 6:11

GIVE US OUR DAILY BREAD

The next part of Jesus' prayer was for our physical needs. He said,

"Give us today our daily bread."

This part of the prayer focuses on God's faithfulness and our neediness. Without God we have nothing. He is the One who gives us all we have, including our minds and our ability to do things. Some may say that the food they have is what *they* worked for, but they forget that God gives us all we have. As David said to the Lord, "You are my Master! Every good thing I have comes from You" (Ps. 16:2, NLT).

If we don't ask God to provide for us, it may be because we don't believe that everything comes from Him. It could also be that we simply expect God to provide for us because that's part of what He does. And so, when we don't ask we take the goodness of the Lord for granted and become ungrateful.

Yet when we pray for ourselves, it should be about the basic things we *need* – not a list of the things we *want*. And always be thankful for everything.

REMEMBER Every good thing comes from God (James 1:17).

Even strong young lions sometimes go hungry, but those who trust in the LORD will lack no good thing.

~ Psalm 34:10, NLT

For forty years, the Lord sent bread from heaven daily to feed thousands and thousands of people (Exod. 16:4, 35).

Matthew 6:12

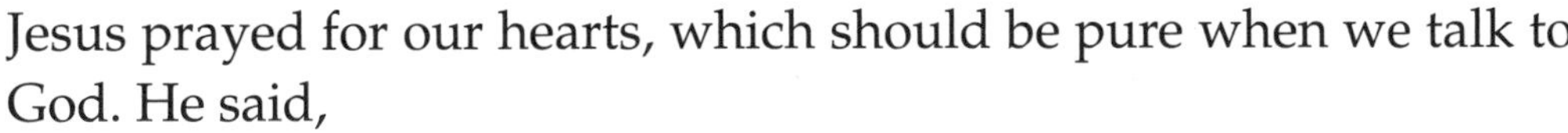

FORGIVE US AS WE FORGIVE OTHERS

Jesus prayed for our hearts, which should be pure when we talk to God. He said,

> "Forgive us our debts,
> as we also have forgiven our debtors."

Coming to God with a sinful heart is like coming to Him all dirty and smelly. If we know of unforgiven sin in our hearts, we cannot expect God to simply ignore it. The psalmist said, "If I had not confessed the sin in my heart, the Lord would not have listened" (Ps. 66:18, NLT).

This part of the Lord's prayer is not only about forgiving others, although it includes that. It is about asking God to forgive us for the sin we have committed against Him *in the same way* that we forgive others for the wrongs they have done to us.

When we are in debt to someone, we owe them until we can pay back the full amount. But when we sin against God we can never, ever pay Him back or make up for the wrong we have done. All we can do is ask God to forgive us, and because Jesus has paid our debt, He takes our sin away and makes us pure.

Lord, please forgive my sin and make me clean. Amen.

Be kind and compassionate to one another, forgiving each other, just as in Christ God forgave you.

~ Ephesians 4:32

If we do not forgive others for the wrongs they've done to us, our heavenly Father will not forgive our sins (Matt. 6:15).

Matthew 6:13

LEAD US NOT INTO TEMPTATION

We do wrong if we fail to meet God's standards when facing a tough situation or temptation. Jesus prayed,

"And lead us not into temptation,
but deliver us from the evil one."

Temptation itself is not sin. It is only when we do what the devil tempts us to do that we sin. God doesn't want us to do wrong, so He wouldn't tempt us to sin. "God is never tempted to do wrong, and He never tempts anyone else" (James 1:13). So why would Jesus ask Him not to lead us into temptation?

God sometimes allows us to be in a situation where our faith is put to the test; either to prove what is in our hearts (Deut. 8:2), or to strengthen our faith (James 1:3). Although God's trials and temptations help us to grow, Jesus prays that those temptations will not be too great for us, and that the devil will not use those temptations to trap us.

Lord, help me to be strong and do what is right. Amen.

The temptations in your life are no different from what others experience. And God is faithful. He will not allow the temptation to be more than you can stand. When you are tempted, He will show you a way out so that you can endure.

~ 1 Corinthians 10:13

When you are tempted, resist the devil (say "no" to the devil) and he will run away from you (James 4:7).

PRACTICAL PRAYING

Jesus gave us an example of a short prayer in Matthew 6:9-13, but this is not the only prayer we should pray. Prayer is talking to God with ordinary words that we would use when talking to a friend. You can pray at any time, wherever you are.

Our prayer should begin with worship and praise.

We can tell God …

- how holy and powerful He is
- how loving and kind He is.

After this we should thank God for the many things He has done for us and given us. We can thank Him for …

- our food, clothes, and homes
- our parents, family, and friends
- our health and protection.

Then we can pray for others …

- our leaders and teachers
- our friends who need Jesus in their lives
- those who are poor or sick.

And lastly, we can pray for ourselves. We can …

- ask the Lord to forgive us
- ask for help, wisdom, and guidance
- ask the Lord to use us and make us to be more like Him.

You can add to this list and change it. Why not write your own list and leave it in your Bible as a bookmark!

Never stop praying.

~ 1 Thessalonians 5:17

Matthew 6:16-18

A HUNGER FOR GOD

Fasting means choosing to go without food (or water) for a certain time to show one's need for God.

Some people made it pretty obvious that they were fasting. They made themselves look miserable because they wanted others to feel sorry for them and admire them for their commitment. But Jesus said, "When you fast, don't look all gloomy. Wash your face so that it isn't obvious that you are fasting. Then, your Father in heaven, who sees all things, will reward you."

Sometimes people fast …

- While praying about something important
- In order to know what God wants them to do
- To show that they are sorry for their sins
- To humble themselves and become more sensitive to God's will.

Fasting is a personal choice that should always be done for the right reason – to please God, and not to impress people.

Fasting is not something we do for ourselves.

So we fasted and earnestly prayed that our God would take care of us, and He heard our prayer.

~ Ezra 8:23, NLT

The wicked people of Nineveh fasted to show that they were sorry for their sins, so God changed His mind about destroying them (Jonah 3:4-10).

Matthew 6:19-21, 24

HEAVENLY TREASURE

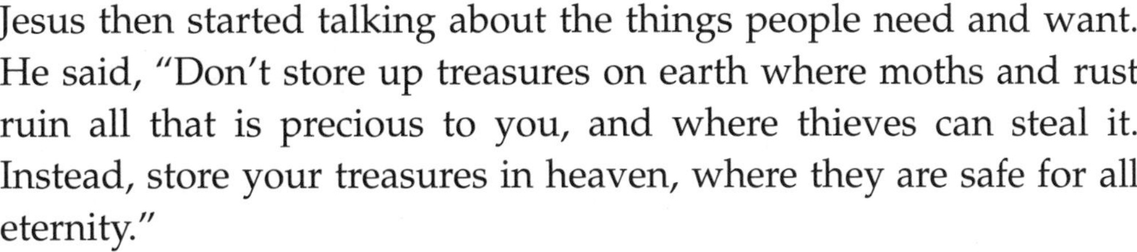

Jesus then started talking about the things people need and want. He said, "Don't store up treasures on earth where moths and rust ruin all that is precious to you, and where thieves can steal it. Instead, store your treasures in heaven, where they are safe for all eternity."

The Bible says, "Be wise enough not to wear yourself out trying to get rich" (Prov. 23:4).

People talk about things lasting a lifetime, and adverts tell us to buy this and that. But in the end, each of us leaves this earth, and our earthly belongings stay behind.

We have to keep our focus on God and not on earthly things like clothes or the latest smartphones.

The sad part for some won't be that everything they owned has been left behind, but realizing that their heart had been in the wrong place. They were so busy wanting more things on earth that they forgot to store up treasures in heaven. Store up treasures in heaven by reading your Bible, praying and living the way God wants you to.

What could I do for God to send treasure to heaven?

Command them to do good, to be rich in good deeds, and to be generous and willing to share. In this way they will lay up treasure for themselves as a firm foundation for the coming age.

~ 1 Timothy 6:18-19

Those who put their trust in money will fall, but the godly flourish like leaves in spring (Prov. 11:28).

Matthew 6:22-23

GOOD EYES AND BAD EYES

"The eye is the lamp that gives light to the body," Jesus said. "If your eyes are good, your whole body is filled with light. But when your eyes are bad, your whole body is dark."

Think of your eyes as windows. When the sun is shining and the shutters are open, the light streams in and brightens up the room. When the shutters are closed, the room is dark. Jesus was saying that when the eyes of our hearts are open to God's Truth, His light shines in. From the inside, the light shining through our eyes makes them look like lamps.

People whose eyes are open to the Truth, understand the things of God: people who shut out the light of God are blind to the Truth.

Although God is patient and longs for everyone to come to Him through Jesus, He eventually shuts the eyes and hardens the hearts of those who refuse to believe in Him (John 12:37-40).

Lord, help me to keep the eyes of my heart open to receive Your light. Amen.

I pray that the eyes of your heart may be enlightened in order that you may know the hope to which He has called you.

~ Ephesians 1:18

The evil god (Satan) of this world has made people's minds blind so that they cannot see the light of the Good News about Jesus (2 Cor. 4:4).

Matthew 6:25-30

DON'T WORRY!

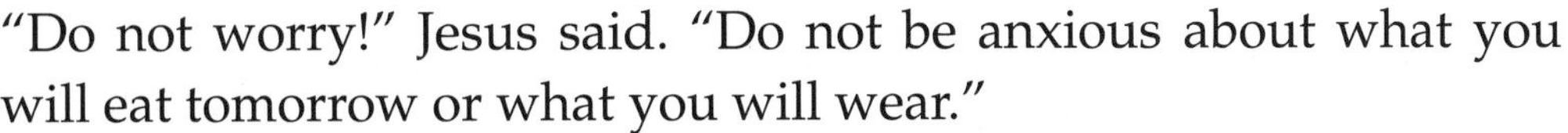

"Do not worry!" Jesus said. "Do not be anxious about what you will eat tomorrow or what you will wear."

"Isn't life more important than food? Look at the birds; they don't sow or reap, yet your heavenly Father feeds them. Surely you are far more valuable than they are. Isn't your body more important than the clothes you put on? Look how the lilies of the field grow. If that is how beautifully God clothes the grass how much more will your heavenly Father clothe you."

Jesus wasn't saying that we shouldn't work, or plan, or save. But if we worry and fuss about these things all the time, it shows that we don't trust God to take care of us.

When God's Kingdom, and becoming more like Him is more important to us than our everyday needs, He takes care of all these other things for us. So, do not worry about what may or may not happen tomorrow, for each day has challenges of its own!

REMEMBER Worry can't add a single hour to our lives.

Do not be anxious about anything, but in everything, by prayer and petition, with thanksgiving, present your requests to God.

~ Philippians 4:6

God used ravens to bring Elijah bread and meat twice a day in the desert (1 Kings 17:2-6).

Matthew 7:1-5

[NOT] JUDGING OTHERS

"Do not judge, or you too will be judged," Jesus warned. "For in the same way you judge others, you will be judged."

Jesus then used a strange example to make a point. Imagine your brother has a speck of sawdust in his eye and you want to help him get it out, but you can't see because you have a plank in your own eye.

Jesus' earthly father was a carpenter and Jesus may have gotten some sawdust in His eyes while helping him. He knew that one needs to see clearly and work carefully to get that small speck out.

The person who criticizes someone for something small that's wrong in their lives, while being guilty of something much worse, is like the person with the plank in his eyes, trying to help the one with the small speck.

We all have faults, but we are not the ones to judge others. God is the One who will judge people for what they do (Eccles. 12:14).

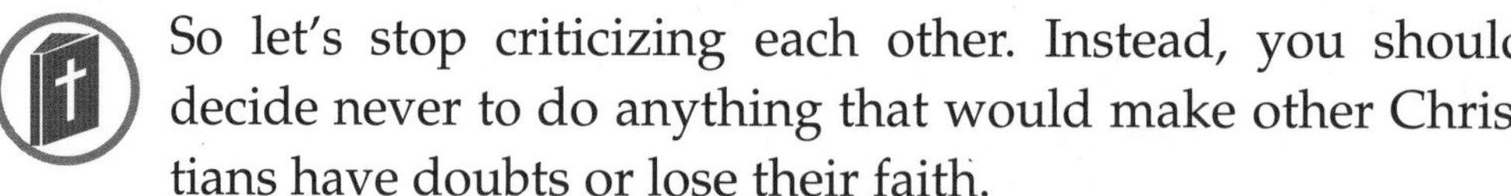

REMEMBER The standard you use for others will be applied to you.

So let's stop criticizing each other. Instead, you should decide never to do anything that would make other Christians have doubts or lose their faith.

~ Romans 14:13

INSTRUCTION Instead of judging someone for doing wrong, we must gently and humbly help that person back onto the right path (Gal. 6:1).

Matthew 7:7-8

ASK, SEEK, KNOCK

Jesus went on to teach about prayer and asking God for something. "Keep on asking, and you will receive what you ask for. Keep on seeking, and you will find. Keep on knocking, and the door will be opened to you" (Matt. 7:7, NLT).

Yes, it is okay to ask the Lord for something. In fact, it shows that we rely on Him and trust Him to help us. But this is not the kind of asking that you tag onto the end of a prayer and forget about.

This kind of asking takes effort. If it is really important to you, it is important to God, but He wants to see whether you are serious about what you're asking. So don't be surprised if God doesn't answer immediately.

If you desperately want something, you will keep on asking. If you need to find something very important, you will keep looking until you find it. If you go to your best friend who is playing outside at the back, you will keep on knocking until the door is opened.

In the same way, keep on praying to the Lord. He will see your faith and reward you for not giving up.

REMEMBER God may not answer in the way we expect.

This is the confidence we have in approaching God: that if we ask anything according to His will, He hears us.

~ 1 John 5:14

We cannot please God when we doubt Him, but when we believe in Him, He rewards our faith (Heb. 11:6).

Matthew 7:9-11

OUR FATHER GIVES GOOD GIFTS

Jesus used examples to show us how willing our Father is to give us good things. He asked, "Which parent, if their children ask for bread, would give them a stone? Or if they ask for a fish, would give them a snake instead? If parents, who aren't perfect, know how to give good things to their children, how much more will your heavenly Father, who is perfect, give good gifts to those who ask Him?"

God alone knows what is really good and so He only gives us the very best. He will only give us what we ask for if we ask for the right thing. "We are confident that He hears us whenever we ask for anything that pleases Him" (1 John 5:14).

If God doesn't give you what you're asking for, perhaps you are asking for the wrong thing. Perhaps He wants to teach you to be content with what you have, or perhaps He wants you to be patient because He has something better for you. But ask anyway, because that way you start finding out what God's best is.

Aren't you glad not all prayers are answered?

He who did not spare His own Son, but gave Him up for us all – how will He not also, along with Him, graciously give us all things?

~ Romans 8:32

Every good and perfect gift comes from God our heavenly Father (James 1:17).

Matthew 7:12

THE GOLDEN RULE

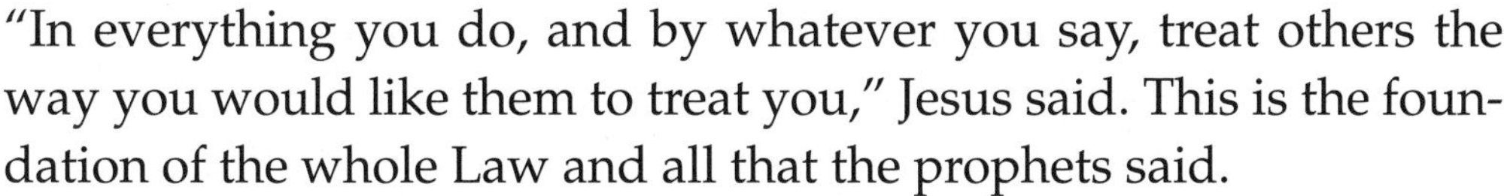

"In everything you do, and by whatever you say, treat others the way you would like them to treat you," Jesus said. This is the foundation of the whole Law and all that the prophets said.

Put yourself in the other person's place and imagine what it would feel like if you were him or her. Would you feel embarrassed, scared, pushed away or lonely?

Perhaps you'll be the first one to imagine what it feels like to be "that person" in your school.

This command of Jesus has two parts to it: firstly, don't treat someone badly, for you can imagine what that feels like. Secondly, don't simply do nothing.

Be friendly and kind to the person who really needs a friend, for you can imagine how good it feels to have at least one friend on your side.

So, be careful what you say about others and the way you treat them. Always ask yourself, "Is that what I would like others to do to me?"

Complete the first line of this verse.

____, so love fulfills the requirements of God's law.

~ Romans 13:10, NLT

When we do something for someone it is like doing it for Jesus (Matt. 25:40).

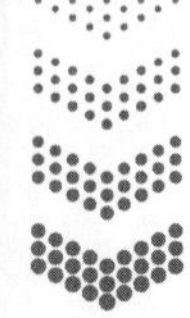

Matthew 7:13-14

THE NARROW AND WIDE GATE

"You can only get into God's Kingdom through the narrow gate," Jesus said. "Wide is the gate and broad is the road that lead to eternal doom, for there are many who choose that way. But it is the small gate and the narrow road that lead to life, and only a few find it."

Although Jesus wasn't talking about an actual gate and an actual road, what He was saying is that the way that leads to eternal life is difficult. Sometimes the way will get so tricky that you need to follow God's warning signs carefully. Jesus didn't promise His followers an easy road (John 16:33), but in our short lives, it's not the condition of the road that's important; it's where the road leads.

The wide road is easy and has no warning signs. There are so many on that road that it feels quite safe to go along with the crowd … until the road ends.

But it all starts at the gate, where you decide which it will be – the wide gate with the wide road that ends in destruction, or the narrow gate with the narrow road that leads to eternal life.

REMEMBER If you're on the road of Life (eternal life with Jesus) never turn back.

Those who are good travel a road that avoids evil; so watch where you are going – it may save your life.

~ Proverbs 16:17

People who believe that there is no God and that God did not create us, think they are on the right track, but their road leads to death (Prov. 14:12).

Matthew 7:15-23

A TREE AND ITS FRUIT

Jesus told His followers to watch out for false prophets who speak as though they have a message from God, but instead their hearts are evil.

"Does one pick grapes from thornbushes, or will you find figs growing on thistles?" Jesus asked. "In the same way, every good tree bears good fruit, but a tree that bears bad fruit is cut down and thrown on the fire. You will know a good tree from a bad tree by its fruit [by the way people live]."

Who were these false prophets that Jesus was talking about? He was telling His followers not to be confused by the religious leaders who proudly kept their many laws but were continually arguing with Him and finding fault with what He did.

There are still false prophets today – people who twist what the Bible says and add their own ideas. The way we know who to trust is to watch for good or bad fruit. The way we know if they're telling the truth is to compare what they say to what the Bible says.

Start writing important Bible verses in a small book.

The fruit of the Spirit is love, joy, peace, patience, kindness, goodness, faithfulness, gentleness and self-control.

~ Galatians 5:22-23

In the Old Testament, the test to know whether a prophet was from God or not was to see if what he predicted actually happened (Deut. 18:22)

Matthew 7:24-29

THE WISE AND FOOLISH BUILDERS

By this time, many people had gathered to hear Jesus. He ended His teaching by telling them a parable – a story to help them understand a spiritual truth.

"Everyone who hears what I have taught, and does what I have said, is like a wise man who built his house on a solid rock. When the rain came, and the wind blew, and the floodwaters rose, the house stood firm because it was built on a rock. But the person who hears My teaching and doesn't obey it, is like a foolish man who built his house on sand. When the rains came and the floodwaters rose, his house collapsed with a mighty crash."

Jesus compares living our lives to building a house. *What* we build our lives on is really important. Without a foundation everything we do in this life is worthless in eternity. All that we value now will be lost.

But if we believe in Jesus and do what He says, we are adding eternal value to our house as we live out God's purpose for our lives.

Draw a picture of the two houses and hang it up as a reminder of the wise man and the foolish man.

Listen to advice and accept instruction, and in the end you will be wise.

~ Proverbs 19:20, NLT

King Solomon was said to be the wisest man of his time. Other kings came from far away to hear his wise words (2 Chron. 9:22-23).

BE WISE

Wisdom is not cleverness or knowledge, and it isn't necessarily experience (although experience can help one make a wise choice). Wisdom is not a natural talent either, or something that comes simply from learning.

- The wisdom that the Bible talks about comes from God. His wisdom helps us know the right thing to do and the best thing to say in a certain situation.
- Wisdom comes from reading the Bible and doing what it says (Matt. 7:24).
- God gives special wisdom to some people as a spiritual gift. "To one person the Spirit gives the ability to give wise advice; to another the same Spirit gives a message of special knowledge" (1 Cor. 12:8).
- Godly wisdom isn't selfish or proud. "The wisdom from above is first of all pure. It is also peace loving, gentle at all times, and willing to yield to others. It is full of mercy and good deeds. It shows no favoritism and is always sincere" (James 3:17). In other words, wisdom from God will not let you make a decision that favors you while putting others at a disadvantage.
- If we are in a tricky situation where we don't know what to do, we should ask God to give us wisdom. "If you need wisdom, ask our generous God, and He will give it to you" (James 1:5).

The Lord gives wisdom, and from His mouth come knowledge and understanding.

~ Proverbs 2:6

The book of Proverbs speaks a lot about wisdom. Reading a few verses each day will be a great way to increase your wisdom.

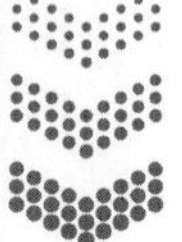

Matthew 8:1, 5-13; Luke 7:1-10

THE CENTURION'S SERVANT

When Jesus had finished speaking, He came down from the mountainside and a large crowd followed Him. As He entered Capernaum, a Roman officer came to Him asking for help: "Lord, my servant is sick at home. He cannot move and is in terrible pain."

Jesus replied, "I will go and heal him."

But the officer said, "Lord, I am not worthy to have You come into my home. Just say the word from here, and my servant will be healed."

When Jesus heard this, He was amazed and said to those around Him, "I tell you the truth, I have not seen faith like this in all of Israel." Then He said to the officer, "Go back home. What you have asked for has been done." And the servant was healed at that moment.

The Roman officer understood how authority works. He could order someone to do something, and they would obey immediately. The officer knew that Jesus has the authority over sickness, evil and the devil. When Jesus gives the word, it happens!

Thank You, Lord, that Your words have such power. Amen.

By faith in the name of Jesus, this man whom you see and know was made strong.

~ Acts 3:16

A centurion was the captain of 100 soldiers in the Roman army. The headquarters of the Roman army in Judea was located at Caesarea.

Luke 7:11-17

THE YOUNG MAN FROM NAIN

Soon after this, Jesus went to the town of Nain. The disciples and a large crowd went along with Him. As they neared the gate of the town, a dead man was being carried out. He was the only son of a widow. When Jesus saw her, His heart overflowed with compassion. "Don't cry," He said.

Then Jesus walked up to the coffin and touched it. Those who were carrying it stood still. Then He said, "Young man, I say to you, get up!" The dead man sat up and began to talk. And Jesus gave him back to his mother. Everyone was amazed and praised God, saying, "God has come to help His people." The news about Jesus spread to the surrounding countryside.

This young man was the first person that Jesus raised from the dead. Jesus didn't do this to become popular among the people or to show off His power. He felt a deep sadness and love for the widow. Jesus cares for us in the same way. When we are sad, He feels it; when we are hurt, He knows and understands.

Jesus died so we can be raised to eternal life one day.

For He [God] raised us from the dead along with Christ and seated us with Him in the heavenly realms because we are united with Christ Jesus.

~ Ephesians 2:6, NLT

The first person mentioned in the Bible that was raised from the dead was also the son of a widow (1 Kings 17:17-24).

Luke 7:18-23; Matthew 11:2-5

ARE YOU THE ONE?

Meanwhile John the Baptist was in prison, so his followers told him all that Jesus was doing. Then John sent them to ask Jesus, "Are You the One sent from God, or should we keep looking for someone else?"

At that time Jesus was healing many people, so He told John's followers, "Go back and tell John what you have seen and heard – the blind see, the lame walk, the lepers are cured, the deaf hear, the dead are raised, and the Good News is being preached to the poor."

John had pointed others to Jesus, now he was stuck in prison. Perhaps he wondered why Jesus hadn't come to get him out. And so, John couldn't see Jesus in action and experience all He was doing.

Like John, we cannot see Jesus either, and at times we may start to doubt. We wonder whether God exists or whether the Bible is true. In those times when our faith is weak and we feel discouraged, we may even be tempted to stop meeting with other believers. But that is exactly when we need their support; for it is there among fellow believers that we will see and hear what the Lord is doing.

Lord, thank You for friends who help me to believe. Amen.

So we fix our eyes not on what is seen, but on what is unseen. For what is seen is temporary, but what is unseen is eternal.

~ 2 Corinthians 4:18

Even before the world was created, Jesus was the One chosen by God to save us – the Messiah (1 Pet. 1:20).

Luke 7:36-38

A JAR OF PERFUME

One of the Pharisees invited Jesus to have dinner with him. A woman who had lived a sinful life heard that Jesus was eating there, so she brought a beautiful alabaster jar filled with expensive perfume. She knelt down behind Jesus and began to wet His feet with her tears. Then she wiped them with her hair and poured perfume on them.

The woman did a courageous thing by entering the home of a stranger to show her love for Jesus. Perhaps it was her way of saying sorry to Jesus for the wrong she had done.

It was a beautiful way of showing Jesus that she loved Him – more than the most precious thing she owned. Like the wise men, the woman brought her gift to Jesus, then humbly poured it on His feet.

Incense, which has a sweet smell as perfume does, was also used as a sacrifice to God (Luke 1:8-9). Even though Jesus is no longer on earth, we can still offer Him a sweet smelling gift – the gift of our prayers.

Lord, may my prayers always be a beautiful gift to You. Amen.

Accept my prayer as incense offered to You, and my upraised hands as an evening offering.

~ Psalm 141:2, NLT

The last book in the Bible, Revelation, tells us about golden bowls full of incense, which are the prayers of the saints (Rev. 5:8).

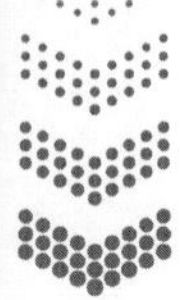

Luke 7:39-50

A HEART THAT LOVES

When the Pharisee saw that the sinful woman poured perfume on Jesus' feet, he said to himself, "If this Man were sent from God, He would know who this woman is."

"Simon," Jesus said to the Pharisee, "I have something to tell you. Two men owed money to a moneylender; one owed him 500 silver coins, the other owed him 50. But neither of them could repay him, so he forgave them both and cancelled their debts. Which one of the two, do you think, loved him more?"

Simon answered, "I suppose the one who had the bigger debt forgiven."

Then Jesus said, "Simon, when I came in, you didn't even give Me water to wash My feet, but this woman wet My feet with her tears. Her many sins have been forgiven, and her actions show her love."

If, every morning, we would stop to think what it cost Jesus to pay for our sins on the cross – a debt we could never repay – we would not want to sin, and we would love Him enough to give Him all we have.

Lord Jesus, I love You so much! Amen.

For the kind of sorrow God wants us to experience leads us away from sin and results in salvation.

~ 2 Corinthians 7:10, NLT

It was a custom in Bible times to give one's visitors water to wash their feet because people wore sandals and walked on dusty roads (Gen. 18:4).

Luke 8:1-3

THE GENEROUS WOMEN

From then on, Jesus and His twelve disciples traveled from town to town telling the people about the Good News of the kingdom of God.

Some women traveled along with them. There was Mary Magdalene, whom Jesus had freed from the evil spirits inside her; there was Joanna, the wife of Herod's manager; Susanna, and many others. These women helped provide Jesus and the disciples with things they needed every day.

Have you ever wondered who cooked for the team of disciples, or if they ever washed their clothes? Here was a group of women who not only helped them but also paid for the team's expenses with their own money.

How different the background was of these women. Each one had their own story to tell of how Jesus had changed their life. Each one had something to offer: practical help, special abilities, money. But they had one thing in common: they loved Jesus and wanted to serve Him in any way they could.

Is there someone you know who serves the Lord whom you could help in a practical way?

Command them to do good, to be rich in good deeds, and to be generous and willing to share.

~ 1 Timothy 6:18

Mary Magdalene became a faithful follower of Jesus, and was one of the first to see the empty tomb after He rose from the dead (Matt. 28:1-10).

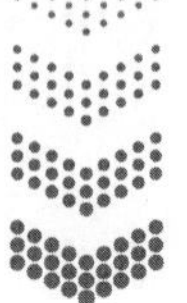

Matthew 8:18-23; Luke 9:57-62

NO PLACE TO SLEEP

One day when there was a crowd around Jesus, He told the disciples to go across to the other side of the lake. Just then, a teacher of religious law said to Him, "Teacher, I will follow You wherever You go."

But Jesus replied, "Foxes have dens and birds have nests, but the Son of Man has no place to lay His head."

Another follower said, Lord, let me first return home and bury my father.

Jesus said to him, "Follow Me now. Let those who are spiritually dead bury their own dead." Then Jesus got into the boat with His disciples.

Following Jesus is not for quitters. Jesus was on the move the whole time, not knowing where He would sleep each night. He didn't have a place He could call home. If someone wanted to be His disciple, Jesus couldn't offer them something He didn't have. The second man wanted Jesus to wait for him, but Jesus gave him a choice – to stay at home or to come with Him. Jesus was leaving in the boat.

Obedience never says *maybe* or *later*.

Lord, I will gladly follow You, even when it is tough. Amen.

To this you were called, because Christ suffered for you, leaving you an example, that you should follow in His steps.

~ 1 Peter 2:21

Jesus called Himself the Son of Man, but He was also the Son of God – completely human and perfectly God (John 3:13; Mark 1:1).

Matthew 8:23-27; Luke 8:22-25

CALMING THE STORM

Jesus and the disciples left the crowd and headed across the lake in a small boat. Suddenly a fierce storm struck and the boat was in danger of sinking. Meanwhile, Jesus was sleeping.

The disciples woke Him up saying, "Lord! Save us, we're going to die!"

Jesus said to them, "Why are you so afraid? You have so little faith." Then He got up and gave an order to stop the howling wind and raging sea, and it all became perfectly calm.

The disciples were amazed and asked, "What kind of a man is this that even the wind and the waves obey Him?"

Jesus showed His complete power over nature, and why shouldn't the One who created everything have the power to control it?

Jesus created you too, and when it feels like there's a storm inside of you with waves of anger, fear or worry, all you need to do is call on the One who is always with you and brings peace.

REMEMBER Jesus is always with you in the boat of life!

You rule over the surging sea; when its waves mount up, You still them.

~ Psalm 89:9

Jonah was on a ship running away from God. So God sent a big storm. Read what the men had to do to Jonah to make the sea calm (Jonah 1).

Galatians 6:9

STORMY TIMES IN YOUR LIFE

Storms in life come and things go wrong. Sometimes the storm is on the outside, like when people are angry with each other or with you. It feels like waves of anger crashing into your life, and there's no way to stop them.

Sometimes the storm is on the inside and it feels like you're swamped with waves of bad feelings. You may struggle to focus on your schoolwork, or you may want to withdraw and not even talk to anyone. But God sees and He cares.

- **Sadness** comes from a longing to be loved, or when we can't be with the person we love. Talk to the Lord about your sadness. He is the best friend you could wish for. He will never leave you nor let you down. Read Psalm 147:3, 2 Corinthians 1:3-4.
- **Anger** usually comes from being treated unfairly, hurt, embarrassed, frustrated, disappointed, or taken advantage of. When we are angry with someone, we should forgive that person and fill our minds with good thoughts. Read Colossians 3:13, Romans 12:19, Philippians 4:8.
- **Fear** is the feeling we get when we're afraid that something bad may happen, or when we're scared of someone. If you are afraid of something in the future, read Philippians 4:6 and Deuteronomy 31:8. If you are scared of a particular person, tell your mom or dad about it.
- **Loneliness** is a longing for a friend – a feeling of wanting to belong and be accepted by others. Ask the Lord to give you a close friend. Read Psalm 68:6.

In every way we're troubled, but we aren't crushed by our troubles. We're frustrated, but we don't give up.

~ 2 Corinthians 4:8

Matthew 8:28-34; Luke 8:26-39

THE MEN ONLY JESUS COULD CALM

When Jesus and the disciples arrived at the other side of the lake, two men with evil spirits came towards them. They were so dangerous that no one dared to go near them.

The evil spirits shouted from inside the men, "What do You want, Son of God? Have You come to torture us before the time set by God?"

The demons begged Jesus, "If You drive us out, send us into the herd of pigs feeding over there." So Jesus did, and they came out of the men and went into the pigs. All the pigs rushed down the mountainside into the lake and drowned.

The two men were controlled by the evil spirits (demons), who made the men destructive and violent. But when Jesus came, the demons recognized Him. They knew that, just as they had power over the men, Jesus had power over them. The power of Jesus sets people free from the devil's hold on them!

Jesus can set us free from sinful habits that control us.

"I will say to the prisoners, 'Come out in freedom,' and to those in darkness, 'Come into the light.' They will be My sheep, grazing in green pastures and on hills that were previously bare."

~ Isaiah 49:9

One day, the Lord will throw the devil and all the demons into a lake of fire, where they will be forever (Rev. 20:10).

Luke 8:40-42

JAIRUS'S DAUGHTER IS SICK

Jesus and the disciples got back into the boat and crossed over to Capernaum. When they got there, a crowd had gathered to welcome them.

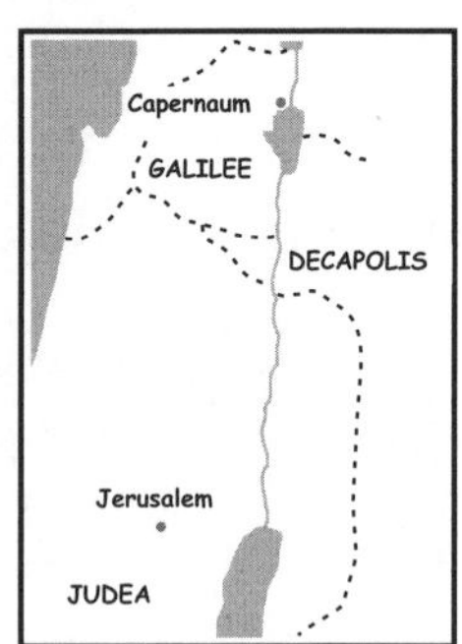

A man named Jairus, a ruler of the synagogue, came up to Jesus and fell at His feet. He pleaded with Jesus to come to his house where his only daughter lay dying. So Jesus made His way through the crowd to Jairus's home.

Jairus was a ruler of the synagogue, like the Pharisees who always argued with Jesus. Even though he was well respected by his fellow Jews for keeping the law, he fell at the feet of Jesus, humbly showing his desperate need. It didn't matter now that he was respected or wore nice clothes, or that he knew every law. He needed Jesus.

Whoever we are, we cannot escape tough times in life. In desperate times, when we feel alone and helpless, Jesus will help us if we humbly come to Him believing that He is able to do what we ask.

REMEMBER Jesus should be the first One we ask for help.

I call on the LORD in my distress, and He answers me.

~ Psalm 120:1

Falling at the feet of Jesus, or kneeling, is a sign of respect and submission - an action to show that we are not worthy to be in His presence (Rev. 1:17).

Luke 8:43-48

A TOUCH, AND SHE IS HEALED

While Jesus was following Jairus through the crowd, a woman who had suffered with bleeding for twelve years came up behind Jesus and touched the edge of His robe. Immediately, the bleeding stopped.

"Who touched Me?" Jesus asked.

Peter said to Jesus, "Master, all these people are pressing up against You."

But Jesus said, "Someone deliberately touched Me, for I felt healing power go out from Me." Realizing that she could not go unnoticed, the woman fell to her knees and told Jesus what had happened.

Then Jesus said to her, "Daughter, your faith has made you well. Go in peace."

Was it the robe that made the woman well? Although the bleeding stopped as she touched the robe, the healing power flowed from Jesus. However, Jesus said to the woman that her faith had made her well. So without Jesus the healing would not have flowed; and without faith, the woman would not have touched His robe.

In faith, may my prayers reach out to touch You. Amen.

Faith is being sure of what we hope and certain of what we do not see.

~ Hebrews 11:1

God did amazing miracles through Paul. Some clothing that Paul had touched was taken to the sick and they were healed (Acts 19:11-12).

MAY

1 WAY
FOLLOW IT

1 TRUTH
BELIEVE IT

1 LIFE
LIVE IT

Luke 8:49-56

A GIRL COMES BACK TO LIFE

While Jesus was still speaking to the woman He had healed, a messenger arrived with the news that Jairus's daughter had died. Jesus heard what had happened and said to Jairus, "Don't be afraid. Just have faith and she will be healed."

When Jesus arrived at the house, everyone there was crying. He went inside with three of the disciples and the girl's parents.

Then Jesus took the little girl by the hand and said, "My child, get up!" At that moment life returned to her body and she stood up! Her parents were amazed, but Jesus ordered them not to tell anyone what had happened.

Jesus was never rushed, and although it seemed as if He was too late to heal the girl, He did an even bigger miracle and raised her from the dead. Sometimes, when we ask the Lord for something and He doesn't answer straight away, or in the way we expect, we may think that He isn't answering at all. Yet He may be doing something bigger first – strengthening our faith.

Lord, help me to trust You even when I don't see an answer. Amen.

"For just as the Father raises the dead and gives them life, even so the Son gives life to whom He is pleased to give it."

~ John 5:21

When we die, our spirit leaves our body, and God gives us a new, perfect body (2 Cor. 5:1; Phil. 3:20-21).

Matthew 9:27-31

TWO BLIND MEN

After Jesus left the home, where He had raised a dead girl, two blind men followed Him calling, "Son of David, have mercy on us!"

When Jesus had gone indoors, the two blind men came to Him. Jesus asked them, "Do you believe that I can make you see?"

"Yes, Lord, we do" they said.

Then He touched their eyes and said, "Because of your faith, it will happen." Immediately, their eyes were opened and they could see.

Jesus gave them a strict instruction not to tell anyone about what had happened. But, they still spread His fame all over.

God has given us an amazing ability to see the colors and shapes of things around us. If we were blindfolded we'd realize what it must have been like for the men.

Yet, just like those blind men who put their faith in Jesus, whom they couldn't see, we put our faith in Jesus, whom *we* cannot see. And because we believe in Him, we, too, will see Him one day; but for now we live by faith, not by sight (2 Cor. 5:7).

Our sight is a precious gift from God.

The LORD gives sight to the blind, the LORD lifts up those who are bowed down, the LORD loves the righteous.

~ Psalm 146:8

Elisha prayed that his servant's eyes would be opened so he would see the invisible army of God around him (2 Kings 6:17).

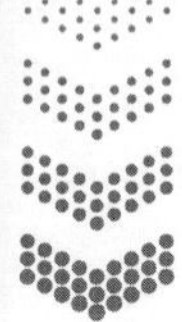

Matthew 9:35-38

THE WORKERS ARE FEW

Jesus continued going through all the towns preaching the Good News of God's Kingdom and healing every sickness. When Jesus saw the crowds of people, He had compassion on them because they were troubled and helpless, like sheep without a shepherd.

Then He said to His disciples, "The harvest is great, but the workers are few. So pray to the Lord who is in charge of the harvest and ask Him to send more workers into His fields."

God our Father is the Lord of the Harvest. The world is His harvest field because He created it and owns it. His purpose for having created everything is that He would have a harvest of people who love and praise Him.

However, as any farmer knows, it takes hard work to get a good harvest. Through His Spirit, God is working in the hearts of people, drawing them to Himself. But there are many who don't know about the Good News of His love. The Lord of the harvest wants us to be His helpers, and to pray for more helpers to join us.

Who can I tell about God's love in my part of the field?

So let's not get tired of doing what is good. At just the right time we will reap a harvest of blessing if we don't give up.

~ Galatians 6:9, NLT

If we sow only a few seeds of good, we will get a small harvest of blessing. If we sow much into God's Kingdom, we will reap much (2 Cor. 9:6).

Luke 9:1-6; Matthew 10:1-10

JESUS SENDS THE DISCIPLES OUT

One day, Jesus called His twelve disciples together and gave them the power and right to heal every sickness and order demons to come out of people. He also told them to spread the message about God's Kingdom.

Then He said, "Don't take anything along with you; not even a walking stick or a traveler's bag for the journey – no money, no food, no extra clothes."

Now that the team had been chosen and trained, Jesus was giving them final instructions before sending them out to put into practice all they had seen Him do. They were now called Apostles (Matt. 9:2), and were given spiritual power over the demons and diseases, which had brought so much suffering.

You may think it is strange that Jesus was sending them out with nothing. Perhaps there were two reasons; one being that Jesus wanted them to learn to trust God for everything; the other being that He wanted the people providing food and shelter for His disciples to experience the blessing of God.

Make a short list of your most basic needs.

This same God who takes care of me will supply all your needs from His glorious riches, which have been given to us in Christ Jesus.

~ Philippians 4:19, NLT

The Heavenly City has twelve gates with the names of the tribes of Israel and twelve foundations with the names of the Apostles (Rev. 21:12-14).

Matthew 10:11-16

AS INNOCENT AS DOVES

Jesus said to His disciples, "As you go out, look for someone who listens to you and makes you feel welcome. Stay with such a person until you leave that town or village. As you go into the home, greet the family with a blessing."

"If you enter a place where people do not welcome you, shake the dust from your feet as you leave [to show that you are taking nothing from them]. So be as wise as snakes and as harmless as doves."

Jesus wasn't only teaching His disciples to be courteous and greet those who took them in, He was telling them to bless the home with the peace of God.

Then Jesus told them to be as quick-thinking as snakes. There are some people in the world who are out to trick and trap anyone who is fooled by their cunning schemes. In our thinking, we must be a step ahead of those who are out to get us. Yet, we are to be as innocent as peaceful doves.

Doves, used as a symbol of peace, remind us that we are spreading the Good News of having peace with God through Jesus Christ (Rom. 5:1).

FIND OUT What greeting also means peace in Hebrew? Sh_l_m

How beautiful on the mountains are the feet of the messenger who brings good news, the good news of peace and salvation, the news that the God of Israel reigns!

~ Isaiah 52:7, NLT

Noah sent a dove out from the ark to look for signs of life (Gen. 8:8-12). In the same way, Jesus was sending His disciples out as doves.

Matthew 10:22-31

TOUGH TIMES AHEAD

Jesus warned the disciples that things would get tough. "Men will hate you because of Me," He said. "But the one who stands firm to the end will be saved. When people hurt and harass you in one place, flee to the next town. But do not be afraid of them!"

"Just think; one can buy two sparrows for a few copper coins. Yet, not a single sparrow falls to the ground without your Father knowing and caring about it. God even knows how many hairs are on your head. So don't be afraid; you are much, much more valuable to God than a whole flock of sparrows."

Jesus knew what lay ahead for the disciples. There would be no surprises for them as they went out to undo the work of the devil. But with the "bad" news came the good news that their heavenly Father would watch over them every step of the way.

If God cared enough to count every hair on their heads, surely He would care enough to protect them. God cares for you as much as He cared for the disciples. So when you face tough times; remember, God knows about everything.

Thank You, Lord, that You know about every detail of my life! Amen.

Everyone who wants to live a godly life in Christ Jesus will suffer persecution.

~ 2 Timothy 3:12

When we are going through tough times, the Lord tells us to be strong and courageous because He will never leave us (Deut. 31:6).

Matthew 10:40-42

DO SOMETHING FOR GOD

The disciples weren't going on a "field trip"; they were being sent out by Jesus.

Jesus said to them, "Anyone who receives you receives Me, and anyone who receives Me receives the Father who sent Me. Anyone who gives you a cup of cold water because you are My disciple, that person will surely be rewarded."

The twelve friends of Jesus would be going out in pairs (Mark 6:7), probably heading off in different directions. Perhaps they were excited; perhaps they were a little nervous.

But there was no question of dropping out of this challenge. With Jesus' power in them, they'd be able to do so much more than Jesus had been doing on His own.

The wonderful truth we learn from Jesus is that whatever we do for one of His followers, we are doing for Him; and whatever we do for Him, we are doing for God the Father. Even for the smallest thing we do – like handing someone a cup of cold water – there is a reward if we do it to please God.

Is there some way you could be a blessing to someone who cannot repay you?

"Truly I tell you, whatever you did for one of the least of these brothers and sisters of Mine, you did for Me."

~ Matthew 25:40

There was an old couple who built on a room so that Elisha the prophet could stay there. As a result, the Lord blessed them with a son (2 Kings 4:8-17).

Matthew 11:20-26

TRUTHS YOU'LL UNDERSTAND

Jesus had done many miracles in the towns of Galilee, but the people's hearts had not changed. They weren't sorry for their sins and had not turned to God. They continued with what they were doing as if Jesus had never come.

Because they wouldn't accept His teaching or believe that He is the Son of God, Jesus warned them that the people from certain wicked cities long ago would be better off than them on Judgment Day.

Then Jesus said a prayer, "O Father, Lord of heaven and earth, thank You for hiding these things from those who think themselves wise and clever, and for making them plain and simple to those who are like children."

What *things* was Jesus talking about in His prayer? Jesus was talking about the truths He'd been teaching. Those who thought they knew everything couldn't understand the simplest of teachings, because spiritual things can only be understood by those who have the Holy Spirit in their hearts.

Jesus praised His Father for letting the humble grasp heavenly truths that the proud and couldn't understand.

Humility is the key that unlocks heavenly wisdom.

You have taught children and infants to tell of your strength, silencing your enemies and all who oppose you.

~ Psalm 8:2, NLT

However clever a person may be, without God's Spirit in his heart, he cannot understand even the simplest Bible truth (1 Cor. 2:14).

Matthew 11:27

KNOWING GOD

Jesus went on to say that His Father has entrusted everything to Him. "Only the Father truly knows the Son. In the same way, no one knows the Father except the Son and those to whom the Son is willing to reveal Him," He said.

There is a big difference between knowing *about* someone and knowing someone. You may know about someone famous from what you've read about the person or seen on TV. Even if you got to meet him or her, you still wouldn't really *know* them.

We can read the Bible and know a lot about God, but without the Holy Spirit in us, we can never truly know God. But to those who come to Jesus to be saved, He gives the Holy Spirit. He makes it possible for them to know God in a personal way.

Jesus, who forgives our sin, is the only way to God; and the Holy Spirit whom God sends into our hearts shows us the truth about Jesus (John 15:26).

Heavenly Father, thank You that I can know You because Jesus, Your Son, is willing to forgive me. Amen.

"If you really knew Me, you would know My Father as well. From now on, you do know Him and have seen Him."

~ John 14:7, NLT

How do we know whether Jesus was also God while He was on earth? Because the Bible tell us so (Matt. 1:23, Isa. 9:6).

Matthew 11:28-30

REST FOR THE WEARY

"Come to Me, all you who are tired from carrying heavy loads, and I will give you rest," Jesus said. "Place My yoke over your shoulders. Let Me teach you, because I am humble and gentle at heart. Then you will find rest for your souls, because My yoke is easy and My burden is light" (Matt. 11:28-30).

Jesus invites those who have become worn-out from carrying a heavy load of guilt, worry, anger and sadness to come to Him. Are *you* carrying a load? It's not going to get any lighter; instead, it will make you weaker and weaker. There's no point in carrying this kind of load through life as it won't be of any use to you where you are going.

Jesus says, "Let Me take your load from you; come rest here with Me. Then, take up My easy yoke that fits you perfectly." Your energy will then be put to good use instead of being used to carry a dead weight.

The rest that Jesus invites us to enjoy comes from His forgiveness that wipes away our guilt; His unfailing help that takes away our anxiety; His peace that calms our troubled hearts, and His love that heals our sadness.

Lord, may my heart always rest in You. Amen.

Find rest, O my soul, in God alone; my hope comes from Him.

~ Psalm 62:5

A yoke is a wooden bar that is fastened over the necks of two animals and attached to a plow or cart that they need to pull.

Matthew 12:46-50; Luke 8:19-21

WHO IS MY FAMILY?

As Jesus was speaking to the crowd, someone came and told Him, "Your mother and Your brothers are outside wanting to speak to You."

Jesus replied, "Who is My mother, and who are My brothers?" Then He pointed to His disciples and said, "Look, these are My mother and brothers. For anyone who does the will of My Father in heaven is My brother and sister and mother!" (Matt. 12:46-50).

One may wonder why Jesus said what He did, and why it seems as though He didn't want to go hear what His family wanted. We get a clue in Mark 3:20-21, where His family tried to take Him out of the public eye because they thought He was out of His mind.

Perhaps they were embarrassed that Jesus was so different and stirred up anger among some people. Perhaps it was because He was the oldest brother in the family and should have been taking care of the needs at home. But Jesus wasn't going to be distracted from what His heavenly Father had sent Him to do.

Isn't it great that Jesus calls us His brothers and sisters?

He is the image of the invisible God, the firstborn over all creation.

~ Colossians 1:15, NLT

Jesus is in the family line of Abraham and King David (Matt. 1:17).

Mark 10:14

WHAT IS THE KINGDOM OF GOD?

Jesus spoke often about the kingdom of God, and at times He would use a parable to explain what the kingdom of God is like. But what is the kingdom of God, and if it is a place, where is it?

The kingdom of God is a spiritual kingdom which reaches every place in creation where God reigns. It certainly includes heaven where God sits on His throne. It includes the universe, which God created, and this beautiful earth we live on … but, not all of it. The devil, who is called the prince of this world, took what didn't belong to him. It's not that he just took it from God; it was given to him (Luke 4:5-6).

Although the devil was on earth when Adam and Eve were in the garden of Eden, the earth was perfect and belonged to the Lord. But when Adam and Eve sinned by disobeying God, they gave the devil permission to come and rule in their hearts and, by doing that, allowed him to bring death and destruction to the world through sin. After sin came, God could no longer have a close friendship with people.

As people spread all around the world, so did sin and the devil's reign (Gen. 6:5). But God sent Jesus to earth to take back what belongs to Him. Jesus came to redeem us (buy us back from the devil) with His blood. When we ask Jesus to forgive us and allow Him to reign in our hearts, we become part of His Kingdom on earth (Luke 17:20-21). That's how God's Kingdom is growing – like a tree getting bigger and bigger as people turn to Him (Luke 13:18-19).

For He [God] has rescued us from the dominion of darkness and brought us into the kingdom of the Son He loves.

~ Colossians 1:13

Matthew 13:1-4, 18-19; Luke 8:4-5

SEED ON THE PATH

One day Jesus left the house and went down to the Sea of Galilee. Soon, the crowd that gathered around Him was so large that He went to sit in a boat at the water's edge and taught the people from there.

He told many stories that taught a heavenly truth, such as this one: A farmer went to plant seed. As he scattered them across his field, some seeds fell on a footpath, and the birds came and ate them.

Jesus often spoke about seed; and in this story called a parable, the seeds are the truths He was teaching, or the Word of God (Mark 4:14). Our hearts are compared to the soil on which the seeds of truth fall.

If a person's heart is hard, like the soil in Jesus' story, the seed doesn't even start to grow. Instead those truths are quickly snatched away by other thoughts and activities, and some get trampled on by people's worldly opinions.

And soon, after hearing a challenging Word from God, the person decides to forget what he heard.

Lord, please help me never to let my heart get hard. Amen.

They made their hearts as hard as flint and would not listen to the law or to the words that the Lord Almighty had sent by His Spirit through the earlier prophets.

~ Zechariah 7:12

We make our own hearts hard when we hear God's Word and deliberately ignore what He says (Heb. 3:15).

Matthew 13:5-6, 20-21

SEED ON ROCKY PLACES

As the farmer in Jesus' story carried on sowing, some seed fell on rocky places. The plants sprouted quickly because the soil wasn't deep.

But when the sun came up, the plants soon wilted; and because they didn't have deep roots, they died.

The seed falling on rocky ground is like the person who hears the Word and gladly accepts it straight away. But since he doesn't have any roots, he lasts only a little while.

When problems and hardship come along because of the Word, he starts to lose his faith and goes back to living a sinful life.

This is the person who perhaps hears a preacher or friend tell him about Jesus. He knows that what he hears is true and that he needs to change his life, so he makes a decision to follow the Lord.

But when he realizes that his wants, goals, attitudes and habits need to come under the Lord's control, he just gives up and no longer wants to follow Jesus.

Faith and obedience make your roots grow deep.

Let your roots grow down into Him ... Then your faith will grow strong in the truth you were taught, and you will overflow with thankfulness.

~ Colossians 2:7

Beware of the devil's lies! Paul was astonished how quickly some believers had turned away from the Gospel that they had heard (Gal. 1:6).

Matthew 13:7, 22

SEED AMONG THORNS

Jesus' story of the farmer who sowed seed continued with some of the seed falling among thorns. As the tender plants grew up, the weeds twisted around them and strangled them.

The seeds that fall among thorn bushes are like those who hear God's Word; but before long, the message is overgrown by the worries of this life along with the trap of riches that chokes the Word in our hearts.

These seeds started growing well, but they were in the wrong place – among weeds, like the rich man who wanted to follow Jesus but didn't (Luke 18:18-23).

This kind of person wants to follow God; but the attractions of the world are so powerful that they crush the heart's longing to live for Him. It's not so much about the *amount* of money one has, but whether one's heart is willing to let go of earthly things and put God first. It is also about trusting Him instead of crowding out His Word with our busy thoughts and worries.

Lord, may my heart not grow in the wrong place – among worldly things that crowd You out. Amen.

In the paths of the wicked lie thorns and snares, but he who guards his soul stays far from them.

~ Proverbs 22:5, NLT

Thorny weeds are a curse which came as a result of Adam's sin (Gen. 3:18). The devil now uses "weeds of the heart" to try and choke our love for the Bible.

Matthew 13:8-9, 23

SEED ON GOOD SOIL

"There is a fourth kind of heart which is like good soil that is ready to hear the Word of God," Jesus said. When the seeds of truth fall on that soil, it grows and grows because the person believes and understands it.

As a person allows the Word to change him, and does what it says, there is a harvest of thirty, sixty, or even a hundred times as much as was planted.

Some give back more than others do. It could be because they are older, or because of the kind of work they do; or perhaps they've been willing for God to use them in a special way to reach others.

The important thing is that your heart must be like good soil that is soft with no weeds. God is the One who makes you grow (1 Cor. 3:7), and as you allow Him to use you by telling others about Him, the seed that was planted in *your* heart may take root in someone else's heart.

And so, with every life that is changed, the harvest for the Lord becomes greater.

Grow some seeds in a seed tray. You could also grow some bean seeds in a saucer with moist cotton wool.

When the ground soaks up the falling rain and bears a good crop for the farmer, it has God's blessing.

~ Hebrews 6:7, NLT

God's Word will always get results, it will always bring about that which the Lord has planned for it (Isa. 55:10-11).

Matthew 13:10-17

WHY PARABLES?

The disciples came to Jesus and asked, "Why do You use parables when You talk to the people?" Even the disciples didn't always understand what Jesus was saying (John 10:6). They probably thought that if Jesus would just say things plainly, everyone would understand and want to follow Him.

However, Jesus was only speaking to those who *really* wanted to know the truth; but He kept the meaning from those who chose not to believe in Him and those who only listened in order to find fault with His teaching.

Jesus called these treasures of truth *the secrets of the kingdom of heaven*. As we think about the parables, and figure out their meaning, we start to understand what the kingdom of God is like.

One could say that Jesus used parables as a code that makes no sense to those who don't believe, yet is perfectly clear to those who have the Holy Spirit. He guides our thinking and leads us to discover the secrets of God's Kingdom.

Lord, give me an understanding heart (Ps. 119:34). Amen.

This fulfilled what God had spoken through the prophet: "I will speak to you in parables. I will explain things hidden since the creation of the world."

~ Matthew 13:35

At first, many things weren't clear to the disciples; but just before Jesus went back to heaven, He let them understand God's plan (Luke 24:45).

Matthew 13:24-30, 36-43

THE WEEDS

Jesus told them another parable: "The Kingdom of Heaven is like a farmer who planted good seed in his field. But that night, his enemy came and planted weeds in the field. When the wheat came up, the weeds also appeared. So the owner's workers asked him, 'Do you want us to pull up the weeds?'"

"'No,' he replied, 'you'll uproot the wheat if you do. Let both grow together until the harvest. Then I will tell the harvesters to burn the weeds and bring the wheat into the barn.'"

This is what the parable means: The farmer who sowed the good seed is Jesus, and the seeds are His followers. The field is the world, and the enemy is the devil.

When the end comes, God will send His angels as harvesters. They will weed out of the Kingdom everything that causes sin and all who do evil. But the children of God will be brought into His Kingdom.

Why doesn't God take all believers to heaven now? We don't have all the answers now, but one day we will know.

Those who live only to satisfy their own sinful nature will harvest decay and death … But those who live to please the Spirit will harvest everlasting life from the Spirit.

~ Galatians 6:8

On judgment day, the Lord will separate those who love Him from those who don't love Him (Matt. 25:32).

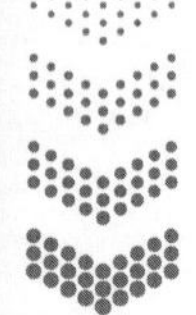

Mark 4:26-29

THE GROWING SEED

"The Kingdom of God is like a man who scatters seed on the ground," Jesus said. "All day, and even at night while the man is sleeping, the seeds sprout and start to grow. First a leaf blade pushes through; then the heads are formed, and finally the grain ripens, even though the man has no idea how that happens."

Have you ever wondered how a seed that's been lying in a packet for months can suddenly come alive when it is planted and watered? If you've planted seeds, you've probably gone out every day to see if they've come up. Then, after a few days, when you've almost forgotten about them, there they are!

God's Kingdom is like that. When we tell others about Jesus, perhaps nothing seems to happen. Like the seed under the soil, we cannot see that God is working in the hearts of our friends. But after a while, one friend and then another starts to change. That's the mystery of how the Kingdom of God grows.

REMEMBER Seeds need time and patience to grow (not force).

God has now revealed to us His mysterious plan regarding Christ – which is to fulfill His own good pleasure.

~ Ephesians 1:9, NLT

When a seed starts to germinate, no matter which way it is positioned, the roots will always go down and the stem will always go up.

Luke 13:6-9

THE FRUITLESS FIG TREE

Jesus told another parable: "A man planted a fig tree in his garden. He came again and again to see if there was any fruit on it, but he was always disappointed. After three years, he said to his gardener, 'I've waited and waited, and there hasn't been a single fig! Cut the tree down. It's just taking up space in the garden.'"

"The gardener answered, 'Sir, give it one more chance. Leave it another year and I'll dig around it and give it plenty of fertilizer. If we get figs next year, great! If not, then we can cut it down.'"

You may think that this is a strange parable; however, Jesus was helping us to see how disappointed God is when He looks at His garden (the world) and sees no fruit on the tree He planted. He is looking for the fruit that comes from people being saved and doing right (Phil. 1:11).

Instead of cutting down the tree that bears no fruit, the Lord is giving people more time to turn to Him and bear the fruit of goodness.

Thank You, Lord, that You are patient and merciful with me. Amen.

The Lord isn't really being slow about His promise [to come back for us], as some people think. No, He is being patient for your sake. He does not want anyone to be destroyed, but wants everyone to repent.

~ 2 Peter 3:9, NLT

Our lips bear fruit for God as we offer Him our praises (Heb. 13:15).

Matthew 13:31-32

THE MUSTARD SEED

"The kingdom of heaven is like a mustard seed," Jesus said. "A man planted a small mustard seed in his field. Though it is one of the smallest seeds, when it grows, it becomes a tree that is large enough for birds to nest in its branches."

This parable shows that the beginnings of the Gospel were small – like a delicate seedling, when there was just a small team of disciples who had no money, no power, and still needed to learn a lot.

But through their faithfulness, the message of Jesus has spread all over the world.

Have you seen a tree that is hundreds of years old? There are trees that have a stem so thick that it would fill your bedroom. Imagine how big the Gospel tree has become – like a tree that is 2, 000 years old. Wow!

Just as a huge tree is a blessing to those who rest in its shade, and a shelter for animals, God's tree of faithful followers is a blessing to the world.

If you are a child of God, you are part of that tree which is growing bigger every day.

Do not despise these small beginnings, for the LORD rejoices to see the work begin.

~ Zechariah 4:10, NLT

Mustard can be made by grinding mustard seeds and adding a bit of salt and vinegar. One can also add some honey for flavor.

Matthew 13:33-35

THE WOMAN'S YEAST

Jesus told another story with a truth to the large crowd that had gathered at the lake. "The kingdom of heaven is like a little bit of yeast that a woman took and mixed into a large amount of flour until it worked all through the dough."

We learn from this parable that the kingdom of heaven is growing quietly, steadily, and is spreading to every place on earth. We are like the yeast that the woman mixed into the dough. She made sure that there was some yeast in every part of it.

The yeast needs to be *in* the flour for it to work. Yeast on its own is just yeast but it doesn't grow. The Gospel on its own is, and will always be, the Gospel (the Good News of Jesus), but without people it cannot grow.

Just as the yeast changes the dough, the Gospel changes people; and as those changed people carry the Gospel in their hearts and share it, the kingdom of heaven spreads and grows.

1. In a cup, mix 2 tablespoons flour; 1 teaspoon sugar and ½ cup water. Stir until mixture is smooth. (Note that nothing much happens.)
2. Now add 10g instant dry yeast and stir. Cover mixture with a cloth for 1 hour. (Watch how the yeast makes it bubble and grow.)

The word of God continued to spread and flourish.

~ Acts 12:24

Yeast consists of living cells that feed on sugars and turn them into a gas, making dough rise. Then when the bread is baked, it is light and fluffy.

Matthew 13:44

THE HIDDEN TREASURE

Jesus said, "The kingdom of heaven is like a treasure that a man found hidden in a field. He was so excited that he hid the treasure again. Then he went off and joyfully sold everything he owned. When the man had enough money, he went back and bought the field with the treasure."

You may have heard of the word *investment*. That's when someone puts money, time or effort into something in the hope of getting out more than was put in. To this man, the treasure was a good investment. But first, he had to buy the field in order to own the treasure; and the field cost him everything he had. Yet, once he had bought the field, he owned a treasure worth much more than everything he had sold.

What would you give to be the child of a king? What would you give to live forever? What would you give to live in a place of unimaginable beauty one day? You can have all this, and it won't cost you any money. God will give you all these things and more as a free gift when you ask Him to save you and make you His child (Eph. 2:8).

Lord, You are worth more than anything to me! I love You. Amen.

We have this treasure in jars of clay to show that this all-surpassing power is from God and not from us.

~ 2 Corinthians 4:7

Esau made a bad investment. He sold something that would have lasted a lifetime for something that lasted only a few minutes (Gen. 25:29-34).

Matthew 13:45

THE PARABLE OF THE PEARL

Jesus told another parable, similar to the one about the treasure, and said, "The kingdom of heaven is like a merchant on the lookout for choice pearls. Then, one day, he discovered a pearl of great value and sold everything he owned to buy it."

This was the deal of a lifetime for the businessman. Unlike the man who happened to find the treasure in the field, this man went out looking for a rare pearl. That took effort. Once he made his discovery, everything else was worthless compared to it.

What makes a pearl so valuable? Perhaps it is because a pearl is beautiful, lasting and rare. Ordinary stones are lasting too, but they're not as beautiful or rare.

Like the many stones that lie around, people say a lot of things and give a lot of advice. But *only* Jesus speaks words that give us precious, everlasting life. As Peter rightly said, "Lord, to whom shall we go? You have the words of eternal life" (John 6:68).

Lord, thank You that You helped me find the precious Pearl of the Kingdom. Amen.

"What do you benefit if you gain the whole world but lose your own soul? Is anything worth more than your soul?"

~ Matthew 16:26, NLT

Yes, the Bible does talk about "pearly gates." In fact, there are twelve gates, each one made of a single pearl (Rev. 21:21).

Psalm 37:4

TREASURE SEEKER

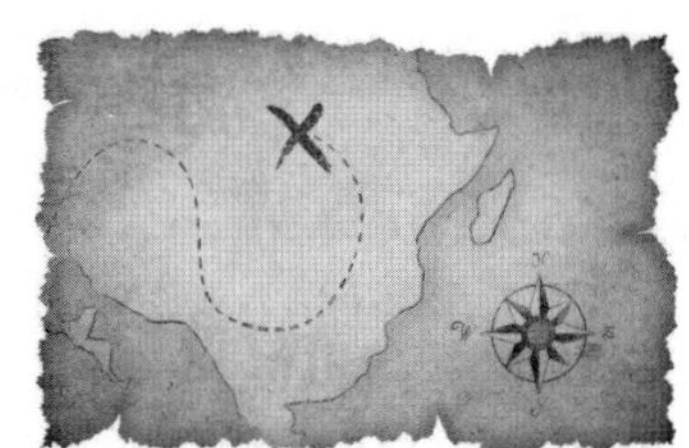

Have you ever dreamed of finding treasure? Just the thought of a buried treasure chest somewhere makes one want to start digging. But without clues, or a map, where does one start?

The good news is that there is a map that points to priceless treasure; and no one can take your treasure away, even if they get there before you.

But before you set off, be aware that you could be distracted by earthly treasures, which look like the real thing but don't last. There will also be signs along the road of life that point to comfort and luxury, so keep using the Bible as your only guide. You will need to give up or share things along the way; like your time, your energy, or something you own.

By helping someone, telling a friend about Jesus, or giving some of your money to grow God's Kingdom, you are storing precious treasure in heaven.

But storing heavenly treasure is not just about *doing* things; it's about our *attitude* when we do things. For example:

- If we do good only to get praise from others, no treasure gets stored (Matt. 6:2).
- If we do good because we love others and we want to please God, we will receive what He has prepared for us (Matt. 6:3-4; Matt. 25:34-36).

So, look for every opportunity to do good (Gal. 6:10).

Wherever your treasure is, there the desires of your heart will also be.

~ Matthew 6:21, NLT

Matthew 13:47-50

DRAWING IN THE NET

Jesus told the people parables because He wanted them to know what God's unseen Kingdom is like. He told another parable, saying, "The kingdom of heaven is like a fishing net that was thrown into the lake. When the net was full of fish, the fishermen pulled it onto the shore and sorted the good fish from the bad ones. That's the way it will be at the end of the world."

The angels will separate the evil people from those who follow the Lord; and the evil people will be judged for their sin.

If you've been to an aquarium, you will know how many different types of fish there are. Similarly, every person in the world is special and different. But Jesus doesn't judge people on what they look like, or who they are.

At the end, when the net is pulled up and judgment time comes, He will look at people's hearts to see whether they are forgiven and made new, or whether their hearts are sinful and rebellious.

The goodness of Jesus in us makes us good.

For we must all stand before Christ to be judged. We will each receive whatever we deserve for the good or evil we have done in this earthly body.

~ 2 Corinthians 5:10

If you have asked Jesus to forgive you, you need not fear God's judgment. Jesus has already taken the punishment for your sin on Him (Rom. 8:1).

Matthew 13:54-58; Mark 6:1-6

JESUS IS REJECTED

When Jesus had finished telling parables to the people, He left the Sea of Galilee and went back to His hometown Nazareth.

He began teaching in the synagogue. The people there were amazed and asked, "Where does He get this wisdom and the power to do miracles? Isn't this the carpenter's son? Isn't His mother's name Mary, and don't His brothers and sisters live here in our town? Where did He learn all these things?"

When the people of Nazareth realized that this was Jesus who had grown up among them as part of an ordinary family, they became upset and wanted nothing to do with Him. And so, because of their unbelief, Jesus could only do a few miracles there.

The people saw only the human side of Jesus. They had seen Him as a boy, a teenager, and a young adult. He wasn't even a Pharisee or a teacher of the law.

To them He was just the carpenter's son. But we know that Jesus is the *Son of God* and that He is the only One who can give us eternal life.

REMEMBER Jesus was completely human and completely God.

No one who denies the Son has the Father; whoever acknowledges the Son has the Father also.

~ 1 John 2:23

James, the brother of Jesus, became an Apostle (Gal. 1:19) and probably wrote the Bible book called James.

Mark 6:14-20; Matthew 14:1-5

NEWS OF JESUS GETS TO HEROD

Herod, ruler of Galilee, heard news reports about Jesus, and who people thought He was. So he said, "This is John, the man I killed, who has come back to life." (Herod was the one who gave orders to have John arrested and put in prison, and later end his life, because John had dared to speak against his sinful behavior.)

John wasn't the first or only one to be put to death. Many prophets had died, and later on, many Christians would die as martyrs. A martyr is someone who suffers greatly or is killed for his faith and for witnessing. Jesus said that if people persecuted Him, they would persecute His disciples too (John 15:20), and we know that Jesus was crucified.

Remember, an easy life of blessing can be a greater enemy than the people who make life hard for us. When life is easy all the time, our spiritual muscles don't grow. But when life is tough because we are good and believe in Jesus, our character grows strong (Romans 5:3-4).

Lord, help me to be bold for You and to do what is right. Amen.

Do not be afraid of those who kill the body but cannot kill the soul.

~ Matthew 10:28

John was the last to die for his faith under the law covenant. Stephen was the first martyr of the New Testament - after Jesus' death (Acts 7:54-60).

Matthew 14:13-16; Luke 9:12-13

HE PROVIDES IN OUR NEEDS

When Jesus heard what had happened to John, He left in a boat and went to a place where He could be alone. But the crowds from the surrounding towns heard where He was going and followed Him on foot along the shore.

When Jesus landed and stepped ashore, He saw a large crowd and had compassion on them. As the sun started setting, the disciples came to Him and said, "No one lives around here, and it's already late. Send the crowds away to the villages to buy food for themselves."

But Jesus said, "They don't need to go away. You feed them!"

When we are faced with a problem, we tend to think practically and try to find a solution that makes the most sense. We focus on trying to make the problem go away. When Jesus faced a problem, He saw an opportunity to glorify His Father.

Jesus' thinking wasn't held back by what is possible; He knew that His Father specializes in the impossible. We have the same Father who is willing to answer our prayers for help!

We please God by putting our complete trust in Him.

When He saw the crowds, He had compassion on them, because they were harassed and helpless, like sheep without a shepherd.

~ Matthew 9:36

Instead of sending people away, Jesus invites everyone in the world to come to Him and receive eternal life (Rev. 22:17).

John 6:8-15; Matthew 14:17-21

JESUS FEEDS 5,000

Andrew, one of the disciples, said to Jesus, "Here is a young boy with five small loaves of bread and two fish. But what good is that for this huge crowd?"

"Tell everyone to sit down," Jesus said. Then He took the loaves and fish, and gave thanks to God. He broke up the loaves and passed the bread to the disciples who handed it to the people. He carried on doing this with the bread and the fish until everyone had eaten as much as they wanted.

The boy gave all his food to Jesus not expecting to get any of it back. He gave all he had, not knowing that he'd bless over five thousand people.

Even though Jesus was the One who supplied the food, He gave thanks to His Father for it. Jesus showed that it is right and good to thank the Lord for every meal He provides (even when someone else buys and prepares the food we eat).

Thank You, Lord, for giving us food every day. Amen.

Give, and you will receive. Your gift will return to you in full – pressed down, shaken together to make room for more, running over, and poured into your lap.

~ Luke 6:38

The Lord fed more than 603,550 people in the desert for forty years (Num. 1:45-46). So a meal for 5,000 wasn't a problem for Him!

Matthew 14:22-27; John 6:16-20

JESUS WALKS ON WATER

Straight after Jesus had fed the crowd, He told the disciples to get back into the boat and go ahead of Him. After sending the people home, He went up a mountain to be alone to pray.

Meanwhile a strong wind was blowing across the lake, and the disciples in the boat were being thrown around by the waves. In the early hours of the morning, while it was still dark, Jesus came walking toward them on the water. The disciples were terrified because they thought they were seeing a ghost.

But Jesus said to them, "Take courage! It is I. Don't be afraid." What wonderful words of hope Jesus spoke to the fearful disciples. They had been rowing half the night, fearing that their boat would sink … and then they thought they were seeing a ghost!

When life gets stormy and it feels like you're about to get swamped by waves of trouble, you fear the worst. You struggle on your own until you're exhausted; and just when you think you can't carry on, things get worse. Just stop! Put down the oars of your boat and pray. Jesus is coming to help you. Do not fear!

Lord, You know my struggles and fears. Help me, Jesus! Amen.

He alone stretches out the heavens and treads on the waves of the sea.

~ Job 9:8

Jesus walking on water went against the laws of nature. The prophet Elisha had faith to make a metal axhead float on water (2 Kings 6:5-7).

JUNE

1 WAY
FOLLOW IT

1 TRUTH
BELIEVE IT

1 LIFE
LIVE IT

Matthew 14:27-32

SAVE ME!

The disciples were crossing the Sea of Galilee when a fierce storm came up. Jesus came walking towards them on the water, and while He was still some distance from the boat, He called to them, "Don't be afraid. It is I."

"Lord, if it is You," Peter replied, "tell me to come to You on the water."

"Yes, come," Jesus said. So Peter climbed out of the boat and walked on the water toward Jesus.

But when Peter saw the stormy sea, he was terrified and began to sink. "Save me, Lord!" he shouted.

Jesus reached out and grabbed Peter. "You have so little faith," Jesus said. "Why did you doubt Me?" When they climbed back into the boat, the wind stopped.

Peter was the only disciple who had enough courage to ask if he could go to Jesus on the water. But he looked at the circumstances around him and probably thought, *What am I doing out here?* Doubt often comes once we've made a decision to step out in faith and obey God. But remember, Jesus will be there for you!

Jesus, Savior, You're the One who rescues me! Amen.

He reached down from on high and took hold of me; He drew me out of deep waters.

~ Psalm 18:16

Our salvation is not dependent on our weak faith, but on God's power and grace (Eph. 2:8).

John 6:21; Matthew 14:32-36

THE BOAT TRIP

When Jesus and Peter climbed into the boat, the wind died down, and the disciples worshiped Jesus, saying, "Truly, You are the Son of God."

The boat reached the shore where they'd been heading – a place called Gennesaret. The word quickly spread that Jesus was there, and the people brought the sick to be healed.

The disciples had spent the previous day handing out food to 5,000 people. At the end of a hard day's work, they got into their boat and headed across the lake. But, there was no sleep for them as that fierce storm had come up and lasted for hours.

What a relief it must have been when Jesus came and calmed the storm! But that meant there was no wind, and instead of using their sails, they'd now have to row all the way to the other side of the lake. So Jesus helped them along, and they landed at the exact place where Jesus wanted them to be.

How that happened, no one knows, except to say that Jesus did a second miracle that night.

When it's stormy, Jesus will get you to the other side.

Lord, there is no one like You! For You are great, and Your name is full of power.

~ Jeremiah 10:6

It doesn't matter how impossible the situation might seem, God is always in control.

Matthew 15:1-9

DIRTY HANDS

Some Pharisees and teachers of the law, who had come from Jerusalem, asked Jesus, "Why do Your disciples disobey our age-old tradition? They don't wash their hands before they eat."

Jesus replied, "And why do you break God's commandments for the sake of your tradition? Isaiah was right about you when he said, 'Their worship of Me is pointless, because their teachings are rules made by humans'" (Isa. 29:13).

There's nothing wrong with washing our hands before we eat. We are just washing off germs that could get onto our food and make us sick.

But the Pharisees were making a big deal of their rules regarding the body; rules that were meant to make one a better person. However, God wants *spiritually* clean hands, which means that when we are forgiven, our hearts are pure, and so whatever we do, we do for Him with clean hands, lifting them up to Him in praise.

Lord, I lift my hands to You in prayer and praise. Amen.

He who has clean hands and a pure heart … will receive blessing from the Lord.

~ Psalm 24:4-5

It's not what we touch that makes our hearts unclean; it's who we are. Jesus touched a man with leprosy (Luke 5:13), yet He never sinned (Heb. 4:15).

Mark 7:14-23; Matthew 15:10-20

CLEAN OR UNCLEAN

Jesus told the Pharisees that keeping their petty rules and traditions was more important to them than having a clean heart before God.

Then He turned to the people who were listening, and said, "Nothing that goes *into* a person from the outside can make him unclean. It's what comes *out* of a person that makes him unclean."

Jesus explained that it doesn't matter [to God] what we eat, because food itself cannot make our hearts unclean (sinful). What does make a person's heart unclean is the evil that comes from the heart – the bad thoughts and attitudes inside a person.

The devil doesn't mind people keeping some rules to ease their conscience. He fools them into thinking that they are pretty good – not like criminals who need God's forgiveness. Meanwhile, he gets those same people to think of all kinds of evil that no one knows about. But God looks at our hearts where our thoughts are formed, not at what we eat.

When bad thoughts come into your mind, pray.

Search me, O God, and know my heart; test me and know my anxious thoughts. Point out anything in me that offends You, and lead me along the path of everlasting life.

~ Psalm 139:23-24, NLT

TRUTH

Our body is the temple of the Holy Spirit. God lives in us through His Spirit (1 Cor. 6:19). That's why it is important to keep our hearts pure.

Matthew 15:21-28; Mark 7:24-30

THE WOMAN'S FAITH

Jesus left Galilee and went north to the area of Tyre and Sidon. A Canaanite woman who lived there came to Him, pleading, "Have mercy on me, O Lord, Son of David! For my daughter has an evil spirit that makes her suffer terribly."

But Jesus gave her no reply. When the woman kept begging Jesus to help her, He said to the woman, "I was sent only to God's lost sheep – the people of Israel."

But she knelt down and pleaded, "Lord, help me!"

"Dear woman," Jesus said to her, "you have great faith. What you have asked for will be done." So the woman went home and found her daughter healed.

It is hard for us to imagine that Jesus wouldn't want to help someone. But Jesus didn't want to be distracted from His mission to reach the Jews first (Rom. 15:8). They were lost sheep that needed to be brought back. When Jesus left earth, the Jews who became followers of Jesus then spread the Gospel to the Gentiles – the rest of the world (Eph. 3:6-8).

God loved us while we were sinful (Rom. 5:8).

He sent out His word and healed them, snatching them from the door of death.

~ Psalm 107:20

The Good News is for everyone (Matt. 24:14).

Mark 7:31-37

A MAN HEARS AGAIN

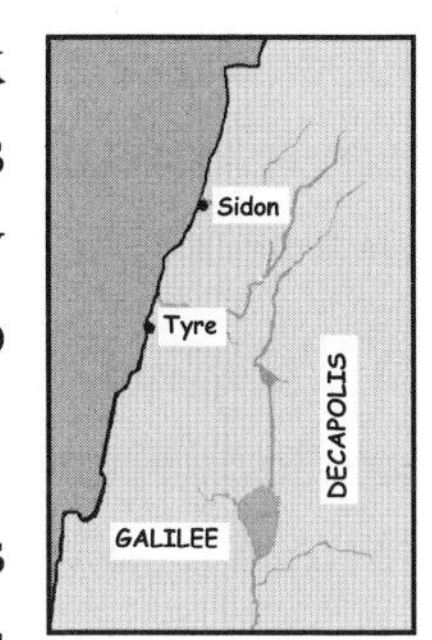

Jesus left Tyre and went up to Sidon before going back to the Sea of Galilee and the region of the Decapolis (the Ten Towns). There, a deaf man who could hardly talk was brought to Him. The people begged Jesus to lay His hands on the man to heal him.

So Jesus took the man away to one side. He put His fingers in the man's ears and also touched the man's tongue. Jesus said, "Be opened!" Immediately, the man could hear and was able to speak again.

Jesus told the crowd not to tell anyone, but they kept talking about Him, and so the news of what Jesus had done spread. They were amazed and said, "Everything He does is wonderful. He even makes the deaf hear and the mute speak!"

This was Jesus' last visit to the Decapolis region. He never went back. Some had heard Jesus speak, but others missed out on what Jesus had to offer because they didn't come to Him while He was there. The Lord is saying, *now* is the time to come to Him (2 Cor. 6:2).

The miracles of Jesus show His love and power.

Seek the LORD while you can find Him. Call on Him now while He is near.

~ Isaiah 55:6

Paul told King Agrippa about Jesus, but Agrippa delayed making a decision and possibly missed his last opportunity to be saved (Acts 26:28).

Matthew 8:17

DOES THE LORD STILL HEAL?

Does God still heal people today? The short answer is yes! God's power displayed through Jesus on earth has not changed, and will never change!

After Jesus left earth, the book of Acts tells of many who were healed (Acts 5:12-16). There are also verses in the New Testament letters that encourage us to pray for healing (James 5:14-16).

Perhaps you may be wondering why we don't see as many people miraculously healed nowadays.

Firstly, for the same reason that Jesus often told those He had healed not to tell anyone about it; God doesn't want people to come to Him only for the healing of their bodies. His main purpose for us is that we come to Him to be saved so that we may have eternal life, and have new, perfect bodies in heaven one day.

Secondly, there are many doctors, hospitals, and medicines that help people become well again, and so the need for miraculous healing isn't as great as it was in Bible times.

However, there are situations where there is no cure, or where a person is paralyzed, or deaf, or blind. That's when people can pray by faith and expect a miracle. To some, the Lord has even given a *gift of healing* (1 Cor. 12:9).

When we are feeling sick, the Lord doesn't mind if we ask Him to make us well again. He may choose to help us get better with medicines, or simply heal our sickness, but He will always answer our prayer in the best way.

Lord my God, I called to You for help, and You healed me.

~ Psalm 30:2

Matthew 15:32-38; Mark 8:1-10

FOOD FOR 4,000

Around that time, another large crowd had gathered around Jesus at the Sea of Galilee. So Jesus said to His disciples, "I feel sorry for these people. They've been here with Me for three days and have nothing left to eat. If I send them home hungry, they will feel weak and perhaps faint along the way."

His disciples said, "Where would we get enough food in this deserted place to feed the crowd?" (They only had seven loaves and a few small fish.)

So Jesus took the loaves and the fish, thanked God for them, and broke them into pieces. He gave them to the disciples, who passed the food to the crowd. They all ate as much as they wanted, and afterward, the disciples picked up seven large baskets of leftover food. There were over 4,000 people there.

Jesus could have done a miracle without the disciples. But He always takes what we give Him, and then chooses us to be part of His blessing to others – and perhaps, part of a miracle.

FIND OUT How many leftover baskets were there? ___

He gives strength to the weary and increases the power of the weak.

~ Isaiah 40:29

Elijah told a starving widow to share her last meal with him. She did so in faith, and her flour and oil lasted until the end of the drought (1 Kings 17:8-16).

Matthew 15:39, 16:1-4; Mark 8:11-13

THE PHARISEES WANT A SIGN

After Jesus had fed the people He sent them home. Then He crossed over to the region of Magadan in a boat. The Pharisees and Sadducees came to test Jesus, asking Him to show them a sign from heaven (to prove His authority for saying the things He did).

Jesus replied, "You are able to forecast the weather by looking at the sky, yet you don't know what's happening around you! Only an evil and unfaithful generation would demand a miraculous sign, but the only sign I will give you is the sign of the prophet Jonah."

The Pharisees, who had been following Jesus around, had seen many miracles. They had become used to people being healed and still wanted Jesus to give them a sign to prove that God had sent Him.

Instead of believing easily, like the people of Nineveh who were sorry for their sins when Jonah preached to them, the Pharisees had hardened their hearts and would not believe in God's own Son. Today, many people who don't believe want proof that God is real. But God wants us to simply believe that He exists; and when we do, He rewards our faith (Heb. 11:6).

Some people don't believe that there is a God even though they see miracles in nature every day.

You are the God who performs miracles; You display Your power among the peoples.

~ Psalm 77:14

Although creation does not use words, it speaks across the universe telling us that there is a Creator - the God we serve (Ps. 19:1-4).

Mark 8:22-26

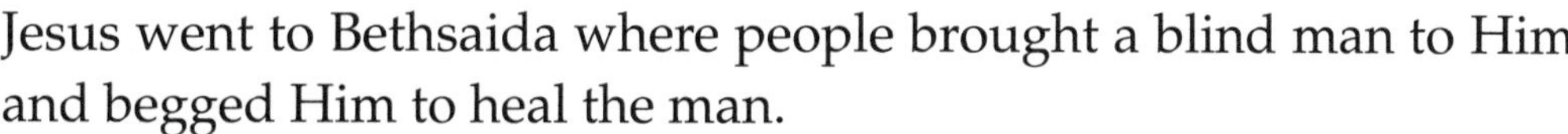

ONE DAY WE WILL SEE GOD

Jesus went to Bethsaida where people brought a blind man to Him and begged Him to heal the man.

Jesus spat on the man's eyes, put His hands on him and asked, "Can you see anything?"

The man looked around. "Yes," he said, "I see people, but I can't see them clearly. They look like trees walking around."

Then Jesus placed His hands on the man's eyes again, and the man could see everything clearly, even at a distance.

Have you noticed the different ways that Jesus healed people? This time, He asked the man if he could see anything, as though He knew that the healing wasn't complete. At first, it was dark. Then, it was dim and fuzzy. Finally, the man could see perfectly.

That's how we start seeing (understanding) things about Jesus. Before we knew Jesus we were in the dark; now we can see things, but not clearly. Yet one day we will see God face to face and know all things.

REMEMBER As we read the Bible we start seeing more clearly.

Now we see but a poor reflection as in a mirror; then we shall see face to face. Now I know in part; then I shall know fully, even as I am fully known.

~ 1 Corinthians 13:12

No one can see God and live, yet after we die, we will have new bodies, and with those bodies we will see God (Exod. 33:20).

Matthew 16:13-16; Mark 8:27-30

WHO IS JESUS?

From Bethsaida, Jesus and the disciples went to the villages around Caesarea Philippi. Then Jesus asked His disciples, "Who do people say the Son of Man is?"

The disciples answered, "Some say that You are John the Baptist, others say Elijah, still others say Jeremiah or one of the prophets."

Then He asked them, "But who do you say I am?"

Simon Peter answered, "You are the Messiah, the Son of the living God."

Jesus often called Himself the *Son of Man*, even though He was and is the *Son of God*. He was born on earth as a human, and so He used this name, which means *human being*.

Most people had realized that Jesus was more than an ordinary person because of the miracles He did. They thought that perhaps He was like one of the great prophets that lived in Old Testament times. But Peter knew in His heart that Jesus is the Son of God, not because of all the miracles he saw, but because God Himself had helped Peter to believe this.

Lord, You are Jesus Christ, the Son of the living God! Amen.

For in Christ lives all the fullness of God in a human body.
~ Colossians 2:9

The name *Messiah* is a Hebrew term meaning "anointed one" or "chosen one." The same word in English is *Christ* (John 1:41).

Matthew 16:17-18

BUILDING THE CHURCH

Jesus said to Peter, "I say to you that you are Peter, and upon this rock [truth] I will build My church, and all the powers of hell will not overpower it."

Jesus had changed Simon's name to Peter (which means *rock)*, when they first met (John 1:40-42). When Jesus said, "On this rock I will build My church," what was He saying?

Firstly, Jesus was probably talking about what Peter had just said, "You are the Son of God, the chosen One."

Jesus is building His church on this important truth! Jesus is the Rock on which we can stand and be sure that we are saved and safe (Acts 4:11-12).

Secondly, the church is not a building, but is made up of all those who are saved. Peter took a lead role when the church started (Acts 2:14, 41) and so, in a way, he became part of the foundation.

Jesus said that all the powers of hell put together could not stand against His church, or conquer it!

Get a stone to remind you of 1 Peter 2:5 that reads: "You are living stones that God is building into His spiritual temple."

For who is God besides the Lord? And who is the Rock except our God?

~ Psalm 18:31

Every believer is a brick in the living church (Eph. 2:19-22).

Matthew 16:19-20

THE KEYS OF THE KINGDOM

Jesus said to Peter, "I will give you the keys of the kingdom of heaven. Whatever you bind on earth will be bound in heaven, and whatever you loose on earth will be loosed in heaven."

What keys was Jesus talking about? The key is the Gospel message, which opens the way to heaven and eternal life. Peter was entrusted with two keys: the first was for the Jews to enter the kingdom of heaven, and the second, for all other people to be brought into God's kingdom (Acts 10:34-48).

The part where Jesus talks about binding means that when someone in the church does something wrong that everyone can see, and if he carries on doing it, his evil deeds must be bound by the church, and he will be judged in heaven (Matt. 18:15-18).

But if someone in the church has sinned publicly and asks to be forgiven, he will be loosed (untied) from his guilt. God will forgive him, and the church is there to help him (Gal. 6:1).

Thank You, Lord, that the Gospel is the key that opens hearts. Amen.

This mystery is the Good News that people who are not Jewish have the same inheritance as Jewish people do. They belong to the same body and share the same promise that God made in Christ Jesus.

~ Ephesians 3:6

Jesus has the keys of death and Hades (hell). He gives eternal life to those who love Him, and locks up the evil that belongs in hell (Rev. 1:18).

Matthew 16:21-23

JESUS TELLS OF HIS MISSION

From that time on, Jesus started telling the disciples about His mission – the main purpose for Him coming to earth.

He told them that He would go to Jerusalem, where He would suffer many terrible things. He would even be killed, but on the third day He would be raised from the dead.

But Peter took Jesus aside and said, "Never, Lord! This shall never happen to You!"

Jesus turned and said to Peter, "Get out of My way, Satan! You are a dangerous trap to Me. You aren't thinking the way God thinks, but the way humans think."

The disciples, and most of Jesus' followers, thought that Jesus was on earth to do good, fight evil, and perhaps even get rid of the Romans, who had taken over their land.

So when Jesus talked about dying, just when things were going so well, Peter wanted to stop Jesus from talking that way. But now we know that because Jesus *did* die for us, we can have eternal life!

Jesus could have taken the easy way out and let His followers make Him their earthly king.

"For I have come down from heaven to do the will of God who sent Me, not to do My own will."

~ John 6:38, NLT

From the beginning, Jesus never allowed Himself to get distracted from doing what His Father had sent Him to do (John 4:34).

Matthew 17:1-9; Luke 9:28-36

JESUS SHINES!

One day, Jesus took Peter, James and John, and led them up a mountain where they could be alone. Suddenly, Jesus' face became as bright as the sun and His clothes as white as light. Just then, Moses and Elijah appeared and began talking with Jesus.

Peter said to Jesus, "Lord, it is good that we're here. If you want, I will put up three tents here – one for You, one for Moses, and one for Elijah."

While He was still speaking, a bright cloud covered them, and a voice from the cloud said, "This is My dearly loved Son, who brings Me great joy. Listen to Him."

The disciples were terrified and fell face down on the ground. But Jesus came and touched them, saying, "Get up, and don't be afraid!"

For a moment, it seemed to the disciples as though they were in heaven. God allowed them to see the glory of His Son Jesus, and even spoke to them. This was like heaven on earth; terrifying, yet so wonderful that Peter wanted to make the moment last.

Think about how wonderful heaven is going to be!

For God, who said, "Let there be light in the darkness," has made this light shine in our hearts so we could know the glory of God that is seen in the face of Jesus Christ.

~ 2 Corinthians 4:6, NLT

After Moses had met with God, his face shone so brightly that he had to cover it (Exod. 34:29-35).

CAN WE SEE GOD?

Some people in the Bible spoke to God and were close to Him, but no one, except Jacob, has ever seen God the Father. And even Jacob was surprised that he had survived it, saying, "I have seen God face to face, yet my life has been spared" (Gen. 32:30).

This is what the Bible says:

- God said, "You cannot see My face, for no one may see Me and live" (Exod. 33:20).
- Jesus said, "No one has ever seen God. But the unique One, who is Himself God, is near to the Father's heart. He has revealed God to us (John 1:18).
- "He [God] lives in light so brilliant that no human can approach Him. No human eye has ever seen Him, nor ever will" (1 Tim. 6:16).

People like Moses, Elijah, Isaiah, and John may have seen the brightness of God's glory, or perhaps a vision of God, but not God Himself.

Our eyes are made to see the physical world around us, not the spiritual world. God is Spirit (John 4:24), that's why we cannot see Him. We cannot see that which is invisible, even though it is very real.

If you want to know what God is like, look at Jesus (John 14:9). From reading the Bible, we know what Jesus is like, and that's how we know what the Father is like.

Let us go right into the presence of God with sincere hearts fully trusting Him. For our guilty consciences have been sprinkled with Christ's blood to make us clean.

~ Hebrews 10:22, NLT

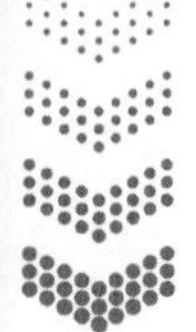

Matthew 17:14-20; Luke 9:37-43

NOT ENOUGH FAITH

As Jesus and three of His disciples came down the mountain, they met a man who knelt before Jesus and said, "Lord, have mercy on my son. He is suffering terribly. I brought him to Your disciples, but they couldn't heal him."

"Bring the boy here to Me," Jesus said. Then He ordered the demon to come out of the boy, and from that moment the boy was well.

Afterward the disciples asked Jesus privately, "Why couldn't we drive that demon out?"

"You don't have enough faith," Jesus replied.

Sometimes we simply expect things to happen because it's the way certain things are. We switch on a light and expect the room to light up. But unlike the physical world, we cannot simply expect things to happen the way we want in the spiritual world. When we pray, we must believe that God hears our prayer, and that He is able to do what we ask.

Lord, I believe! Please help my lack of faith (Mark 9:24). Amen.

Without faith it is impossible to please God, because anyone who comes to Him must believe that He exists and that He rewards those who earnestly seek Him.

~ Hebrews 11:6

By faith, Joshua prayed for the sun to stand still and the sun stopped in the middle of the sky for about a day (Josh. 10:12-13).

Matthew 17:24-27

A COIN IN THE FISH'S MOUTH

When Jesus and the disciples arrived in Capernaum, the collectors of the temple tax came to Peter and asked, "Doesn't your Teacher pay the temple tax?"

"Yes, He does," Peter replied.

Then Peter went into the house, and Jesus asked Him, "What do you think? From whom do kings collect taxes? From their children or from others?"

"They collect tax from others," Peter replied.

"Then the children don't need to pay!" Jesus said. "However, we don't want to offend them, so go down to the lake and throw in a line. Open the mouth of the first fish you catch, and you will find a large silver coin. Take it and pay the tax for both of us."

Temple taxes went towards the upkeep of the temple, but Jesus, being *God's Son*, shouldn't have had to pay for *God's house*. Jesus was making the point that He is the Son of God! Yet for us, it is right and good to bring our offerings to God's house.

When we give money to the church, we are not paying the church, we are bringing a gift of love to God.

If you are eager to give, God will accept your gift on the basis of what you have to give, not on what you don't have.

~ 2 Corinthians 8:12

Temple tax was paid once a year and was, more or less, what a working man would earn in two days.

Mark 9:33-37; Luke 9:46-48

WHO IS THE GREATEST?

Jesus and the disciples were still in Capernaum and had come back to the house where they were staying. Jesus turned to them and asked, "What were you arguing about on the road?"

But they didn't answer because they had been arguing about which of them was the greatest.

Jesus sat down and called the twelve disciples around Him. Then He said, "Whoever wants to be first must take the last place and be the servant of everyone else."

Then He took a little child in His arms and said, "Anyone who welcomes one of these little children in My name welcomes Me, and whoever welcomes Me also welcomes My Father who sent Me."

Wanting to be the greatest, and wanting to be first, is not the way of the Kingdom. Whoever people are, whatever they can do, or whatever they may know, they can learn about having a kingdom attitude from a little child. Little children are happy to just be, even if no one thinks they are important.

Thank You, Lord, that I am important to You. Amen.

"Anyone who becomes as humble as this little child is the greatest in the Kingdom of Heaven."

~ Matthew 18:4, NLT

If children are taught about the Bible, and shown how to live for God, they will want to follow the Lord for the rest of their lives (Prov. 22:6).

Mark 9:38-41; Luke 9:49-50

FOR OR AGAINST

When the disciples argued about who was the greatest, Jesus told them how to be truly great. Then John, changing the subject, said, "Master, we saw someone using Your name to drive demons out of people, but we told him to stop because he isn't one of us."

But Jesus said, "Don't stop him! For no one who does a miracle in My name will in the next moment say anything bad about Me. Anyone who is not against us is for us. If anyone gives you even a cup of water because you belong to the Messiah, that person will surely be rewarded."

At the time that Jesus chose His team of twelve disciples, there were many others following Him, and that number had grown. But John had fallen into the "*us* and *them*" trap, feeling that only their group had the right to do miracles.

However, Jesus told John that if someone does good in His name, he is obviously on their side. That goes not only for those who fight against the powers of evil, but all those who are kind to any of His followers. We are all part of that team, each one working together for God's Kingdom.

Our faithfulness is more important than our task.

Let us think of ways to motivate one another to acts of love and good works.

~ Hebrews 10:24, NLT

We are part of the body of Christ. Each one of us has a specific purpose and everyone's job is important to the whole body (1 Cor. 12:14-20).

Matthew 18:6-10

KNOW RIGHT FROM WRONG

Jesus said, "If anyone causes one of these little ones who trusts in Me to sin or lose faith, it would be better for that person to be drowned in the sea. How terrible it will be for the world because it tempts people to sin. Situations that cause people to sin are sure to come up, but how terrible it will be for the person who causes one of these little ones to sin!"

Why did Jesus use such strong words about those who mislead children? Because children are tender in their faith: Firstly, they are trusting and usually believe whatever an adult tells them (even if it isn't the truth). Secondly, small children can't figure out right from wrong, especially if they haven't been taught.

Harsh punishment is waiting for the person who causes a child to doubt, tempts him to do wrong, or leads him away from the Lord. If someone has encouraged you to do wrong, ask the Lord to forgive you. If someone has confused you about God, remember that you can trust every word in the Bible.

REMEMBER Even if you do wrong, you are still a child of God!

But you belong to God, my dear children. You have already won a victory over those people, because the Spirit who lives in you is greater than the spirit who lives in the world.

~ 1 John 4:4, NLT

Even as a child, you can get to know right from wrong by reading the Bible (2 Tim. 3:14-17).

Matthew 18:10-14

THE LOST SHEEP

Jesus had called a little child to stand among them, and said, "Be careful that you don't look down on one of these little ones. For in heaven their angels are always in the presence of my heavenly Father."

He continued, "What do you think? Suppose a man has 100 sheep and one of them goes missing. Won't he leave the 99 sheep to look for the one that has strayed? In the same way, your Father in heaven does not want one of these little ones to be lost."

Do you sometimes think that God is so busy with grown-ups that He wouldn't even miss you? Well, just imagine how worried your parents would be if you got lost. They would leave everything to look for you until they found you. Our heavenly Father would be even more worried about you if you decided to wander away from Jesus the Shepherd and went your own way. He knows the dangers that tempt those who are far from Him. So rather stay close to Jesus where you can hear His voice, and He will lead you safely through life until you are home with Him in heaven.

Lord, always keep me close to You. Amen.

He will feed His flock like a shepherd. He will carry the lambs in His arms, holding them close to His heart.

~ Isaiah 40:11, NLT

All of us have strayed away like sheep. We have left God's path to follow our own. But God has taken our sins and put them on Jesus (Isa. 53:6).

Matthew 18:15-17

CORRECTING ANOTHER BELIEVER

Jesus then said, "If a believer wrongs you, go privately to that person and point out his fault. If he admits he did wrong and says sorry, you have helped that person get back on the right path. But if he doesn't listen, take two or three others with you to sort out the problem. If he still refuses to listen, tell the church what happened. If he then ignores what the church says, treat him as an unbeliever."

If the church did nothing to stop a believer from sinning, others may begin to think that it is okay to do the same. Yet Jesus teaches us a positive way to sort out wrongs that break down the unity in the church. The first thing to do is give the person the chance to say sorry in private. (It isn't right to go tell everyone what the person did, because that could lead to criticism and gossip in the church.)

However, if the person is rebellious and won't say sorry, he should be seen as an unbeliever, because as Christians, we know that we must never follow the example of unbelievers.

One rotten apple in a pile makes all the apples rotten.

If someone is caught in a sin, you who are spiritual should restore him gently.

~ Galatians 6:1

When David the king of Israel sinned, God sent a prophet to tell him that he had done wrong. Then David asked for forgiveness (2 Sam. 12:1-13).

Matthew 18:19-20

JESUS IS WITH US

Jesus said, "I also tell you this: If two of you on earth agree about what you are asking for, My Father in heaven will do it for you. For where two or three have gathered together as My followers, I am right there with them."

Jesus was with His disciples when He said this, but He also meant it for the groups who would get together once He had gone back to heaven. Jesus said that even two are enough to form a group!

God is faithful and will answer our private prayers, but when we pray with others, our faith combines with theirs, and so the power of prayer is increased, and our faith is encouraged. When Jesus said that God will do whatever we ask, we should remember that He only does for us what He knows is best (1 John 5:14-15).

We know that Jesus lives in our hearts by His Spirit (Eph. 3:16-17), yet when we get together with another believer, or in a group, Jesus meets with us in a special way. How exciting is that!

Find someone you can encourage and pray with.

Let us not neglect our meeting together, as some people do, but encourage one another, especially now that the day of His return is drawing near.

~ Hebrews 10:25, NLT

Jesus can be with every believer at one time because He has the nature of God who is everywhere (Col. 1:15).

Matthew 18:21-35

THE UNMERCIFUL SERVANT

Peter asked Jesus, "Lord, how often should I forgive someone who sins against me? Seven times?"

"Not just seven times, but seventy times seven!" Jesus replied. He then told this story: "There was a king who called in his servants to pay back the money they had borrowed from him. One servant had borrowed a huge amount of money and couldn't pay it back. The king wanted to throw him in jail, but the servant begged for mercy.

The king felt sorry for him and forgave his debt. But the servant then went to another man who owed him a few coins and ordered him to pay the money back. The man didn't have the money, so the servant had him jailed. The king was very angry when he heard about this and did to the servant what he had done to the man."

Jesus compared our huge debt of sin that has been forgiven with the few small things we need to forgive others. If God the King has forgiven us so much, how can we not forgive someone else?

Thank You, Lord, that my huge debt of sin is forgiven. Amen.

There will be no mercy for those who have not shown mercy to others. But if you have been merciful, God will be merciful when He judges you.

~ James 2:13

The record of our debt (sin) has been nailed to the cross of Jesus and forgiven (Col. 2:14).

John 6:35-37

THE BREAD OF LIFE

One day, Jesus told some unbelieving Jews, "I am the Bread of Life. Whoever comes to Me will never be hungry again. Whoever believes in Me will never be thirsty. Everyone whom the Father gives Me will come to Me. I will never turn away anyone who comes to Me."

The reason Jesus talked about bread was that many were following Him only because of the bread He had given to the crowds (John 6:26).

They wanted Jesus to keep feeding them as God had fed the Israelites with bread for 40 years (John 6:30-31).

But Jesus told them that they were missing the point of life. Life is not about working for food that spoils, but living on food that lasts forever. Jesus said that if anyone comes to Him, He would fill their hearts with God's goodness so that they will never feel empty inside again.

Jesus was offering them food – not just for forty years, but for eternity. Just as the food we eat becomes part of us, when Jesus comes into our lives His eternal life also becomes part of us.

FIND OUT What did the Israelites call the bread God had given them in the desert? (Exod. 16:31)

"The true bread of God is the One who comes down from heaven and gives life to the world."

~ John 6:33, NLT

Jesus is in us and we are in Him (John 14:20).

John 8:12, 9:4-5

THE LIGHT OF THE WORLD

Jesus said, "I am the light of the world. Whoever follows Me will never walk in darkness, because you will have the light that leads to life."

In the beginning, God separated the light from the darkness. He made the light more powerful than the darkness so that the light always drives the darkness away (Gen. 1:3-5). The blackest darkness cannot dim the smallest light.

John said this about Jesus, "In Him was life, and that life was the light of all mankind" (John 1:4). Although we have the sun to give us light, John was saying that when His light shines into our hearts, we have eternal life. The *Life* that was in Jesus became the *Light* of hope to everyone on earth.

Sin brought darkness to our hearts because it separated us from God, who is Light (1 John 1:5). Without God, we were in spiritual darkness. People stumbled around in the darkness and couldn't find their way back to God (John 11:10). But then Jesus came to earth to be the Light that shows us the way to God.

Thank You, Jesus, for shining Your light into my heart. Amen.

"I have come into the world as a light, so that no one who believes in Me should stay in darkness."

~ John 12:46

Jesus is described as the rising Sun that comes to us from heaven (Mal. 4:2; Luke 1:78).

John 10:7-10

JESUS IS THE GATE

At another time, Jesus said, "I tell you the truth, I am the gate for the sheep. Anyone who comes in through Me will be saved. They will come in and go out, and find pasture. The thief comes only to steal and kill and destroy; I have come that they may have life, and have it to the full."

In the days when Jesus was on earth, shepherds didn't have nice sheep pens fenced off with wire or poles. Instead, the shepherds would make a wide circle of thorn branches that would keep the sheep in, and keep the wolves out. There was a narrow opening in the hedge where the sheep could enter. At night, once all the sheep were safely inside, the shepherd would lie down across the entrance. If any animal dared to come in, the shepherd would wake up and chase it away or kill it. While the sheep were inside, they were safe.

As we enter through Jesus the Gate, we are saved and become part of His flock. We are safe in Him – safe from the attacks of the devil, and safe from "thieves" that would lead us astray. We are His sheep because He laid down His life for us at the entrance.

Jesus is the only way to God (John 14:6).

This is the gate of the LORD through which the righteous may enter.

~ Psalm 118:20

The sheep don't stay in the sheep pen all the time; the shepherd leads them out to green pastures every day (Ps. 23:1-3).

John 10:11-15

THE GOOD SHEPHERD

"I am the Good Shepherd," Jesus said. "The Good Shepherd lays down His life for the sheep. A hired person isn't a shepherd and he doesn't own the sheep. When he sees a wolf coming, he leaves the sheep and runs away. So the wolf drags the sheep away and scatters the flock. The man runs away because he's working only for money and doesn't care about the sheep. I am the Good Shepherd; I know My own sheep, and they know Me, just as My Father knows Me and I know the Father. So I give My life for My sheep."

Whenever Jesus said *"I am"* He wasn't just saying I am like ..., but I AM. This is the name God used for Himself when He spoke to Moses (Exod. 3:14).

Sheep cannot look after themselves – they need to be led and protected. Without a shepherd, sheep wander off and get lost, and wild animals scatter and kill them. Jesus is the Good Shepherd who has given His life for His sheep. Someone who is paid to look after the sheep, won't risk his life to protect them. But when you belong to Jesus, He will protect you.

Lord, thank You for holding me safe in Your arms. Amen.

Even if I go through the deepest darkness, I will not be afraid, LORD, for You are with me. Your shepherd's rod and staff protect me.

~ Psalm 23:4

David rescued his father's sheep from lions and bears (1 Sam. 17:34-35).

John 11:23-25

THE RESURRECTION AND THE LIFE

Martha's brother had died, and Jesus comforted her by saying that Lazarus would rise again. Martha answered, "I know that he will come back to life on the last day, when everyone comes back to life."

Jesus said to her, "I am the Resurrection and the Life (the One who brings people back to life, and Life itself). Anyone who believes in Me will live, even when they die."

Jesus is Life – He is eternal. He always was and always will be, and so He gives to us the eternal life that is in Him. Even though Jesus is Life, He didn't cling to His own life, but gave it up willingly when He went to the cross for us. But death could not overpower the life in Him and He rose again. That's why Jesus could say that He is the Resurrection *and* the Life.

Sin brought death to our spirits and our bodies. But the moment we ask Jesus to forgive us and come into our hearts, He puts a new spirit in us that has eternal life (Ezek. 36:26). And even though our body (the outer part) dies, He will raise our bodies to life again when He returns (1 Cor. 15:51-52).

Jesus lives in your spirit (your spiritual heart) (Eph. 3:17).

If Christ is in you, your body is dead because of sin, yet your spirit is alive because of righteousness.

~ Romans 8:10

Jesus doesn't only promise us a life that lasts for ever and ever, but also a life that is full and satisfying (John 10:10).

JULY

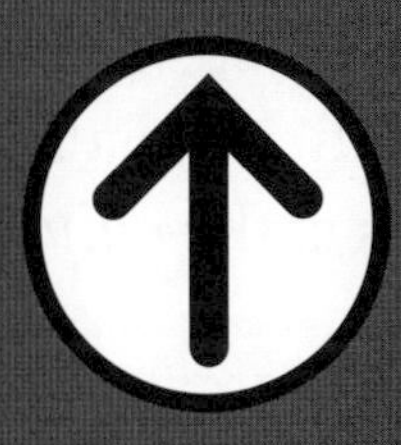

1 WAY
FOLLOW IT

1 TRUTH
BELIEVE IT

1 LIFE
LIVE IT

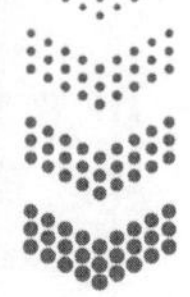

John 14:2-6

THE WAY, THE TRUTH, AND THE LIFE

When Jesus was explaining to the disciples that He is going back to His Father in heaven, and that they know the way, Thomas became worried, and said, "Lord, we don't know where You are going, so how can we know the way?"

Jesus replied, "I am the Way, the Truth, and the Life."

There is a right way and a wrong way. Those who follow along the sinful way of the world are on the wrong path. Proverbs says that; "There is a way that seems right to a man, but in the end it leads to death." But Jesus is the path to life – the narrow road that leads to eternal life in heaven with God (Matt. 7:14). The early church even called their faith in Jesus "The Way" (Acts 24:14), because they knew that Jesus is the *only* Way.

Jesus doesn't only *speak* words of truth – He *is* the Truth. But people of the world would rather believe the lies of the devil than know the truth. The devil is the father of lies for he cannot speak a single word of truth. But the words of Jesus are truth and they are life (John 6:63), so when He speaks, His words bring life.

Fill in the letters to complete the Scripture verse.

"I tell you the _ _ _ _ _, he who believes has everlasting _ _ _ _."

~ John 6:47, NLT

We should walk in His truth (2 John 1:4), and in His light (Ps. 89:15) along the path of life (Ps. 16:11).

John 15:1-8

THE TRUE VINE

One day, Jesus was talking to the disciples, and said to them, "I am the True Vine, and My Father is the gardener. He cuts off every branch of Mine that doesn't produce fruit, and He prunes the branches that do bear fruit so they produce even more."

"Live in Me, and I will live in you. A branch cannot grow fruit by itself; it has to stay attached to the vine. In the same way, you cannot produce fruit unless you live in Me. Anyone who does not stay connected to Me is thrown away like a dry branch."

Jesus used an example of a vine to show how we are in Him, and He is in us. He is the strong stem with deep roots; we are the branches that grow from the stem and bear fruit.

God is the Gardener who prunes the branches (trims the bushy growth) so that the sap from the roots can go into growing fruit instead of only growing leaves. When God sees things like selfishness, pride and unforgiveness, He cuts them away so that fruit like love, joy and peace can grow in our lives.

Lord, help me to bear more fruit for You. Amen.

The person who is joined to the Lord is one spirit with Him.
~ 1 Corinthians 6:17, NLT

The fruit of the Spirit is love, joy, peace, patience, kindness, goodness, faithfulness, gentleness and self-control (Gal. 5:22-23).

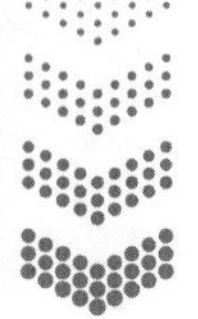

John 7:1-10

THE FEAST OF TABERNACLES

Jesus was going around in Galilee because He wanted to stay out of Judea, where the Jewish leaders were looking for a way to kill Him. But when the Jewish Festival of Tabernacles was near, Jesus' brothers said to Him, "Leave Galilee and go to Judea, so that Your followers there can see the miracles You do. You can't become famous if You hide like this!"

Jesus replied, "Now is not the right time for Me to go; but for you any time will do." But after His brothers left for the festival, Jesus also went, though secretly, staying out of public view.

At the Feast of Tabernacles, the Jews celebrated the harvest (Exod. 23:16), and also remembered how God provided for them in the desert for 40 Years (Deut. 2:7).

For Jesus, the right time was God's time. He knew that if He went to Jerusalem too soon, word would get around that He was there and the Jews would try to arrest Him before God's time had come. Jesus showed us how important it is to wait for the right time – God's time.

Jesus trusted His Father completely, and so can we.

There is a time for everything, and a season for every activity under the heavens.

~ Ecclesiastes 3:1

A Tabernacle is like a tent, and during the Feast of Tabernacles, people would build flimsy shelters and live in them for a week (Lev. 23:42-43).

John 7:14-19

THE TEACHING OF JESUS

Halfway through the Feast, Jesus then went up to the temple area and began to teach. The people were amazed when they heard Him, and asked, "How does He know so much when He hasn't been trained?"

So Jesus told them, "My message is not My own; it comes from God who sent Me. Anyone who wants to do the will of God will know whether My teaching is from God or My own."

At the age of twelve, Jesus was at the same temple talking to the teachers. Already then, temple leaders were amazed at His answers (Luke 2:46-47). Jesus knew and understood the scriptures so well that the teachers of the law could never catch Him out. He was teaching the teachers without having been taught.

As a boy of twelve, Jesus really impressed the leaders. But now something had changed. Jesus was saying that He is the Son of God, and many believed Him. This made the Jewish leaders angry. They wanted to put a stop to His teaching and get rid of Him.

When we talk about Jesus with those who don't believe, it makes them feel uncomfortable because they know that it could be true.

Why didn't the leaders like Jesus healing people?

Jesus said, "Anyone who loves Me will obey My teaching."
~ John 14:23

When Jesus spoke to people, He mainly quoted from these Old Testament books: 1. Psalms 2. Deuteronomy 3. Isaiah 4. Exodus, in that order.

John 7:25-30

WHO IS THIS MAN?

As the people talked about Jesus, they asked, "Isn't this the Man they are trying to kill? Why then is He speaking in public and the leaders aren't saying anything to Him.

Is it because they now believe that He *is* the Messiah? But how could He be, for we know where He comes from. When the Messiah comes, no one will know where He comes from."

While Jesus was teaching in the temple courtyard, He said, "Yes, you know Me, and you know where I come from, yet I didn't decide to come on My own."

Then the leaders tried to arrest Him; but they couldn't because God stopped their plan.

People had different ideas of what the Messiah would be like and how God would send His promised One. Yet, Jesus did, in fact, come from heaven; but because He came as a man so that He could be like us, He was far 'too ordinary' in the minds of people, so they missed out on the biggest privilege anyone could have – meeting the King of kings.

Did the people really know where Jesus came from?

Jesus said in a loud voice, "Whoever believes in Me believes not only in Me but also in Him who sent Me."

~ John 12:44

One day when Jesus comes back, every eye will see His glory and every knee will bow down to Him (Rev. 1:7; Rom. 14:11).

John 7:37-39

LIVING WATER TO QUENCH YOUR THIRST

On the last and greatest day of the feast, Jesus said in a loud voice, "Let anyone who is thirsty come to Me and drink. Whoever believes in Me, as the Scripture has said, rivers of living water will flow from his heart."

When Jesus talked about *living water*, He was speaking of the Holy Spirit, who would be given to everyone who believes in Him. Up to that time the Spirit had not yet been given to believers, because Jesus had not yet been glorified [returned to His Father].

Once before, Jesus had talked about living water, when He spoke to the woman at the well. Now the invitation was to everyone. Jesus waited for the high point of the festival, and spoke loudly to make sure that His offer of living water was heard by all. When we believe in Jesus, we drink of the life-giving water He gives us. This water is the Holy Spirit who fills us to overflowing so that our hearts become a spring of living water, flowing over to eternal life (John 4:13-14).

Thank You, Lord, for the spring of eternal life in my heart. Amen.

The LORD will guide you always; He will satisfy your needs in a sun-scorched land and will strengthen your frame. You will be like a well-watered garden, like a spring whose waters never fail.

~ Isaiah 58:11

The Holy Spirit was given to believers at the Feast of Pentecost, about 10 days after Jesus returned to heaven (Acts 2:1-5, 2:32-33).

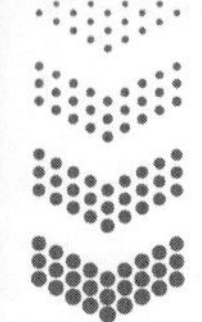

John 7:40-52

NO ONE EVER SPOKE LIKE THIS!

When the crowds heard Jesus offer them living water, some of them declared, "Surely this Man is the great Prophet." Some said, "He is the Messiah." But others weren't so sure, so the crowd was divided about Him.

Meanwhile, the temple guards who had been sent to arrest Jesus, returned without Him. So the Pharisees demanded, "Why didn't you bring Him in?"

"We have never heard anyone speak like this!" they replied.

So the Pharisees mocked them; "It seems like you've been led astray, too!"

Guards are supposed to be tough and unfeeling; they aren't meant to have their hearts touched by someone's words.

Yet even though they were Jewish and worked for the temple officials, they realized that the words of Jesus had life-giving power. And so they returned to the Pharisees having failed in their mission, but having discovered who Jesus really is.

The Pharisees were religious but spiritually blind.

They were amazed at His teaching, because His words had authority.

~ Luke 4:32

Temple guards were the 'police force' of the temple. They could arrest Jews who disobeyed or disrespected their Jewish laws and customs.

John 8:1-11

JESUS AND THE UNFAITHFUL WOMAN

Early the next day Jesus went to the temple area again and started teaching the people who had gathered around Him. The Pharisees brought a woman to Jesus and said, "Teacher, this woman was caught sleeping with a man who is not her husband. The law of Moses commands that a woman who does this be stoned. What do you say we should do?" They were trying to trap Jesus into saying something they could use against Him, but Jesus bent down and wrote in the dust with His finger.

They kept demanding an answer, so He stood up and said, "All right, but let the one who has never sinned throw the first stone!" One by one, the scribes and Pharisees left until Jesus was left alone with the woman. Then Jesus asked her, "Woman, where are they? Has no one condemned you?"

"No, Lord," she replied. So Jesus said, "Neither do I. Go and sin no more."

The woman had done something bad that deserved death. But Jesus saved her from death and forgave her sin, just as He has done for us.

Lord, thank You for saving me and forgiving me. Amen.

"God did not send His Son into the world to condemn the world, but to save the world through Him."

~ John 3:17

Because we have sinned, we deserve God's punishment; but because Jesus took our punishment, we are forgiven and set free (Rom. 6:23).

John 8:12-19

TWO WITNESSES

When Jesus spoke again to the people at the temple. He said, "I am the Light of the world."

The Pharisees replied, "You are saying that about Yourself, so what You are saying proves nothing."

Jesus answered, "Even though I say things about Myself, what I say is trustworthy and true because I know where I came from and where I am going. Your own law says that if two people agree about something, what they say is as good as fact. I am one witness, and My Father who sent Me is the other."

The Jews were saying to Jesus that whatever He says counts for nothing: He is like someone in a court of law who has no witnesses. A witness is someone who tells about what he has seen or knows. Well, Jesus had seen His Father in heaven, where He came from.

His other witness is His Father, who said, "This is My Son, whom I love; Listen to Him!" (Mark 9:7). Jesus sure proved His point! His Father and Him are witnesses, and so what they agree on is true.

FIND OUT Where did God say those same words? (Matt. 17:5).

Jesus Christ, the witness, the trustworthy one, the first to come back to life, and the ruler over the kings of the earth.

~ Revelation 1:5

In Old Testament times, one witness wasn't enough to convict someone of a crime, offense, or sin he may have committed (Deut. 19:15).

John 8:21-30

I AM GOING AWAY

Jesus then said to the Jews, "I am going away. You will look for Me but you will die in your sin. You cannot come where I am going."

This made them ask, "What does He mean when He says, 'You cannot come where I am going'?"

So Jesus said to them, "When you have lifted up the Son of Man on the cross, then you will understand that I am the One sent from God. The Father who sent Me is with Me – He has never left Me alone, for I always do what pleases Him."

When Jesus said, "I am going away," He meant that He was going back to His Father in heaven. And, by saying to the unbelieving Jews that they could not go where He was going, He was saying that they cannot get into heaven because they don't believe. But all who do believe in Jesus will go to be with Him in heaven.

Jesus only did what pleased His Father, even if it meant being lifted up (dying) on a cross. And we know that His Father was pleased with Him, because He said so when Jesus was baptized.

Thank You, Jesus, for being obedient to Your Father. Amen.

"But I, when I am lifted up from the earth, will draw all men to Myself."

~ John 12:32, NLT

Jesus went back to His Father in heaven, 40 days after He had risen from the grave (Acts 1:3).

John 8:31-36

THE TRUTH WILL SET YOU FREE

Jesus said to the Jews who did believe in Him, "You are truly My disciples if you remain faithful to My teachings. Then you will know the Truth, and the Truth will set you free."

"But we are descendants of Abraham," some said. "We have never been slaves to anyone. What do You mean, 'You will be set free'?"

Jesus replied, "I tell you the truth, everyone who sins is a slave to sin. A slave isn't part of the family, but a son is. So if the Son sets you free, you are truly free!"

Jesus was saying that those who believe the Truth He teaches would be set free from their life of sin. Sin won't have power over them as a master has power over his slaves. Some Jews didn't understand what Jesus was saying and argued that they had never been slaves. But the truth is that we are all slaves to sin until the Truth of Jesus unlocks the chains that keep us trapped. Yet, Jesus does more than free us from sin; He makes us part of God's family!

We are no longer slaves of the devil. We have been adopted as God's own children (Rom. 8:15).

So you are no longer a slave, but God's child; and since you are His child, God has made you also an heir.

~ Galatians 4:7

Slaves were owned by their masters. They were made to work hard and could be disciplined. They were given food but were not paid for their work.

John 8:37-41

SONS OF ABRAHAM

"Yes, I realize that you are descendants of Abraham," Jesus said. "Yet, some of you are trying to kill Me because there's no room in your hearts for My message. I speak about what I've seen in My Father's presence. But you are following the advice of *your* father."

"Our father is Abraham!" they declared.

"If you were Abraham's children, you would do what Abraham did," Jesus replied. "Instead, you are trying to kill Me because I told you the Truth, which I heard from God. Abraham would never have done that!"

When the Jews said that Abraham is their father, they meant that the Jewish nation came from one person, Abraham, who lived 2,000 years before.

Abraham had faith in God and was obedient to Him. If the Jews who were arguing with Jesus had the kind of faith Abraham had; and were obedient as Abraham was, they would not only have been children of Abraham, but children of God.

Thank You, heavenly Father, that I am Your child. Amen.

The real children of Abraham, then, are those who put their faith in God.

~ Galatians 3:7, NLT

If we love and trust God, we are children of Abraham because he is the father of all who believe (Gen. 15:5; Rom. 4:16).

John 8:42-47

THE FATHER OF LIES

Jesus told the Jews, "If God were your Father, you would love Me because I have come to you from God. I am not here on My own, for My Father has sent Me.

"But you can't even hear Me for you are the children of *your* father the devil, and you love to do the evil things he does. He has always hated truth, because there is no truth in him. He is a liar and the father of lies. So when I tell you the truth, it is in your nature not to believe Me!"

The devil uses different ways to prevent people from believing the truth.

- He tries to keep people away from hearing the Truth and so discover the Good News of Jesus.
- When people *do* hear the Truth, he twists thoughts in their minds to make them doubt God's Word.
- He blinds the minds of people so that they don't recognize the Truth (2 Cor. 4:4).

Just because people say so, it doesn't mean it's true.

So now we can tell who are children of God and who are children of the devil. Anyone who does not live righteously and does not love other believers does not belong to God.

~ 1 John 3:10, NLT

When the devil tempted Eve, he made her doubt what God had said by twisting God's instruction into a lie (Gen. 3:1-5).

John 8:56-59

"I AM"

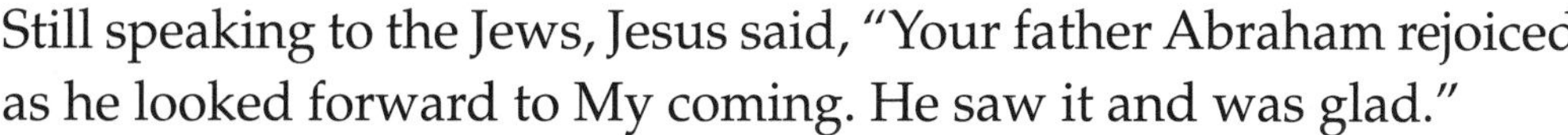

Still speaking to the Jews, Jesus said, "Your father Abraham rejoiced as he looked forward to My coming. He saw it and was glad."

The Jews said to Jesus, "You're not even fifty years old. How could You have seen Abraham?"

Jesus answered, "I tell you the truth, before Abraham was even born, I Am!"

At that point they picked up stones to throw at Him. But Jesus hid Himself from them and left the temple grounds.

Even though Abraham lived 2,000 years before, Jesus knew him because He had watched him from heaven. Jesus saw the longing in Abraham's heart, and the faith that made his heart glad as he thought about the promise of God (John 8:56).

Jesus was there before the world was created, yet He was also right there speaking to the Jews. He is alive at this very moment, and He lives in eternity. That is why Jesus called Himself I AM. It doesn't matter what day it is on our calendar, HE IS (always there).

To Jesus there is no time – with Him it is always now.

Jesus Christ is the same yesterday and today and forever.

~ Hebrews 13:8

Jesus promised to be with us every day while we are on earth (Matt. 28:20), and then we'll go to live with Him forever (John 14:3).

John 9:1-7

THE MAN BORN BLIND

As Jesus went along, He saw a man who had been blind from birth. His disciples asked Him, "Teacher, whose sin caused him to be born blind? Was it his own sin or his parents' sin?"

"It was not because of his sin or his parents' sin," Jesus answered. "This happened so that the power of God could be seen in his life." Then He spread mud over the blind man's eyes and said to him, "Go wash yourself in the pool of Siloam." So the man went and washed, and came back seeing!

People in Bible times had the idea that God punished people for their sins by means of sickness or disaster. While the Old Testament does give examples of God's punishment for disobedience, the punishment was mainly as a warning to others.

Yet, God is merciful and will not punish us as we deserve but is willing to forgive us when we ask Him to.

So, if something has gone wrong, or is going wrong in your life, it could be that this happened so that the power of God can be seen in your life.

Lord, thank You so much for Your love and grace! Amen.

He does not punish us as we deserve or repay us according to our sins and wrongs.

~ Psalm 103:10

Jesus healed the blind man using mud He made with His own saliva, and the dust. Do you know that God formed man out of dust? (Gen. 2:7)

John 9:13-25

"NOW I CAN SEE"

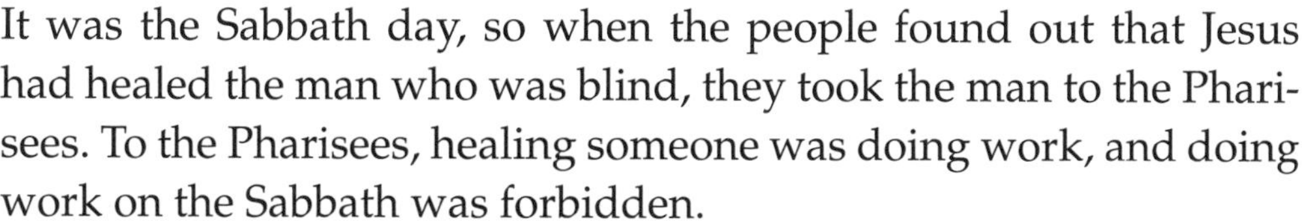

It was the Sabbath day, so when the people found out that Jesus had healed the man who was blind, they took the man to the Pharisees. To the Pharisees, healing someone was doing work, and doing work on the Sabbath was forbidden.

They questioned the man to find out exactly what had happened. They even asked his parents about him to make sure that he really had been blind.

Then they spoke to the man again; "Give glory to God by telling the truth," they said. "We know this man Jesus is a sinner."

"I don't know whether He is a sinner," the man replied. "But I know this: I was blind, and now I can see!"

The man born blind didn't know exactly who Jesus was or what He taught, yet he became a witness by telling the Pharisees what Jesus had done for him. You might not be able to answer every question about God and the Bible, but you do know who Jesus is; and like this man, you can tell others what He has done for you.

I once was blind, but now I see!

We cannot help speaking about what we have seen and heard.

~ Acts 4:20

God made the Sabbath day a day on which people should rest; not a day filled with rules about what one is not allowed to do (Mark 2:27-28).

John 9:35-38

"LORD, I BELIEVE"

The Pharisees became angry with the man who had been healed, and they threw him out. When Jesus heard what had happened, He found the man and asked, "Do you believe in the Son of Man?"

The man replied, "Sir, tell me who He is so that I can believe in Him."

Jesus said, "You have now seen Him; in fact, He is the One speaking to you."

Then the man said, "Lord, I believe," and he worshiped Jesus.

The first miracle happened when Jesus let the man see for the first time in his life. The second miracle happened when the man wanted to know who Jesus was, and Jesus said, "You have now seen Him." The man could now use his healed eyes to see Jesus standing there; and the moment he saw Jesus, the eyes of his heart were opened too! Meanwhile the hearts of the Pharisees, who could see with their eyes, became blind.

Lord, I believe! Thank You that I can see! Amen.

Then Jesus said, "I have come into this world to judge: Blind people will be given sight, and those who can see will become blind."

~ John 9:39

If you believe in Jesus - that He died for you and rose again - you will be saved from your sin and have eternal life (Rom. 10:9-10).

John 10:22-30

SAFE IN THE FATHER'S HAND

It was winter, and the time of the Feast of Dedication at Jerusalem. The Jews gathered around Jesus and asked, "How long are You going to keep us in suspense? If You are the Messiah, tell us plainly."

Jesus replied, "I have already told you, and you don't believe Me. The proof is the work I do in My Father's Name. But you don't believe Me because you are not My sheep. My sheep listen to My voice; I know them, and they follow Me. I give them eternal life, and they will never be lost. No one can snatch them away from Me, for My Father has given them to Me, and He is more powerful than anyone else."

Isn't it great to know that no one can snatch you away from Jesus, because God the Father won't let that happen. And He is greater than all! You are the Lord's sheep and you recognize His words of Truth. He is the Good Shepherd who gathers the lambs in His arms and carries them close to His heart (Isa. 40:11).

You are my Shepherd, and You hold me tight! Amen.

I am convinced that nothing can ever separate us from God's love. Neither death nor life, neither angels nor demons, neither our fears for today nor our worries about tomorrow – not even the powers of hell can separate us from God's love.

~ Romans 8:38-39, NLT

The Feast of Dedication (Hanukkah), is usually in December, and lasts for eight days. It is also called the Feast of Lights.

John 10:37-39

DO NOT BELIEVE ME ...

Jesus said to the unbelieving Jews who were arguing with Him, "Do not believe Me ... unless I am doing the things My Father wants Me to do. Yet, if you refuse to believe *Me*, then believe the *miracles* I am doing so that you will realize that the Father is in Me and that I am in the Father."

Once again the Jews tried to arrest Jesus, but He got away and left them.

Jesus was patient with the unbelief of the Jews. He was saying to them; okay, don't believe Me just because I say that I am in the Father and that He is in Me. But at least, believe that the miracles I do are the miracles of God the Father. Perhaps then you'd be able to figure out that I can only do these miracles if the Father is in Me.

The problem was that the Jews were seeing so many miracles, that to them there was nothing special about the miracles anymore; and so there was nothing special about Jesus either.

The more we stop to look at God's creation, the more we see His miracles.

Although they had seen Jesus perform so many miracles, they wouldn't believe in Him.

~ John 12:37

Although God had rescued the Israelites from the Egyptians and parted the Red Sea for them, they soon forgot about those miracles (Ps. 106:7-13).

John 10:40-42

JESUS LEAVES JERUSALEM

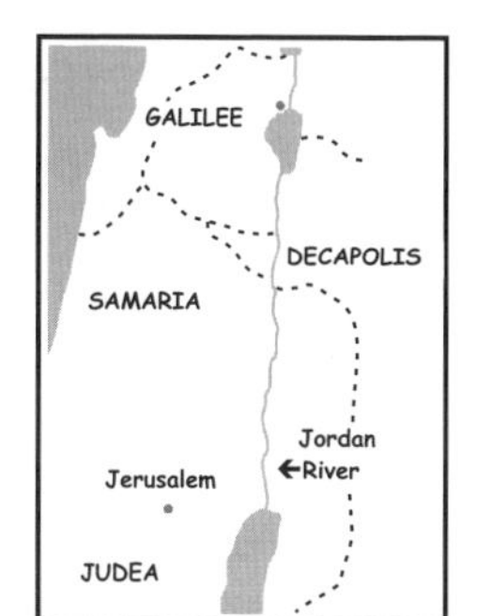

Jesus had completed His work in Galilee and was spending the last few months of His earthly ministry in Judea. He spent some time in Jerusalem, the capital of Judea, but the Pharisees had tried to kill Him.

So Jesus left Jerusalem and went back across the Jordan River to the place where John had baptized people. Many came to hear Jesus, and said, "John didn't perform any miracles, but everything John said about this man is true." And they believed in Jesus.

The seeds of truth that John the Baptist had planted in the hearts of the people, had grown. From time to time, they may have heard a bit about what Jesus was doing, and their hearts were ready to believe! Yet, simply hearing about the miracles wasn't enough to save the people from their sins, so Jesus went to tell them about God's plan of forgiveness and eternal life. Jesus came to earth to be more than just a miracle worker – He came to earth to be our Savior.

The bad news is sin; the Good News is forgiveness.

John said, "Look, the Lamb of God, who takes away the sin of the world!"

~ John 1:29

The area of Judah was called Judea by the Romans. This was where the tribe of Judah settled when they entered the promised land (Josh. 15:1).

Luke 10:1-3, 16

JESUS SENDS OUT THE 72

The Lord chose 72 other disciples and sent them ahead to all the towns and places He planned to go. They were to travel in pairs.

Jesus told them, "As you go, remember that I am sending you out as lambs among wolves." Then He said to them, "Anyone who listens to your message also listens to Me. Anyone who walks away from you also walks away from Me. And those who reject Me reject God, who sent Me."

Just as Jesus had sent out the 12 disciples to tell people about Him and to heal the sick, so He was now sending out 72 disciples, giving them the same instructions. The disciples were to go ahead to the places Jesus would visit before His crucifixion in order to prepare the way for Him, as John the Baptist had done.

The Good Shepherd sent His lambs to places where there were wolves. These weren't real wolves, but people who'd want to scatter and scare the disciples, and perhaps harm them. So the disciples needed to trust Jesus' promise that He would protect them, as a shepherd protects his sheep.

Work out how many pairs of disciples went out: _____

The Lord is my shepherd; I have all that I need.

~ Psalm 23:1, NLT

The Bible tells us that two are better than one (Eccles. 4:9-10). That's why Jesus sent the disciples out in pairs.

Luke 10:17-20

THE 72 COME BACK

When the 72 disciples returned, they joyfully told Jesus what had happened, "Lord, even the demons obey us when we use Your Name!"

Jesus said to them, "I saw Satan fall from heaven like lightning. Look, I have given you the authority to trample snakes and scorpions and to destroy the enemy's power. Nothing will hurt you. However, don't be happy that evil spirits obey you. Be happy that your names are written in heaven."

The disciples were happy and excited to be part of the team that was growing God's Kingdom. Jesus had given them the power to heal the sick and drive out evil spirits from people.

Up to that time, they had only seen Jesus do such miracles; now they were doing the same. As they went, they broke down the barriers of the devil and crushed his work (Rom. 16:20). The God of Peace was fighting a war against His enemy in order to free those who were trapped in sin!

God has given us the victory! (1 Cor. 15:57).

They will come to their senses and escape from the devil's trap. For they have been held captive by him to do whatever he wants.

~ 2 Timothy 2:26, NLT

When we believe in Jesus, our names are written in the 'Lamb's book of Life' (Rev. 21:27).

Genesis 3:1

DID GOD CREATE THE DEVIL?

In the beginning, there were angels in heaven who worshiped God and served Him. There was one heavenly being who was the chief of the angels. He was beautiful and wise, but he became proud and decided to take God's place. So God threw him down to earth, together with the other angels who rebelled (Isa. 14:12-15).

On earth Satan continued his rebellion against God. He decided to use man (created in God's likeness) to get back at God. Even though Satan had failed to become like God, he lied to Eve and told her that she could become like God. But instead, when Adam and Eve fell for Satan's trick and disobeyed God, sin entered the world (Gen. 3:1-5).

So did God create the devil? Yes, He created all heavenly beings, but one of them rebelled. God didn't create evil and He doesn't tempt anyone to do wrong; but because the angels were given a free will, just as we have, some decided to turn against God. However, God is in charge and He has everything under control!

- The devil's first punishment came when God threw him and his angels out of heaven (Rev. 12:9).
- The devil's second and final punishment is coming when God will throw him into a burning pit, where he will be tortured forever! (Rev. 20:10).
- If we are on God's side, we are stronger than the devil (1 John 4:4).
- God has made a way for our sins to be forgiven (John 3:16).

For Christ must reign until He humbles all His enemies beneath His feet.

~ 1 Corinthians 15:2, NLT

Luke 10:25-28

THE CORRECT ANSWER

One day an expert in religious law stood up to test Jesus by asking Him this question: "Teacher, what should I do to have eternal life?"

Jesus replied by asking him a question; "What does the law of Moses say? How do you understand it?"

The man answered,

> "You must love the Lord your God with all
> your heart, all your soul, all your strength,
> and all your mind (Deut. 6:5).
> and, Love your neighbor as yourself" (Lev. 19:18).

"You have answered correctly," Jesus replied. "Do this and you will live."

We can only love God with all that we are if there's been a change in our hearts. True love comes from God, and it is only when His Spirit comes into our hearts that we can love with God's kind of love (Rom. 5:5). The test of whether we have, in fact, been made new on the inside is whether we love others (1 John 3:14).

Write out this Scripture verse and memorize it:
Deuteronomy 6:5

This is His command: to believe in the name of His Son, Jesus Christ, and to love one another as He commanded us.
~ 1 John 3:23

Love can be seen by how we *act* towards others; and by how we *react* when people mistreat us (1 Cor. 13:4-8).

Luke 10:29-32

A PARABLE OF THE BAD GUYS

Jesus agreed with the man He was talking to that one should love one's neighbor; So the man asked Him, "Who is my neighbor?"

Jesus answered with this parable: "A man was going down from Jerusalem to Jericho, when he was attacked by robbers. They stripped him of his clothes, beat him and went away, leaving him half dead.

By chance a priest came along. But when he saw the man lying there, he crossed to the other side of the road and passed him by.

A temple assistant walked over and looked at him lying there, but he also passed by on the other side."

There are those in the world who hurt others, and those who don't care. But Jesus' story isn't really about the robbers, it's about the people who walked down the road and saw the injured man. Perhaps the one man avoided getting involved in other people's lives, and the other was just too busy to help. But the parable doesn't end there because there are good people too, and that's what the story is about.

Lord, help me to see how I can help someone in need. Amen.

Remember, it is sin to know what you ought to do and then not do it.

~ James 4:17, NLT

In Bible times, the steep, winding road from Jerusalem down to Jericho was dangerous because of robbers who attacked and stole from travelers.

Luke 10:33-37

A PARABLE OF THE GOOD GUY

In a story that Jesus told, a man had been robbed and beaten. Two temple officials had passed that way, seen him lying there, and just walked on.

Jesus continued His story; "But a Samaritan, as he was traveling along, came across the man. When the Samaritan saw him, he felt sorry for the man, went to him, and bandaged his wounds. Then he put the man on his own donkey, took him to an inn, and made sure he was taken care of.

Which of these three would you say was a neighbor to the man who was attacked?" Jesus asked.

The man replied, "The one who showed him mercy."

Then Jesus said, "Yes, now go and do the same."

The Jews hated the Samaritans, and in the story that Jesus told the Jewish expert, He lets the good guy be a Samaritan. Maybe the point Jesus was making is that whether the injured man was a Jew or a Samaritan, any one of the three passing by the man lying on the road was in a position to show real love – the kind of giving love that comes from God.

Will I show kindness to the unpopular kid in class?

Owe no one anything, except to love each other, for the one who loves another has fulfilled the law.

~ Romans 13:8

The Jews hated the half-Jewish Samaritans because they had not stayed true to God. They worshiped idols and married the heathen Assyrians.

Luke 10:38-42

MARTHA AND MARY

As Jesus and the disciples made their way to Jerusalem, they came to the village of Bethany where a woman named Martha welcomed Him into her home.

Her sister, Mary, sat at the Lord's feet, listening to what He taught. But Martha was upset about all the work she had to do. So she asked, "Lord, don't You care that my sister has left me to do the work all by myself? Tell her to help me!"

But the Lord said to her, "Martha, Martha! You worry and fuss about a lot of things. There is only one thing worth worrying about. Mary has made the right choice, and that one thing won't be taken away from her."

Martha was preparing a special meal for Jesus while Mary was just sitting there, listening to Him. Why would Jesus tell Martha not to become distracted by all her work?

Jesus wasn't going to be on earth much longer, and when time is precious, one wants to spend that time doing what is most important. Mary wanted to hear Jesus' words, and to Jesus, that was far more important than preparing a special meal.

May Your words be the most important thing to me. Amen.

Whom have I in heaven but You? And earth has nothing I desire besides You.

~ Psalm 73:25

Bethany was a small village about an hour's walk from Jerusalem (John 11:18).

Luke 11:5-10

THE FRIEND AT MIDNIGHT

One day, when Jesus was helping the disciples learn more about prayer, He used this story:

"Suppose you went to a friend's house at midnight, wanting to borrow three loaves of bread because you have an unexpected visitor and you have nothing for him to eat. Your friend might answer you from inside his house, 'Don't bother me! I can't get up to give you anything.'"

"I tell you this," Jesus said. "Although he won't get up just because you are his friend, he will get up and give you whatever you need because you kept on asking."

This story is not about God being slow to answer our prayers; it's about us having a bold faith that keeps trusting God because we know that He is able to give us (or do for us) what we're asking.

Faith doesn't grow in a world where everything is easy, available and instant. Our roots of faith only go down deep when God doesn't send showers of blessing on us all the time, and we start looking with expectation to heaven.

What is the one thing you'd like to trust God for?

For everyone who asks receives; the one who seeks finds; and to the one who knocks, the door will be opened.

~ Luke 11:10

You can pray to God at any time, day or night, because He never sleeps (Ps. 55:17, 121:1-4).

Matthew 12:38-41; Luke 11:29-30, 32

THE SIGN OF JONAH

As more people gathered around Jesus, He said, "The people living today are evil. They are looking for a miraculous sign. But the only sign they will get is the sign of Jonah. Just as Jonah was a miraculous sign to the people of Nineveh, so the Son of Man will be a sign to the people living today."

"On judgment day the people of Nineveh will condemn you, because they repented of their sins when Jonah preached to them. Now someone greater than Jonah is here, but you refuse to turn from your sins."

Jonah became a miraculous sign because he was in the dark belly of a huge fish for three days before being spat out onto land (Jonah 1:17). In the same way Jesus, the Son of Man, was soon to be buried in the darkness of the earth, and then rise again. This miraculous sign proves that Jesus is the Son of God!

When Jonah preached to the people in the wicked city of Nineveh, they believed and repented (Jonah 3:4-10). Yet even though the *Son of God* had preached to the Jews, they were rebellious and refused to believe.

Two hearts: a R_p_ntant heart and a R_b_llious heart.

Repent, then, and turn to God, so that your sins may be wiped out, that times of refreshing may come from the Lord.

~ Acts 3:19

Jonah ended up in the fish's belly because of his *disobedience* (Jonah 1); Jesus was buried in a tomb because of His *obedience* (Phil. 2:8).

Matthew 12:42; Luke 11:31

THE QUEEN OF SHEBA

Jesus went on to tell the unbelieving Jews that, at the end of time, the Queen of Sheba would condemn them too. "She came from the ends of the earth to hear Solomon's wisdom," He said, "and now, someone greater than Solomon is here!"

The Queen of Sheba traveled from a far-off country to hear the wise words that God had put in King Solomon's heart. Though Solomon was just a man, she brought him camel-loads of spices, gold and precious stones.

She talked with him about the many things she had on her mind. Nothing was too hard for Solomon to explain, and he answered all her questions.

The Queen of Sheba went to find Solomon; Jesus came to earth to find us. Solomon was an ordinary man; Jesus is the Son of God.

Solomon had the answers to all the queen's questions; Jesus *is* the answer to all of life's problems. Solomon spoke wise words; Jesus spoke life-giving words of Truth.

Lord, Your words bring hope and joy to my life. Amen.

For what seems to be God's foolishness is wiser than human wisdom, and what seems to be God's weakness is stronger than human strength.

~ 1 Corinthians 1:25

When the Lord said to King Solomon that he could ask for whatever he wanted, Solomon asked for wisdom (1 Kings 3:5-12).

Luke 11:37-41

DIRTY DISHES

When Jesus had finished speaking, a Pharisee invited Him home for a meal. The Pharisee was surprised to see that Jesus didn't rinse His hands before the meal, which was one of the Jewish customs.

So Jesus said to him, "You Pharisees are so careful to clean the outside of the dish, but inside you are dirty – full of greed and wickedness! Didn't God make the inside as well as the outside? So clean the inside by giving to the poor, and you will be clean all over."

What's the point of cleaning a bowl on the outside and leaving the inside packed with crusty, rotten leftovers? Yuck! That's what the Pharisees were like. They made sure they looked good on the outside, but their hearts were filled with selfishness and wrong motives. On the outside they seemed to be friends with Jesus, but inside they were thinking of a way to trap Him.

God sees us inside and out, and if we are dirty on the inside, He can't use us to bless others.

Lord, make me clean and fill me with Your goodness. Amen.

If you keep yourself pure, you will be a special utensil for honorable use. Your life will be clean, and you will be ready for the Master to use you for every good work.

~ 2 Timothy 2:21, NLT

Guard your heart, for everything you do flows from it (Prov. 4:23).

AUGUST

1 WAY
FOLLOW IT

1 TRUTH
BELIEVE IT

1 LIFE
LIVE IT

Luke 11:46, 52

A HEAVY LOAD, AND NO KEY

Jesus also had something to say to the experts in religious law, "How terrible things will be for you! You burden people with loads that are hard to carry. But you won't lift a finger to help them.

"What sorrow awaits you, for you have taken away the key of knowledge from people. You have not entered the kingdom yourselves, yet you've kept out those who wanted to enter."

The experts made it difficult for people to understand the truth because they confused them with all their petty rules. They made people believe that keeping the rules is all that matters to God. But instead, God looks at the thoughts and attitudes of the heart. Rather than helping people *believe the Truth,* the experts weighed them down by making them feel guilty.

Jesus told them that they have also taken away the key that helps people *understand the Truth.* The key is a person's respect and love for God that unlocks the treasure of salvation (Isa. 33:6).

Lord, thank You for those who teach me the truth. Amen.

Give your burdens to the LORD, and He will take care of you. He will not permit the godly to slip and fall.

~ Psalm 55:22, NLT

Jesus, the King of kings has the key to eternal life. Right now, Jesus holds open the door of Salvation, and no one can shut it (Rev. 3:7).

Luke 12:4-5

DO NOT BE AFRAID!

Thousands of people had gathered around, but Jesus spoke first to His disciples, saying, "I tell you, My friends, don't be afraid of those who want to kill your body; they cannot do any more to you after that. Fear God, who, after you have died, has the power to throw you into hell (or save you from hell)."

Perhaps the disciples were becoming a bit nervous, or even afraid of the Pharisees, who had been trying to find a way to kill Jesus. What if they did? Would they be next? But instead of assuring them that nothing bad would happen, Jesus tells them to focus on God rather than people.

People may be able to harm your body, but that's all they can do. They have no power over where you will spend eternity – in heaven or in hell. Only God has! So if we fear God (meaning that we should respect and obey Him), we are trusting Him to take us to heaven to be with Him forever. Even so, no one can harm our bodies without God knowing and caring (Luke 12:6-7). God is the One who protects, and He is the only One who can take us safely to heaven.

Thank You, Lord, that my life is in Your hands! Amen.

The righteous person faces many troubles, but the LORD comes to the rescue each time.

~ Psalm 34:19, NLT

The disciples, *and* those who persecuted them, have died. The difference is the disciples are celebrating their eternal life in heaven (John 11:25).

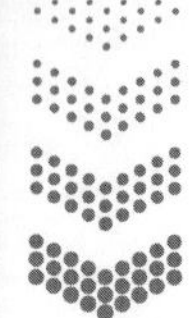

Luke 12:13-21

THE RICH FOOL

Someone in the crowd said to Jesus, "Teacher, tell my brother to give me my share of the inheritance that our father left us."

Jesus replied, "Friend, who made Me a judge to decide things like that? Be careful! Guard against every kind of greed."

Then He told them a story: "A rich man had a farm that produced fine crops. He said to himself, 'I don't have enough room for all my crops. But I know what I'll do. I'll tear down my old barns and build bigger ones to store all my grain. Then I'll have plenty of grain stored up for many years so that I can take life easy.'

"But God said to him, 'You fool! You will die this very night. Then who will get everything you worked for?' That's how it is when a person has earthly riches, but is not rich in his relationship with God."

Storing or saving wasn't this man's problem: being proud and greedy was! The rich man thought he didn't need God in his life; but he found out that he was wrong.

Life isn't measured by how much we own (Luke 12:15).

Do not brag about tomorrow, because you do not know what another day may bring.

~ Proverbs 27:1

"A person may plan his own journey, but the LORD directs his steps" (Prov. 16:9).

Luke 12:29-31; Matthew 6:33

SEEK GOD'S KINGDOM FIRST!

Jesus turned to His disciples, and said, "Don't become anxious about your everyday needs! Those who don't believe in God fill their minds with such things, but your heavenly Father knows that you need them. Instead, seek His Kingdom first, and all these things will be given to you as well."

Jesus had just told a story where a very rich man held on to what he owned, but when he died, he couldn't take a single thing with him.

So Jesus assured His flock that if they put God first in their lives and do what pleases Him, they don't need to worry about the future because God can make a plan with our problems.

At this point, Jesus and the disciples had been on the road for well over two years, yet God had always provided food for them. Twice, He provided more than enough food for thousands of followers.

When we depend on God to help us, we learn to trust Him more, and we are more likely to be grateful to Him for supplying our need.

Thank You, Lord, that You give me what I need. Amen.

Wherever your treasure is, there the desires of your heart will also be.

~ Luke 12:34, NLT

A godly life has a great reward for those who are content with what they have (1 Tim. 6:6-8).

Luke 12:35-36

BE READY TO SERVE!

Jesus told His followers, "Be dressed and ready for service. Keep your lamps burning as though you were waiting for your master to return from a wedding feast. Then you will be ready to open the door and let him in the moment he arrives back home."

This is the first part of a parable, in which Jesus tells us to be ready for Him when He, the Master, comes back. The disciples didn't really understand what Jesus meant because He was right there with them. It was only when Jesus went back to heaven that they understood that He would be returning to earth one day.

However, Jesus wasn't speaking only to His disciples; He was also telling us to be dressed and ready for Him when He comes back. This means we should expect Jesus to return at any time, and be clothed with (show) compassion, kindness, humility, gentleness and patience (Col. 3:12). We must also keep our "lamps" burning as we let the Holy Spirit shine God's goodness through us (Matt. 5:16).

REMEMBER Live your life as if Jesus were coming back today.

Jesus said, "Whoever serves Me must follow Me; and where I am, My servant also will be. My Father will honor the one who serves Me."

~ John 12:26

Whatever you do, work at it with all your heart, as though you were working for the Lord rather than for people (Col. 3:23-24).

Luke 12:37-38

THE MASTER WHO SERVES

Jesus said, "Blessed are the servants who are awake and ready when the master comes home late. I tell you the truth: He will let them sit down at the table and then serve them. He may come in the middle of the night or just before dawn. But when he comes, he will reward the servants who are ready."

That just doesn't seem right! In the story, the master comes home late at night and is probably ready for bed. Yet, he tells his servants to go sit at his table, and then he serves them a meal?

Jesus, our Master, is coming back at any time, but we don't know when. That's why we should be ready all the time. When He comes, He will reward those who have been faithfully waiting for Him to come back.

Jesus said, "Look, I am coming soon! My reward is with Me, and I will give to each person according to what they have done," (Rev. 22:12). So what should we be doing? As servants of Jesus, we should be living godly lives, telling others about Him, and doing good because we love Him (Titus 2:11-13).

Lord, may I always do what pleases You. Amen.

For even the Son of Man did not come to be served, but to serve, and to give His life as a ransom for many.

~ Mark 10:45

A crown is waiting for all those who long expectantly for Jesus to come again (2 Tim. 4:8).

Luke 13:1-5

SIN AND SUFFERING

Jesus was told that Pilate had murdered some people from Galilee as they were offering sacrifices at the temple. So Jesus asked, "Do you think those Galileans were worse sinners than the other people from Galilee? And what about the people who died when the tower in Siloam fell on them? Were they the worst sinners in Jerusalem? Not at all! But I tell you that unless you repent, you will perish, too."

Some seemingly good people had been killed at the temple, and some were killed when a tower collapsed. Life seems so unfair. Good people die, and wicked people seem to get away with their evil deeds. But this wasn't a punishment from God. Good *and* bad things happen to everyone. But for believers, God always makes good come from the bad.

Jesus used this opportunity to tell the people listening to Him that something unpleasant could happen to anyone at any time; so we need to be sure that we are saved and ready to meet God when we die.

Pray for a friend who is having a hard time.

We know that if the life we live here on earth is ever taken down like a tent, we still have a building from God. It is an eternal house in heaven that isn't made by human hands.

~ 2 Corinthians 5:1

God causes everything to work together for the good of those who love Him (Rom. 8:28).

Luke 13:10-17

THE CRIPPLED WOMAN

It was the Sabbath day and Jesus was teaching in a synagogue (a place of worship). He saw a woman who had been crippled for 18 years and couldn't straighten up at all. So He called her to come to Him and said, "Woman, you are free from your disability." Immediately, she stood up straight and praised the Lord.

But the leader in charge of the synagogue was irritated because Jesus had healed her on the Sabbath. So Jesus said, "You hypocrites! Each of you works on the Sabbath day! Don't you untie your ox or donkey on the Sabbath and lead it out for water?

This descendant of Abraham has been bound (tied up) for 18 years. Isn't it right to free her on the day of worship?" This shamed His enemies, but others were happy because of the wonderful things He did.

Have you noticed how those who don't believe in God hate it when He gets the glory for things that are good and beautiful? But let *your* heart rejoice when a sick person gets better, or when you see God's beautiful creation. Tell the Lord how wonderful He is!

Make a list of ten things you can praise God for.

Sing to Him, sing praise to Him; tell of all His wonderful acts.

~ Psalm 105:2

God will judge and punish those who say that evil is good and good is evil (Isa. 5:20).

Luke 13:22-27

THE NARROW DOOR

Jesus went through the towns and villages, teaching as He made His way toward Jerusalem. Someone asked Him, "Lord, will only a few be saved?"

Jesus replied, *"Do everything you can* to enter through the narrow door. When the master of the house has locked the door, it will be too late! You will stand outside knocking and pleading, 'Lord, open the door!' But He will reply, 'I don't know you or where you come from. Get away from Me, all you who do evil.'"

Long ago, God sent a great flood to destroy the wickedness that was spreading on earth. However, He had a plan to save anyone who would believe Noah's warning and enter through the door into the ark. But those who laughed at Noah, all drowned.

Right now, the door into the kingdom of God is open. Anyone may enter and be saved from the judgment to come. But, like the day when God shut the door of the ark, a day will come when the door to eternal life will be shut, and it will be too late to enter.

Thank You, Lord Jesus, that You have saved me. Amen.

Let us make every effort to enter that rest, so that no one will perish by following their example of disobedience.

~ Hebrews 4:11

God told Noah to build a huge boat. Once Noah and his family were safely inside, *God shut the door.* Then He sent a great flood (Gen. 6:13-17).

Luke 13:31-34; Matthew 23:37

JESUS LONGS TO GATHER HIS PEOPLE

Some Pharisees said to Jesus, "Leave this place because Herod wants to kill You."

Jesus said to them, "Tell that fox that I will keep on driving out demons and healing people until My work is finished; besides, a prophet can only die in Jerusalem! O Jerusalem, the city that kills prophets and stones God's messengers! How often I have wanted to gather your children together as a hen gathers her chicks under her wings, but you wouldn't let Me."

Jesus was saying that it is not in Herod's power to take away His life, or to stop Him from doing God's work until it is complete.

Then Jesus spoke to Jerusalem, where He would soon be killed. He had such a love for the people there. How He longed for the Jews in Jerusalem to gather around Him like children who sit at their father's feet, listening to him. He longed to look after them as a hen protects her chicks with her wings. Jesus also longs for each of your friends to be saved so that they, too, will one day gather around our heavenly Father.

Lord God, You are a kind, wonderful, caring Father. Amen.

He will cover you with His feathers. He will shelter you with His wings. His faithful promises are your armor and protection.

~ Psalm 91:4, NLT

Herod had been given his power by the Romans. Jesus called him a fox because, unlike a lion, a fox lacks strength and captures its prey by being sly.

Luke 14:7-11

THE PROUD GUESTS

One day, when Jesus went to eat at the house of a well-known Pharisee, He noticed that those who had come to the dinner wanted to sit in the places of honor near the head of the table.

So Jesus said to them: "When you are invited to a wedding feast, don't sit in the seat of honor in case the host says to you, 'Give this person your seat.' Then you will be embarrassed, and you'll have to take whatever seat is left at the foot of the table!"

"Instead, take a place at the foot of the table. When your host sees you, he will say to you, 'Friend, we have a better place for you!' Then you will be honored in front of all the other guests. For …

Those who honor themselves will be humbled,
but those who humble themselves will be honored."

The world teaches us to push and shove in order to get ahead of the next person. The world tells us that we have rights to demand certain things. Jesus shows us how to put others first and serve them.

Be polite. Be kind. Be generous. Be humble.

Don't be selfish; don't try to impress others. Be humble, thinking of others as better than yourselves.

~ Philippians 2:3, NLT

Pride leads to embarrassment, jealousy and anger. Pride causes you to lose your friends, and the Lord hates a proud heart (Prov. 16:5).

Luke 14:12-14

DON'T INVITE YOUR FRIENDS

Jesus once turned to His host and said, "When you invite people for lunch or dinner, don't invite your friends, your brothers or sisters, your relatives, or your rich neighbors. For they will invite you back, and that will be your only reward. Instead, invite the poor, the crippled, the lame, and the blind. Then, on the day that believers rise from the dead, God will reward you for inviting those who couldn't pay you back."

Jesus didn't mean that we should never have our friends around for a meal; He used strong words to make the point that we should also invite those who have no way of inviting us back.

You may be thinking that you can't just invite anyone to your house. Yet there are other ways you can be kind to those who aren't your close friends. Maybe you could share a sandwich at school, or give someone a sip of your water. Jesus said that if you give even a cup of cold water to anyone who loves Him, you will surely be rewarded (Matt. 10:42).

Lord, help me to notice people who need some kindness. Amen.

Don't forget to show hospitality to strangers, for some who have done this have entertained angels without realizing it!

~ Hebrews 13:2, NLT

Abraham offered three strangers some water and prepared a meal for them, not realizing that they were God's messengers (Gen. 18:1-8).

Luke 14:15-17

PREPARING FOR THE GREAT FEAST

A man sitting near Jesus heard what He said, and exclaimed, "What a blessing it will be to attend the banquet in the Kingdom of God!"

Jesus replied with this story: "A man planned to have a great feast and sent out many invitations. When the preparations were done, he sent his servant to tell the guests, 'Come, the banquet is ready.'"

At the dinner table, Jesus had been talking about true discipleship – living the life that is pleasing to God. He then told this story to help the guests understand that they have been invited to take part in God's Kingdom. In the story, the Man preparing the feast is God. The invited guests are His people.

A lot of planning and effort goes into preparing a feast. God had prepared the way through the prophets; through John the Baptist; and through the disciples that were sent to prepare the way for Jesus. Now everything was ready and the people were invited to come.

Design a dinner invitation for this feast with your name written on it.

"Look! I stand at the door and knock. If you hear My voice and open the door, I will come in, and we will share a meal together as friends."

~ Revelation 3:20, NLT

The following types of food were common at that time: lamb, fish, bread, vegetables, eggs, olives, nuts, grapes, figs and herbs.

Luke 14:18-20

EXCUSES, EXCUSES!

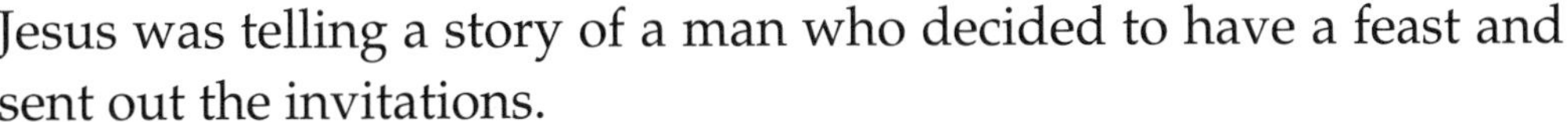

Jesus was telling a story of a man who decided to have a feast and sent out the invitations.

"The invited guests all began making excuses," Jesus told them.

"One said, 'I have just bought a field and I must go and see it. Please excuse me.'"

"Another said, 'I have just bought five pairs of oxen, and I want to try them out. Please excuse me.'"

"Still another said, 'I just got married, so I can't come.'"

How silly to choose to miss out on a wonderful feast (which they had known about)!

Isn't it amazing how easily we find excuses for things we don't want to do. Excuses seem to pop into our heads from nowhere; and they actually seem quite reasonable to us because we see things from our small view of life. But making an excuse to turn down God's invitation of a feast is just plain stupid! These guests didn't need to pay; or work hard; or struggle to get there. All they needed to do was *go*.

What plan could each of the three guests have made?

If I had not come and spoken to them, they would not be guilty of sin; but now they have no excuse for their sin.

~ John 15:22

No one has an excuse for not believing in God (Rom. 1:20).

Luke 14:21-24

THE DAY OF THE GREAT FEAST

The story Jesus was telling, ends like this: "The servant returned and told his master that all the guests had made excuses. The master was furious and said, 'Go quickly into the streets and alleys of the town and invite the poor, the crippled, the blind, and the lame.'

"After the servant had done this, he reported, 'There is still room for more!'

"So his master said, 'Go out into the country lanes and behind the hedges and urge anyone you find to come, so that the house will be full. For none of those I first invited will get even a small taste of my feast.'"

There is room enough in heaven for everyone on earth to have a place! Jesus has gone ahead to prepare a beautiful place for us (John 14:2-3). How sad if only a few accepted His invitation to be saved and to enjoy eternal life. That's why God – the Master of the feast – is sending us out to every part of the world to invite people to come to Him.

God has put you in a certain place on earth to tell the people that you know about His invitation.

He [Jesus] said to them, "Go into all the world and preach the Gospel to all creation."

~ Mark 16:15

Paul and Barnabas preached to the Jews; but when the Jews refused to listen to them, they shared the Gospel with the Gentiles (Acts 13:46).

Luke 14:28-30

COUNTING THE COST

Jesus turned to the crowds who were following Him and said, "Suppose you want to build a tower. You would first sit down and figure out what it costs. Then you would see if you have enough money to finish it. Otherwise, you might complete only the foundation before running out of money, and then everyone would laugh at you. They would say, 'There's the person who started that building and couldn't afford to finish it!'"

Jesus wanted to make sure that the crowds that were following Him were doing so for the right reason. Had they counted the cost of being a disciple? Did they know what it would cost them to follow Him and not give up halfway?

Counting the cost may have included the following:

- Am I willing to sell all I have? (Matt. 19:21)
- Am I willing to leave my family? (Matt. 19:29)
- Am I willing to give up my comforts? (Luke 9:57-58)
- Am I willing to suffer for Jesus? (Matt. 5:11)

Lord, help me to be loyal to You and never give up. Amen.

Jesus said, "If any of you wants to be My follower, you must turn from your selfish ways, take up your cross, and follow Me."

~ Matthew 16:24, NLT

Jesus said that no person who decides to follow Him and then keeps turning back to his sinful ways is of any use in the kingdom of God (Luke 9:62).

Luke 15:8-10

THE LOST COIN

Some tax collectors and sinners had gathered around Jesus to listen to Him. The Pharisees and teachers of religious law started to mutter and complain that Jesus was spending time with bad people.

So Jesus said to them, "Suppose a woman has ten silver coins and loses one. Wouldn't she light a lamp and sweep the entire house and search carefully until she finds it? And when she finds it, she would surely call her friends and neighbors and say, 'Come celebrate with me: I have found my lost coin!'"

Searching takes effort. There's a difference between having a quick look and really searching high and low for something. Unsaved people are lost in sin. It's not that Jesus doesn't know where they are, it's that *they* don't know how to find their way to God.

Jesus came as the Light of the world to search for the heart of each one and save them. Every person on earth is important to Jesus, including bad people. That's why Jesus was spending time with sinners, whom the Jewish leaders thought of as being just "too bad" to care about.

Lord, help me never to judge someone who doesn't know You, but rather, to show them the way to You. Amen.

"For the Son of Man came to seek and to save the lost."

~ Luke 19:10

The silver coin that Jesus spoke about was a Greek coin called a *drachma*, which was what a person would earn for a day's work.

Luke 15:11-16

THE LOST SON

Jesus told another parable to help the religious Jews understand that God loves even the worst of sinners and wants to forgive them. He said to them:

"One day, a man's younger son said to him, 'Father, give me my share of the property.' So the father divided the property between his two sons. The younger son then packed his bags and set off for a distant country, where he wasted all his money living foolishly. At that time there was a famine, and he began to starve. So the son went to work for a farmer who sent him to look after the pigs. He became so hungry that even the pig food looked good to him. But no one gave him anything."

Why did this son leave home? Was it that he was tired of having to do things for his father? Was it that he was bored with life at home? Perhaps. But it's more likely that the reason lay deeper – in his heart. He was *rebellious* and *selfish*. He wanted to push away the restrictions of home life and enjoy the "pleasures" of the real world. However, living it up in the real world soon changed to living alongside real pigs!

Sometimes, when we insist on our way, we get it.

We have sinned, done wrong, acted wickedly, rebelled, and turned away from Your commandments and laws.

~ Daniel 9:5

Jews were forbidden to have anything to do with pigs because they were unclean animals according to the law of Moses (Lev. 11:7).

AUGUST 19

Luke 15:17-24

THE RETURN OF THE LOST SON

Jesus told a parable about a rebellious son who demanded his inheritance and then wasted it until he had nothing left.

Eventually, the son in the parable came to his senses, and said to himself, "At home even the servants have enough food to eat, and here I am dying of hunger! I will go back to my father and say to him: Father, I have sinned. I am not worthy to be your son; make me one of your servants." So he got up and went back home. While he was still a long way off, his father – filled with love – ran to him and hugged him.

The father said to the servants, "Quick! Bring the best coat for him, and a ring and sandals as well. Then kill a calf. We must celebrate with a feast, for my son was dead and has now returned to life. He was lost, but now he is found." So they began to celebrate.

The focus of Jesus' story has now changed to the father. What love the father had for his son! He forgave the son and took him back into his home.

Like the son in the story, we too have rebellious hearts and have walked away from God. But God the Father lovingly welcomes us back with open arms!

Heavenly Father, thank You for Your love and mercy! Amen.

"My wayward children," says the LORD, "come back to Me, and I will heal your wayward hearts."

~ Jeremiah 3:22, NLT

God has not taken us back in order to be His servants - He has taken us back to be His sons and daughters (Gal. 4:6-7).

Luke 15:25-32

THE ANGRY BROTHER

In the parable where the rebellious son came back to his loving father, Jesus went on to tell how the older son felt about his brother.

The father was so happy that his son had returned, he organized a big party. Meanwhile, the older son was working in the fields. When he returned home and heard music and dancing, he asked a servant what was going on. "Your brother is back," the servant said, "and your father is celebrating his safe return."

The older brother was angry and wouldn't go in. So his father came out and begged him, but he replied, "All these years I have worked for you and you never gave me even one goat for a feast with my friends. Yet when this son of yours comes back after wasting your money, you celebrate by killing a fattened calf!"

His father said to him, "My dear son, you have always stayed by me, and everything I have is yours. We just had to celebrate this happy day. For your brother was lost, but now he is found!"

Imagine if you were the older brother. How would you have felt? Would you be happy or jealous? The Pharisees were jealous that Jesus welcomed lost, undeserving sinners and brought them back to God.

REMEMBER None of us deserve God's grace and goodness.

"In the same way, I tell you, there is rejoicing in the presence of the angels of God over one sinner who repents."

~ Luke 15:10

The Lord takes great delight in His children - He rejoices over us with joyful songs (Zeph. 3:17).

Luke 16:10-12

TRUSTWORTHY OR DISHONEST?

Jesus said to His disciples, "Those who can be trusted with very little can also be trusted with bigger things. Those who are dishonest in little things, will also be dishonest with greater responsibilities.

If you have not been trustworthy in handling worldly wealth who will trust you with the riches of heaven?"

God sees us all the time and tests our hearts. He gives us small tasks to do and watches whether we faithfully obey Him (even when there's no one around).

He also gives us the Holy Spirit to help us grasp simple truths. As we believe those truths and live by them, He gives us greater wisdom and understanding of His Word (Matt. 13:12, NLT).

God gives us talents and gifts and watches whether we use them for His glory. He also sees how we use our money: whether we use some of it to help others, or whether we keep it all to ourselves. If we are faithful in all these little things, God is able to trust us with bigger things and gives us more to look after.

REMEMBER Faithfulness in small tasks shows a big heart.

Work willingly at whatever you do, as though you were working for the Lord rather than for people.

~ Colossians 3:23, NLT

After Paul the great Apostle was shipwrecked, he was willing to help collect firewood for everyone to warm themselves (Acts 28:1-3).

Luke 16:13-15

THE TWO MASTERS

Jesus said, "A servant cannot serve two masters. He will hate the first master and love the second, or he will be devoted to the first and despise the second. You cannot serve God and riches."

When the Pharisees heard this, they made fun of what Jesus said because they loved their money. So Jesus said to them, "You make a show of how good you are when people are around, but those very things that impress them are disgusting to God."

Imagine having two sports coaches shouting different instructions to the players, or having two teachers who disagree with each other about a certain subject they teach. Whom would you listen to?

Trying to be an eager servant of worldly fortunes as well as a willing servant of God just doesn't work. You cannot run from one master to the other in order to serve both. The real issue isn't having money, but rather, who or what you live for.

Lord, You are the One I love and serve. Amen.

Don't love money; be satisfied with what you have. For God has said, "I will never fail you. I will never abandon you."

~ Hebrews 13:5, NLT

People who long to be rich often do wrong things to get money, and when they have it, they are tempted to use it the wrong way (1 Tim. 6:9).

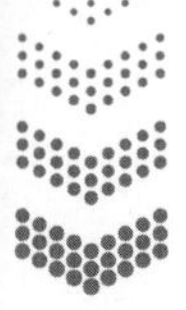

Luke 16:19-25

THE RICH MAN AND THE BEGGAR

Jesus said, "There was a rich man who lived in luxury every day. At his gate lay a poor, hungry man named Lazarus who was covered with sores. Finally, the poor man died and was carried by the angels to be with Abraham.

"The rich man also died and was buried, and his soul went to the place of the dead where he suffered in agony. When he saw Abraham in the distance, he shouted, 'Father Abraham, have pity on me! Send Lazarus here to give me some water. I am in anguish in these flames!' But Abraham replied, 'Son, remember that in your lifetime you received your good things, while Lazarus received bad things, but now he is comforted here and you are in agony.'"

Jesus was comparing this life to the next (once we die). The way things are in the short time we are on earth will be very different when we die. Those who have loved God – even though they have had it hard here on earth – will be blessed and comforted in heaven. Those who have lived selfish lives – not thinking of God or others – will be punished in hell.

I love You, Lord, and one day I will be with You! Amen.

Each person is destined to die once and after that comes judgment.

~ Hebrews 9:27, NLT

In heaven there will be no more sadness or crying or pain. It will be gone forever (Rev. 21:4).

John 11:1-6

LAZARUS IS SICK

Lazarus, a close friend of Jesus, became sick. So his sisters Mary and Martha sent someone to let Jesus know that His dear friend from Bethany was very sick.

When Jesus heard this He said, "His sickness will not end in death. This has happened for the glory of God so that the Son of God will receive glory from this." So although Jesus loved Martha, Mary, and Lazarus, He stayed where He was for the next two days.

One would think that Jesus would have left immediately to go heal His friend. After all, He'd been willing to go to other sick people and heal them. Everything Jesus did He did for the glory of His Father. Although it was probably hard for Jesus to stay and "do nothing," He knew that by waiting, God's Name would be made great in the eyes of the people.

The next time you are delayed for some reason and feel frustrated, remember that God's timing is always perfect. He sees things in the future that you can't.

Thank You, Lord, that my times are in Your hands. Amen.

"My thoughts are nothing like your thoughts," says the LORD. "And My ways are far beyond anything you could imagine."

~ Isaiah 55:8, NLT

Just as God has set certain times and seasons in nature, He has also put in place certain times for things to happen in your life (Eccles. 3:1).

John 11:7, 17-26

LAZARUS DIES

After Jesus had received a message that His friend Lazarus was very sick, He waited two more days.

Then Jesus said to His disciples, "Let us go back to Judea." When Jesus finally arrived at Bethany, He found out that Lazarus had died and that he'd already been in the grave for four days.

Meanwhile, when Martha heard that Jesus was on His way, she went to meet Him. But Mary stayed at home. Martha said to Jesus, "Lord, if only You had been here, my brother would not have died. But even now I know that God will give You whatever You ask."

Jesus told her, "Your brother will rise again. Anyone who believes in Me will live, even after dying."

If only are words of a hopeless wish that things could have worked out differently. "If only You had come straight away," is what Martha was saying to Jesus. Yet her weak faith kept the door of hope open, knowing that it is never too late to ask God for help.

Martha was trying to make sense of something bad that had happened in her life. At that point, things didn't make sense, but by faith she held on to the fact that God can do the impossible.

God uses delays to teach us to trust Him more fully.

Great is our Lord and mighty in power; His understanding has no limit.

~ Psalm 147:5

Although it is okay to ask God *why*, you may never know the reason. Instead, ask Him to help you to trust Him more, even when you don't understand.

John 11:28-35

JESUS COMFORTS THE SISTERS

When Jesus arrived in Bethany, His friend Lazarus had died. Martha, his sister, went to meet Jesus; but the other sister, Mary, stayed at home, weeping.

Martha went back home and called her sister Mary saying, "The Teacher is here and wants to see you."

So Mary immediately got up and went to Him. Jesus had stayed outside the village, at the place where Martha met Him. When Mary arrived and saw Jesus, she fell at His feet and said, "Lord, if only You had been here, my brother wouldn't have died."

When Jesus saw her weeping and saw the other people crying with her, He was deeply moved and troubled. "Where have you laid him?" Jesus asked. So they went to show Him. Then Jesus wept.

When we remember that Jesus was God here on earth, we begin to understand how God the Father feels when He sees man's sin bringing pain and sadness to His children.

Knowing that Jesus wept with His friends helps us to realize that God feels our sadness in the same way. Sin brought pain and death to the world; but because Jesus loves us so much, He took away the hopelessness of sin and death by going to the cross for us (1 Cor. 15:57).

Lord, thank You for knowing what my sadness feels like. Amen.

He [Jesus] was despised and rejected – a man of sorrows, acquainted with deepest grief.

~ Isaiah 53:3, NLT

The Lord cares deeply when one of His loved ones dies (Ps. 116:15).

John 11:38-45

LAZARUS IS RAISED

Jesus' friend Lazarus had died. He was buried in a tomb – which was a cave with a large stone rolled across the entrance.

When Jesus, and those with Him, came to the tomb, He said, "Roll the stone aside."

But Martha replied, "Lord, he has been in there for four days!"

Jesus said, "Didn't I tell you that if you believe, you will see the glory of God?" So they rolled away the stone.

Then Jesus prayed, "Father, I thank You that You have heard Me. You always hear Me, but I said this so that these people will believe You sent Me." After Jesus had prayed, He shouted, "Lazarus, come out!" Then the man who was dead came walking out, still wrapped with strips of linen. When the people saw the miracle Jesus did, many believed in Him.

Jesus had told the disciples that the death of Lazarus would bring glory to God. When the friends of Mary, who had seen the hope that Jesus brought to her life, saw that He could also raise the dead; they, too, wanted that hope. And they believed in Jesus.

Lord, You are my hope in the darkest times! Amen.

The LORD gives both death and life; He brings some down to the grave but raises others up.

~ 1 Samuel 2:6, NLT

When Jesus saves us and makes us new, our old nature dies. Jesus then raises us up to a new life in Him (Eph. 2:6; Col. 2:12-13).

Luke 17:5-10

THE MASTER AND SERVANT

The apostles said to the Lord, "Increase our faith!"

So Jesus said to them, "Suppose a man has a servant who is out plowing or looking after the sheep. When he comes in from his day's work, does his master say, 'Come here and eat with me'? Won't he rather say, 'Prepare my supper, get yourself ready and serve me while I eat. Then you can eat later.'"

"In the same way, when you obey Me you should say, 'We are unworthy servants who have simply done our duty.'"

The disciples had asked Jesus for more faith, which seemed like a good thing to ask. But they were asking for faith, not just enough to be obedient and faithful, but for a faith which would take away all their uncertainty and doubt. They were wanting to have it easy – to have a big serving of faith from their Master before their work was done. But the "increased faith" that the apostles were asking for would only come as they humbly and obediently did their duty.

Great faith should go hand in hand with great humility.

In everything we do we show that we are God's servants by patiently enduring troubles, hardships, and difficulties.

~ 2 Corinthians 6:4

God has given us just enough faith to do the tasks He has planned for us to do while we humbly look to Him for help (Rom. 12:3).

Luke 17:11-19

THE THANKFUL LEPER

One day, Jesus was met by ten lepers, who stood at a distance shouting, "Jesus, Master, have mercy on us!" When Jesus saw them, He said, "Go, show yourselves to the priests." As they went, they were healed of their leprosy. One of them, when he saw he was healed, went back to Jesus, praising God. He fell at Jesus' feet and thanked Him for what He had done.

Jesus asked, "Didn't I heal ten men? Where are the other nine? Has no one come back to give glory to God except this Samaritan?" Then He said to the man, "Stand up and go. Your faith has made you well."

You may struggle at school; you may not have many friends; you may not be great at sports. But if you're the kind of person who is thankful for what you have, and grateful to God for the way He has made you, you are sure to be more positive about life than those who seem to have it all, yet are never satisfied. Being thankful for the little things in life is an attitude we can learn by seeing God's hand in every situation (Phil. 4:12).

Lord, I praise You for life and love! Amen.

Let all that I am praise the Lord; may I never forget the good things He does for me. He forgives all my sins and heals all my diseases.

~ Psalm 103:2-3, NLT

A person cured of leprosy had to go show himself to the priest. Only the priest could check his skin and declare him healed (Lev. 14:3).

Psalm 118:1

BE THANKFUL (LIST 100 THINGS)

Get a blank sheet of paper or a notebook and write down 100 things you are thankful for. Here are some ideas to get you started:

- **Things at home:** things that make you happy
- **Things at school:** your favorite subject and teacher
- **Your body:** eyes, ears, legs, hands
- **Food:** your favorite meals, vegetables and fruit
- **Fresh,** running water and hot showers
- **Family:** parents, brothers, sisters, grandparents
- **Friends:** write down their names
- **The Bible:** to help us become more like Jesus
- **Church:** friends, teachers and leaders
- **Clothes** to wear
- **Nature:** the sea, rain, sunsets, clouds, trees and flowers
- **Animals** and pets
- The **warmth** and light of the sun
- **Love,** hope, peace and safety
- **Hobbies,** sports, books and music
- Your favorite **color**

Use your time with God today to think of all the things that are beautiful and good (Phil. 4:8).

Look around you every day and keep adding to this list. Use it to remind you of all the big and small things that you can thank God for.

Through Jesus we should always bring God a sacrifice of praise, that is, words that acknowledge Him.

~ Hebrews 13:15

Luke 18:1-8

THE WIDOW AND THE JUDGE

Jesus told His disciples a parable to show them that they should always pray and not give up. He said, "In a certain town there was a judge who didn't fear God or care about people. A widow kept coming to him saying, 'Help me against my opponent.'"

"The judge ignored her for a while, but finally he said to himself, 'This woman is driving me crazy! I'm going to see that she gets justice; otherwise, she'll wear me out with her asking.'" Then Jesus said, "Even the dishonest judge made a fair decision in the end to help the woman. So don't you think God will help His people who pray to Him day and night? Of course He will! But when the Son of Man comes back, how many will He find who have faith?"

The only reason the judge helped the woman was that she *kept on asking*. That's the lesson Jesus is teaching. If constant asking worked for the woman, how much more will God answer the prayers of His children whom He loves? But Jesus asks us the question; "When He comes back to earth, will He find those who pray and pray, believing that God, who is fair, will answer?"

Talk to God all the time, about everything!

Pray in the Spirit at all times and on every occasion. Stay alert and be persistent in your prayers for all believers everywhere.

~ Ephesians 6:18, NLT

Unlike the dishonest judge, God is a righteous Judge who does only what is fair (1 Pet. 1:17), yet God is our loving Father too.

SEPTEMBER

1 WAY
FOLLOW IT

1 TRUTH
BELIEVE IT

1 LIFE
LIVE IT

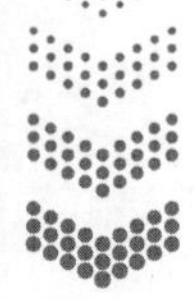

Luke 18:9-14

THE PHARISEE AND THE TAX COLLECTOR

Jesus told this story to some who were sure of their own goodness while they looked down on everyone else. "Two men went to the temple to pray. One was a Pharisee; the other was a tax collector."

"The Pharisee prayed this prayer: 'I thank You, God, that I am not a sinner like everyone else. For I don't cheat, I don't sin, and I am certainly not like that cheating tax collector!'

"But the tax collector stood at a distance and dared not even lift his eyes to heaven as he prayed, 'O God, be merciful to me, for I am a sinner.'"

Then Jesus said, "I tell you, this sinner, not the Pharisee, received forgiveness from God. For those who exalt themselves will be humbled, and those who humble themselves will be exalted."

What makes our hearts right in God's eyes is not the good we do, nor the sins that we don't do. *We are sinners!* All that God wants from us is that we humbly admit that there's nothing good about us; then ask Him to forgive us and make us good with *His* goodness.

Even our good deeds can't make us perfect (Isa. 64:6).

"God resists the proud, but gives grace to the humble."

~ James 4:6

God made Jesus Christ (who had no sin) to be our sin and die on the cross for us, so that we could become righteous - right with God (2 Cor. 5:21).

Luke 18:15-17; Matthew 19:13-15

JESUS BLESSES THE CHILDREN

One day some parents brought their children to Jesus so He could lay His hands on them and pray for them. However, the disciples told the parents not to bother Him. But Jesus called the children and said,

"Let the children come to Me."

"Don't stop them! For the kingdom of heaven belongs to those who are like these children" And He placed His hands on their heads and blessed them.

Jesus loves children! Children's hearts are trusting, carefree, forgiving, sensitive, hopeful. That's what makes children so special to Jesus.

Although children aren't perfect, they are innocent in their thinking and drawn to the Truth: they easily believe in God and want to please Him. Jesus said that the kingdom of heaven belongs to those who are child-like; those who have a gentle attitude and a pure heart.

Lord, thank You that I am special and precious to You! Amen.

"Beware that you don't look down on any of these little ones. For I tell you that in heaven their angels are always in the presence of My heavenly Father."

~ Matthew 18:10, NLT

You are never too young for God to use you! Josiah was eight years old when he became king and reigned for 31 years (2 Chron. 34:1-2).

Matthew 19:16-22; Luke 18:18-23

JESUS AND THE RICH MAN

A man came to Jesus and asked "Teacher, what good deed must I do to have eternal life?"

"Obey the commandments," Jesus told him.

"Which ones?" the man wanted to know. So Jesus mentioned some of the commandments as examples.

"I have obeyed all these commandments," the young man replied. "What else must I do?"

Jesus replied, "If you want to be perfect, sell all your possessions and come follow Me." But when the man heard this, he went away sad, for he was very rich.

Although this man had tried to be good, he felt there was something missing and he needed to do more to get to heaven. So he asked Jesus, "What else must I do?" Perhaps he wanted to 'score a few more points' just to make sure.

But being quite good, or even very good, won't get us to heaven – we must be perfect! Jesus said that this man needed to get rid of an idol in his life! He needed to let go of his money and follow Him, because *Jesus makes us perfect*.

REMEMBER Faith in Jesus makes us right with God (Phil. 3:9).

For the person who keeps all of the laws except one is as guilty as a person who has broken all of God's laws.

~ James 2:10, NLT

Those who are rich should not trust in their money, but their hope should be in God. He gives us everything we need (1 Tim. 6:17).

Luke 19:1-6

ZACCHAEUS MAKES A PLAN

Jesus entered Jericho and was making His way through the town. Many people, including Zacchaeus (Zac-ee-us) a tax collector, lined the street wanting to see Jesus as He passed by.

Zacchaeus tried to get a look at Jesus but he was too short to see over the crowd, so he ran on ahead and climbed a tree. When Jesus came to the tree and saw Zacchaeus, He called to him; "Zacchaeus, come down! I must be a guest in your home today."

Zacchaeus quickly climbed down with great excitement and joy took Jesus to his house.

Seeing the large crowd, Zacchaeus could have thought of a number of excuses to just walk away: "I'm too short; the crowd is so inconsiderate; Jesus doesn't even know me."

But Zacchaeus made a plan! And that's what made Jesus see the longing Zacchaeus had to meet with Him; and so Jesus made a plan too.

As Zacchaeus took Jesus to his home, his heart was filled with ______________ .

May all who seek You rejoice and be glad in You; may those who long for Your saving help always say, "The LORD is great!"

~ Psalm 40:16

Do you make an effort to get closer to Jesus through prayer and reading the Bible? Are you glad when you can go to church? (Ps. 122:1).

Luke 19:7-10

ZACCHAEUS TAKES ACTION

Zacchaeus was very happy and took Jesus to his home. But when the people saw this, they started grumbling, "This man has gone to be the guest of a sinner!"

Meanwhile, Zacchaeus stood up and said to Jesus, "I will give half my wealth to the poor, Lord; and if I have cheated people on their taxes, I will give them back four times as much!"

Jesus said to him, "Salvation has come to this home today. For the Son of Man came to seek and save those who are lost."

Jesus came to earth to search for those who are *lost* in sin and to *save* them from eternal death. Zacchaeus was lost. But he wanted to be found; and so, a very special guest came to his house, and into his life.

Jesus changed his heart from being dishonest and greedy to being joyful and generous. Jesus wants to be your guest too! He wants to make you new inside, and live in you (John 14:23). All you need to do is ask Jesus to forgive you and invite Him to be in charge of your life.

Lord, Your love is great, and Your grace is amazing! Amen.

If we confess our sins, He is faithful and just and will forgive us our sins and purify us from all unrighteousness.

~ 1 John 1:9

Anyone who belongs to Christ has become new on the inside. The old life is gone; a new life lies ahead for them (2 Cor. 5:17).

Matthew 19:27-28

BENEFITS OF FOLLOWING JESUS

Peter the disciple said to Jesus, "We have left everything to follow You! What reward will there be for us?"

Jesus replied, "I assure you that when the world is made new and the Son of Man sits upon His glorious throne, you who have been My followers will also sit on twelve thrones, judging the twelve tribes of Israel."

What's in it for us? When people commit to something, they usually want to know what they'll get out of it. But being a disciple isn't like being a member of a club. In fact, Jesus gave His life so that we could be members of God's *family*.

But there's more! Jesus told the disciples that the best is yet to come; that they will rule over the twelve tribes of Israel. And for us who believe; we will rule over angels when we are made perfect in heaven (1 Cor. 6:3).

But right now, we have the Father's care and protection on earth. His promise to hear our prayers and help us; the peace and joy that Jesus gives; the comfort and guidance of the Holy Spirit, and much more!

See how many promises you can find in Psalm 34.

Out of the fullness of His grace He has blessed us all, giving us one blessing after another.

~ John 1:16

We have been blessed with every spiritual blessing; and every promise of God applies to us (Eph. 1:3; 2 Cor. 1:20).

Matthew 20:1-15

EARLY OR LATE

Jesus told this parable: "The kingdom of heaven is like a master who went out early one morning to hire workers for his vineyard. He agreed to pay them the normal daily wage and sent them out to work. Later that morning he hired more workers, and again at midday, and late in the afternoon.

"At the end of the day, he paid everyone a full day's wage. Those who were hired early in the morning were upset and said, 'Those people over there worked only one hour, yet you've paid them the same as you paid us even though we worked all day.'"

"The master answered them, 'I haven't been unfair! You agreed to work all day for the usual wage. Should you be jealous because I am kind to others?'"

It doesn't really matter how many years we've served the Lord, all of us will receive God's promised reward of eternal life. Although we will be rewarded differently for *how* we have served God, eternal life is given equally to those who have served God from their earliest years, and those who only started later in life.

God our Master is merciful, not unfair.

Never be lazy, but work hard and serve the Lord enthusiastically.

~ Romans 12:11, NLT

The criminal hanging on a cross next to Jesus was saved just a few hours before he died (Luke 23:39-43).

Luke 18:31-34; Matthew 20:17-19

JESUS KNOWS THAT HE WILL DIE

Jesus was getting ready to leave Jericho and go up to Jerusalem. He took the twelve disciples aside privately and told them what was going to happen to Him when they got there.

"Listen," He said, "we are going to Jerusalem, where the Son of Man will be betrayed. They will sentence Him to die. Then they will hand Him over to the Romans to be mocked; flogged with a whip, and crucified. But on the third day He will be raised from the dead."

Jesus was preparing His disciples for what was going to happen to Him in Jerusalem: "I am going to die," He said, "but I will rise again on the third day!" The disciples, however, missed the details of what Jesus had said.

Perhaps they thought this was a parable; for surely no one could take the life of God's Son – the One who lives forever. Yes, Jesus did have the power over everything and everyone, and no one could take His life; yet, dying for us was the reason Jesus came to earth.

Jesus came to bring peace between God and man (Rom. 5:1) in Jerusalem, *The City of Peace*.

"Christ Jesus came into the world to save sinners" – and I am the worst of them all.

~ 1 Timothy 1:15, NLT

Jerusalem gets its name from the city of Salem (*Jerusalem*) or *Shalom*, meaning peace. Jerusalem is also known as *The City of Peace*.

Matthew 20:20-23

PLACES OF HONOR

The mother of the disciples James and John came to kneel before Jesus to ask Him a favor. "What is it you want?" Jesus asked.

She replied, "In Your Kingdom, please let my two sons sit in places of honor next to You, one on Your right and the other on Your left."

Jesus answered by saying to them, "You don't know what you are asking! I have no right to say who will sit on My right or My left. My Father has prepared those places for the ones He has chosen."

What makes one follower of Jesus more special than another? Although James, John and Peter were, at times, the privileged ones (Mark 9:2), they were just as human and imperfect as the others. Sitting on the right hand side of a king is to sit in a place of authority and power.

But power to rule (to be in charge) can make one feel more special than others, and that leads to pride. Jesus the King of kings had just told them that He was going to die for them; and now they were selfishly wanting to sit in places of honor.

Thank You, Jesus, for showing us what true humility is. Amen.

From now on the Son of Man will be seated in the place of power at God's right hand.

~ Luke 22:69, NLT

Jesus humbled Himself by becoming human and dying on a cross for us. Now God has given Him the highest place of honor (Phil. 2:5-11).

Matthew 20:29-34; Luke 18:35-43

JESUS HEALS TWO BLIND MEN

As Jesus and the disciples left the town of Jericho, a large crowd followed them. Two blind men were sitting beside the road. When they heard that Jesus was coming that way, they began to shout, "Lord, Son of David, have mercy on us!"

"Be quiet!" the crowd yelled at them. But they only shouted louder, "Lord, have mercy on us!"

When Jesus heard them, He stopped and called, "What do you want Me to do for you?"

"Lord," they said, "we want to see!" Jesus felt sorry for them and touched their eyes. Instantly they could see! Then they followed Him.

What would have happened if the men had listened to the crowd, thinking that the crowd is probably right? Do *you* sometimes listen to the crowd? The Bible warns us that the crowd is usually wrong (Matt. 7:13).

Jesus asked the men, "What do you want Me to do for you?" It sounded too good to be true – almost like being given a wish! Above all else, these men wanted to see; so Jesus let them see.

What would you like Jesus to do for you? You can just ask Him.

Since we know He hears us when we make our requests, we also know that He will give us what we ask for.

~ 1 John 5:15, NLT

Do not allow the world (unbelievers) to tell you what to do, or you will start thinking like them and becoming like them (Rom. 12:2).

John 12:1-7

MARY ANOINTS JESUS

The Saturday before the Passover celebration, Jesus arrived in Bethany, the home of Lazarus (whom Jesus had raised from the dead). Martha served a dinner for everyone, and Lazarus was there too. Then Mary took a jar of expensive perfume, and poured it on Jesus' feet, and wiped His feet with her hair.

But Judas, who would soon betray Jesus, said, "That perfume was worth a year's wages. It should have been sold and the money given to the poor."

He didn't care about the poor, but being in charge of the disciples' money, he often stole some for himself.

Jesus replied, "Leave her alone. She did this to prepare My body for burial."

Mary didn't know that Jesus would soon die on a cross. If she had thought about her plan with the perfume for another week, it would have been too late.

Sometimes it's better not to think too long and hard about being generous. When giving, we should let our hearts tell us what to do, even when it doesn't make sense to anyone else.

Plan to do something kind and special for someone.

Each of you should give what you have decided in your heart to give ... for God loves a cheerful giver.

~ 2 Corinthians 9:7

In Bible times, oils, spices and perfumes were spread on the body of a dead person. Jesus said that Mary was preparing His body to be buried.

Matthew 21:1-7

TWO DISCIPLES FETCH A DONKEY

Jesus and the disciples set out for Jerusalem. As they neared the village of Bethphage, Jesus sent two of His disciples on ahead, saying to them, "Go into the village and as soon as you enter it, you will see a donkey and a colt tied there. Untie them and bring them to Me."

This took place to fulfill the prophecy in Zechariah 9:9, "Tell the people of Jerusalem,

> 'Look, your King is coming to you. He is humble,
> riding on a donkey – riding on a donkey's colt.'"

The two disciples did as Jesus commanded. They brought the donkey and the colt to Him and threw their garments over the colt for Jesus to sit on.

A king should have been riding a horse, not a borrowed donkey! Riding on a donkey is a sign of humility, gentleness and peace. Kings needed a fast, powerful horse when going into battle.

But Jesus was coming in peace. The battle that lay ahead for Him was against the power of sin and death: a battle He would face without a fight, and yet rise up as the conquering King.

Lord, You have forgiven my sin and given me eternal life! Amen.

The horse is prepared for the day of battle, but the victory belongs to the Lord.

~ Proverbs 21:31, NLT

Jesus has defeated death; but one day He will come from heaven riding on a white horse to conquer the devil (Rev. 19:11; 20:10).

Matthew 21:8-11; John 12:12-15

PALM SUNDAY

When the crowd that had come for the Passover feast heard that Jesus was coming, they took palm branches and went out to meet Him. Some spread their garments on the road; others cut branches from the trees and spread them before Jesus, shouting,

"Hosanna!"
"Blessed is He who comes in the name of the Lord!"

When Jesus entered Jerusalem, people asked, "Who is this?" The crowds answered, "This is Jesus, the Prophet from Nazareth in Galilee."

The crowd had seen the miracles Jesus did (Luke 19:37), and many had seen Him raise Lazarus (John 12:17). They were hoping that as Jesus entered Jerusalem, they would finally be able to make Him king (John 6:15) so that He would free them from the Romans.

But setting them free from the rule of the Romans would have only helped *them*, and only in *this life*. Jesus had a far bigger plan – to set the whole world free from the power of the devil and give *everlasting life* to *all* who believe.

Lord, You deserve all my praise and adoration! Amen.

Praise the Lord, all you nations. Praise Him, all you people of the earth.

~ Psalm 117:1, NLT

The word *hosanna* means "Lord, save us," but *hosanna* also became a joyous shout of praise.

Luke 19:41-44

JESUS WEEPS FOR JERUSALEM

As Jesus came closer to Jerusalem and saw the city ahead, He began to weep, saying, "How I wish today that you of all people would understand the way to peace. But now it's too late, and peace is hidden from your eyes.

"The time will come when your enemies will surround you and close in on you from every side. They will crush you into the ground. Your enemies will not leave a single stone in place, because you did not accept your opportunity for salvation."

How sad the words, *it's too late*. Jesus had come to Jerusalem many times, and He had tried to reach out to the Jews for three years, but they had stubbornly rejected Him. They pushed away the only chance they had of knowing God personally and having eternal life.

Now it was too late! As in the days of Noah, when people could have been saved from the coming flood by entering the ark, the door was now shut for the Jews, and judgment was coming.

The way to real peace is through Jesus (John 14:27).

Just as it was in the days of Noah, so also will it be in the days of the Son of Man.

~ Luke 17:26

In 70 AD, about forty years after Jesus went back to heaven, the Romans conquered the city of Jerusalem, exactly the way Jesus said they would.

Matthew 21:12-13; Mark 11:15-17

JESUS CLEARS THE TEMPLE AGAIN!

In the city (Jerusalem), Jesus entered the temple area and began to drive out all the people buying and selling animals. He knocked over the tables of the money changers and seats of those selling doves.

He said to them, "The Scriptures declare, 'My house will be called a house of prayer,' but you have turned it into a den of thieves!"

This was the second time Jesus cleared the temple by chasing out the traders and businessmen. But what were they doing there? In those days people sacrificed animals at the temple, and the traders made it easy for them to buy an animal right there.

With the Passover feast coming up, business was good. People would come from different countries, so money changers made a profit by exchanging the money from other countries for the money used in Judea.

But things have changed since then. Jesus has sent the Holy Spirit into the hearts of believers. God no longer lives in a temple. He now lives in *us* through His Spirit, and our *bodies* have become His temple (1 Cor. 6:19). That is why we must be very careful to honor the Lord with our bodies.

Lord, what a thought, that You would want to live in me. Amen.

God bought you with a high price. So you must honor God with your body.

~ 1 Corinthians 6:20, NLT

Animal sacrifices were stopped when the temple was destroyed, and for Jewish Christians, when Jesus died and rose again (Heb. 9:27-28).

Matthew 21:14-17

CHILDREN SHOUTING PRAISES

The blind and the lame came to Jesus in the temple, and He healed them. The children were happy and started shouting in the temple courtyard, "Hosanna to the Son of David!"

When the chief priests saw the amazing miracles Jesus performed, and heard what the children were shouting, they were upset and said to Him, "Do You hear what these children are saying?"

Jesus replied, "Yes, I do. Have you never read, 'From the mouths of little children and infants, You have created praise'?" And He left them and went back to Bethany, where He spent the night.

The children were doing what Psalm 150:1-2 tells us to do: "Praise God in His temple! Praise Him for the mighty things He has done."

What was obvious to the children – that Jesus deserves our praise – was upsetting to the temple officials. They were irritated that "noisy" children were drawing people's attention to Jesus. And that is what we still do today when we sing praises: we draw people's attention to Jesus and tell of His greatness.

Read Psalm 148, and count how many times it says *Praise*.

I will praise the LORD all my life; I will sing praise to my God as long as I live.

~ Psalm 146:2

There are two sacrifices that please God: the sacrifice of serving with our lives (Rom. 12:1), and the sacrifice of our praise (Heb. 13:15).

Matthew 21:18-19

THE CURSED FIG TREE

Early the next morning, as Jesus made His way back to Jerusalem, He was hungry. He noticed a fig tree beside the road and went over to see if there were any figs on it, but there were only leaves. Then He said to it, "May you never bear fruit again!" And immediately the fig tree wilted and dried up.

Jesus was acting out a parable for the disciples. The tree in the lesson is the unbelieving nation of Israel. It stood alone next to the road, like Israel standing out among the nations of the world as a sign of God's blessing.

Though the outward signs of the religious Jews showed promise of growth, like the leaves on the tree; there was no fruit! Inside, the Jews were spiritually dead, and so they didn't bear the spiritual fruit of goodness.

The season to be fruitful had come, and the Jews should have been the first to accept Jesus the Messiah. But they didn't. And so God hardened their hearts; like that fig tree, they dried up spiritually. But because God is patient and merciful, they will one day turn back to Him (Rom. 11:25, 31).

God's Spirit inside you gives life and make you fruitful.

"I will pour out a spirit of grace and prayer on the family of David and on the people of Jerusalem."

~ Zechariah 12:10, NLT

The Jewish law allowed a person to pick and eat fruit from a tree that had been planted by someone else (Deut. 23:24).

Matthew 21:23-27; Luke 20:1-8

THE QUESTION ABOUT JESUS' AUTHORITY

When Jesus returned to the temple and began teaching, the chief priests and elders came up to Him and demanded, "By what authority are You doing these things? Who gave You the right?

"I'll tell you by what authority I do these things if you answer one question," Jesus replied. "Did John's right to baptize come from heaven or from humans?"

They talked it over among themselves and finally replied, "We don't know." So Jesus said to them, "Then I won't tell you by what authority I do these things."

Being in charge of the temple, the officials were angry that Jesus had come in as a spiritual teacher and leader and taken over what they were supposed to do.

Although the priests and elders should have had all the answers, when Jesus challenged *them* with a question, they said, "We don't know."

It was a safe answer – an easy way to avoid a personal challenge from Jesus on one hand, and upsetting the crowd on the other. And so the "know-it-alls" admitted before the crowd that they didn't actually know it all.

God's Word shows what's in a person's heart (Heb. 4:12).

Jesus told His disciples, "I have been given all authority in heaven and on earth."

~ Matthew 28:18, NLT

Be ready to give an answer to those who want to know why you believe what you do (1 Pet. 3:15).

Matthew 21:28-32

THE TWO SONS

Jesus said to the Jewish leaders, "A man with two sons went to the first son and asked him to go work in the vineyard. The son answered, 'No, I won't go,' but later he changed his mind and went anyway."

"Then the father asked the other son to go. This son said, 'Yes, sir, I will.' But he didn't go. Which of the two obeyed his father?"

"The first," they replied.

Jesus told them, "Bad people [who turn to God] are entering the Kingdom ahead of you. For John the Baptist showed you the right way to live, but you didn't believe him, yet many bad people did."

Jesus told the priests and elders that they, who should have been the ones to serve God, were disobedient. Like the second son, they had *said* all the right things, but they didn't *do* what God wanted them to do. Meanwhile, bad people who had not obeyed God at first, had changed their minds and were now serving God.

REMEMBER What you *do* means more than what you *say* you'll do.

"Not everyone who says to Me, 'Lord, Lord,' will enter the kingdom of heaven, but only the one who does the will of My Father who is in heaven."

~ Matthew 7:21

Many sinners, tax collectors, and even soldiers asked John what they should do to please God (Luke 3:10-14). But the chief priests and elders didn't.

Matthew 21:33-41; Mark 12:1-9

THE WORKERS IN THE VINEYARD

Jesus told another parable: Jesus said, "There was a landowner who planted a vineyard and rented it to some vineyard workers.

At the time of the grape harvest, he sent his servants to collect his share of the crop. But the workers grabbed his servants, beat one, killed one, and stoned another. Then he sent other servants to them, but the workers treated them the same way.

Finally, the owner sent his son, thinking, 'Surely they will respect my son.' But the workers said to each other, 'He will own the land one day so let's kill him. Then we will own the land.' So they took him outside the vineyard and killed him."

In the past, God had sent His servants, the prophets, to the Jewish people, but they killed the prophets. Then God (the landowner) sent His only Son Jesus to His vineyard.

The chief priests and elders in the story are the wicked workers, who would soon take Jesus outside the city of Jerusalem (the vineyard) and kill Him there.

Lord God, You are so patient and merciful. Thank You! Amen.

The earth is the Lord's, and everything in it. The world and all its people belong to Him.

~ Psalm 24:1, NLT

God *allowed* Jesus to die in our place; Jesus *gave* His life for us because it was the only way that He could save us from sin (Gal. 1:4).

Matthew 21:42-44

THE CORNERSTONE

Jesus asked the chief priest and Pharisees if they had ever read this in the Scriptures:

> "The stone that the builders rejected
> has become the cornerstone" (Ps. 118:22).

"Anyone who stumbles over that stone will be broken to pieces," He said.

Once builders have dug a foundation for a building, the first stone they lay is a big cornerstone. It is the most important stone because the walls are lined up with the sides and measured from its outside corner.

Jesus is our unmovable foundation stone. He is also the foundation on which His church is built. But those who reject Jesus will stumble over that stone because they disobey His message (1 Pet. 2:8).

The same stone that is a firm foundation for those who believe will crush those who reject Him, when Jesus who is our Savior becomes their Judge.

REMEMBER Jesus is your sure foundation (Isa. 28:16).

For no one can lay any foundation other than the one already laid, which is Jesus Christ.

~ 1 Corinthians 3:11

We as living stones are being used in God's building, with Jesus as our cornerstone and foundation (1 Pet. 2:1-5; Eph. 2:20).

Matthew 22:15-22; Luke 20:20-26

THE QUESTION ABOUT PAYING TAXES

The Pharisees met together to think of a way to trap Jesus into saying something for which He could be arrested. So they sent some men to say to Him, "Teacher, we know how honest You are. You teach the way of God truthfully. Now tell us what You think: Is it right to pay taxes to Caesar or not?"

But Jesus knew their evil motives and said, "Why are you trying to trap Me? Show Me the coin used for paying the tax." When they handed Him a Roman coin, He asked, "Whose picture and title are stamped on it?"

"Caesar's," they replied.

Then Jesus said, "So give back to Caesar what is Caesar's, and to God what is God's."

The Jews knew that Jesus hadn't said or done anything for which the Romans could arrest Him. So they tried to trap Jesus into saying that the Jews shouldn't pay taxes to the Roman government.

However Jesus' wise answer showed that by paying taxes, which they should do, they would not be honoring Caesar above God.

Lord, help me to speak words that are kind and wise. Amen.

The mouth of the righteous person reflects on wisdom. His tongue speaks what is fair.

~ Psalm 37:30

God wants us to obey the government of our country, whether we agree with what they are doing, or not (Rom. 13:1-2).

Matthew 23:38-39

JUST A BUILDING

On the Tuesday before He died, Jesus was telling the disciples and the others around Him not to follow the example of the Pharisees. Jesus pointed out to the Pharisees the ways in which they were hypocrites (Matt. 23).

They tried to show off how good they were, yet their hearts were filled with all kinds of evil. This was the last time Jesus spoke to the Pharisees in the temple.

Jesus said to them, "And now, look, your house is abandoned. For I tell you this, you will not see Me again until you say, 'Blessed is He who comes in the name of the Lord!'"

Although the temple had been God's house, now it was *their* house – just a building. Jesus was leaving it to them, empty and deserted. From now on God would no longer live in a man-made temple (Acts 17:24); instead, He would live in the hearts of those who love Him.

Yet, Jesus left the door of hope open to the Jews. He knew that one day they would turn back to Him (Hos. 3:4-5). And so, this harsh chapter closes with a glow of hope and a promise.

Lord, You are welcome to live in my heart! Amen.

The Lord is loving and merciful, slow to become angry and full of constant love.

~ Psalm 145:8

God will one day pour out His Spirit on the Jewish people. They will weep when they see Jesus whom they crucified (Zech. 12:10).

WRONGDOINGS GOD DOESN'T LIKE

God hates all sin because it separates us from Him and spoils our relationship with others. Yet, there are certain sins that Jesus spoke against often – sins that come from an evil heart and a rotten attitude.

- **Being a hypocrite.** A hypocrite is someone who pretends to be good, but those good deeds are a cover-up for a sinful heart. Such people always seem to find fault with others (Matt. 7:3-5). God wants us to be honest about our weaknesses and not look down on others (Rom. 14:1).
- **Worshiping idols.** The second commandment of God tells us not to have idols (Exod. 20:3-4). Anything that takes the place of God in our lives, or becomes more important to us than our relationship with God is an idol (for example, money). God wants us to love Him more than anything or anyone (Mark 12:30).
- **Pride.** People who are proud, think they are so much better than others (Luke 18:9). They also think that everything in life is about them. The opposite of pride is humility. Jesus gave us the perfect example of what it means to be humble and serve others (Phil. 2:5-8).
- **Unbelief.** Unbelief comes from a stubborn heart that refuses to accept the truth. The opposite of unbelief is faith. Without faith we cannot please God (Heb. 11:6).
- **Selfishness.** A person is selfish when he only thinks of himself and doesn't care about others. The opposite of being selfish is being generous and caring. God cares about the weak and the needy and has given us the task of helping others in whatever way we can (Gal. 6:10).

You will never succeed in life if you try to hide your sins. Confess them and give them up; then God will show mercy to you.

~ Proverbs 28:13

Mark 12:41-44; Luke 21:1-4

THE WIDOW'S COINS

Jesus was sitting near the place where the offerings for the temple were put and watched the people as they put in their money. Many rich people put in large amounts, but a poor woman whose husband had died came and put in two very small copper coins.

Jesus called His disciples to Him and said, "I tell you the truth, this poor widow has given more than anyone else. For they gave only a *tiny part* of all the money they have; but this poor widow gave *everything* she had to live on."

The widow was so poor that *she* was the one needing money. Yet, because of her faith and love for God, she gave the little she had left.

A few coins, given as an act of worship, are worth more to God than large amounts of money given with a wrong attitude. God owns everything anyway (Acts 17:24-25), so to Him, seeing us give with a joyful, thankful heart is worth far more than the value of the money.

How about doing a few chores for some pocket money or saving money in a bottle to give to the Lord?

Give generously to the poor, not grudgingly, for the Lord your God will bless you in everything you do.

~ Deuteronomy 15:10, NLT

In Bible times, widows were often poor because they had no work. God expects the church to help these women (Ps. 68:5; 1 Tim. 5:3).

Matthew 24:1-2; Luke 21:5-6

TEMPLE STONES

As Jesus was leaving the temple grounds, His disciples pointed out to Him the various temple buildings. But Jesus said to them, "Do you see these buildings? I tell you the truth, they will be completely broken down. Not one stone will be left on top of another!"

Jesus was telling the disciples what would happen in the future: that the temple with its thick stone walls would be broken down to a heap of rubble.

God has always wanted to be near His people, but because of our sin, the only way He could live among us was by His presence filling the temple (1 Kings 8:11). But even then, only the high priest could get close to God, and only once a year (Heb. 9:7).

Now that Jesus has come to take away our sin, God can live in our hearts through the Holy Spirit because Jesus makes our hearts sinless and pure. All believers together have become the new temple of God, and we are the living stones of His temple (1 Pet. 2:4-5).

Lord, thank You that I can be a stone in Your temple. Amen.

Don't you realize that all of you together are the temple of God and that the Spirit of God lives in you?

~ 1 Corinthians 3:16, NLT

After Jesus left earth, the Jews rebelled against the Roman empire. So the Romans destroyed much of Jerusalem and the temple in 70 AD.

Matthew 24:3-13; Luke 21:7-19

TROUBLE ON THE WAY

As Jesus was sitting on the Mount of Olives, the disciples came to Him and asked, "Tell us, when will all this happen? What sign will signal Your return and the end of the world?"

Jesus replied, "There will be wars, famines and earthquakes in many parts of the world. But all this is only the beginning of the trouble to come. My followers will be persecuted and hated because of their love for Me; and many will give up their faith and turn away from Me. In those last days, the wickedness on earth will become so bad, that many will stop loving altogether."

The disciples knew that, before the end of the world, Jesus would come back and take those who love Him to be with Him in heaven. When Jesus told them that the temple (God's house) would be broken down, this seemed like the end of the world to them.

So they asked Jesus how they'd be able to tell when the end of the world and His coming were near. One of the signs, Jesus told them, was that they could expect trouble (John 16:33). Yet we need never be afraid, because Jesus will be with us to the end, and He will save us.

REMEMBER God is our refuge in times of trouble (Ps. 46:1-2).

He will keep you strong to the end so that you will be free from all blame on the day when our Lord Jesus Christ returns.

~ 1 Corinthians 1:8, NLT

When we see Jesus coming in the clouds, we will all be changed: we will get new, perfect bodies and live forever with God (1 Cor. 15:51-52).

Matthew 24:36, 42-44

BE READY!

Still talking about His coming back, Jesus said to the disciples, "No one knows the day or the hour when these things will happen, not even the angels in heaven or the Son Himself. Only the Father knows."

"Think of it this way," He said. "If a homeowner knew exactly when a burglar was coming, he would keep a lookout all the time. In the same way, you must be ready all the time, for the Son of Man will come at a time when you *don't* expect Him."

Jesus was saying that we must be ready for Him as though He was coming today or tonight. If we are saved and serving Him, we can sleep peacefully, knowing that if Jesus should come, we would go to be with Him in heaven (John 14:1-3).

However, the parable is a warning to those who say that Jesus won't be coming back; those who foolishly live sinful lives, not caring that they are unsafe (not saved). They are the ones who will "wake up" and find that it is too late to make their hearts right with God.

Lord, I love You! Thank You that one day I will be with You. Amen.

For you know quite well that the day of the Lord's return will come unexpectedly, like a thief in the night.

~ 1 Thessalonians 5:2, NLT

When Jesus comes back, all believers will be taken up in the clouds to meet the Lord in the air (1 Thess. 4:17).

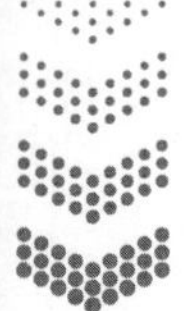

Matthew 25:1-13

THE TEN BRIDESMAIDS

Jesus said, "The kingdom of heaven will be like ten bridesmaids who took their lamps and went to meet the bridegroom. Five of them were foolish and didn't take enough oil for their lamps; but the other five were wise and took along extra oil."

"At midnight they heard a shout, 'The bridegroom is on his way! Come and meet him!' All the bridesmaids got up and prepared their lamps. But the lamps of the foolish ones were going out so they went off to go buy some more oil.

While they were away, the bridegroom arrived. So the five who were ready went in with him to the marriage feast, and the door was locked. When the other five bridesmaids eventually got back, they were locked out and couldn't attend the wedding feast!"

The foolish bridesmaids thought they could arrive at the feast just as they were – unprepared. The wise bridesmaids, however, made sure that their lamps would keep burning.

We prepare ourselves for Jesus when we ask Him to save us, and the Holy Spirit becomes our never-ending supply of oil. He keeps our light shining with goodness in the world (Matt. 5:14-16).

Lord, may my light shine brightly all the time, wherever I am. Amen.

"So you also must be ready, because the Son of Man will come at an hour when you do not expect Him."

~ Matthew 24:44

The church is the bride of Christ (Rev. 19:7-8), and He (Jesus) is the bridegroom (John 3:28-29).

Matthew 25:14-18

PARABLE OF THE TALENTS

Jesus used another parable to help the disciples understand what it will be like when He comes back. He said to them, "A man was going on a trip, so he gave each of his servants some money, trusting them to take care of it for him. He gave five talents to one, two talents to another, and one talent to the last.

"The servant with the five talents began to invest the money and earned five more. The servant with two talents also went to work and earned two more. But the servant who received the one talent dug a hole in the ground and hid his master's money."

God has given each of us certain abilities, like the talents in the story. What we do with them is up to us. Like the servants who invested their talents, we could improve the abilities God has given us so that we can do even *more,* and do things *better*.

The master leaving on his trip is like our Master (Jesus) going back to heaven. We don't know when He'll be back; but we should do the best we can with what He has given us so that we will please Him and be a blessing to others.

How are you using the abilities God has given you?

God in His mercy has given us this work to do, and so we do not become discouraged.

~ 2 Corinthians 4:1

A talent in Bible times was a heavy gold or silver disc worth a large sum of money, which could have taken many years to earn (Ezra 8:26).

OCTOBER

1 WAY
FOLLOW IT

1 TRUTH
BELIEVE IT

1 LIFE
LIVE IT

Matthew 25:14-46

USING OUR TALENTS AND GIFTS

God has invested something special and precious in each of us. He has placed abilities in us that make us valuable for His use, and He trusts us to honor His name. "Now it is required that those who have been given a trust must prove faithful" (1 Cor. 4:2).

Talents

Each of us has certain talents, which are natural abilities we are born with. We may be good at music, gymnastics, writing, art, speaking, numbers and so on. Some people are so talented in one area that they may spend their lives doing what they're good at.

Others may have a number of talents and enjoy using all of them. But even skills and talents need to be developed through disciplined training and practice.

Make a list of the things you are good at:

____

____

____

Gifts

When we are born again and the Holy Spirit comes to live in us, He gives us one or more spiritual gifts. These are spiritual abilities with which we can serve each other.

Here are some: encouraging others; giving to others; caring for people; making wise decisions; being able to lead; helping in some way (Rom. 12:6-8, 1 Cor. 12:8-10).

Think about how you can honor God with your talents.

Think about ways you can serve others with your gift.

God has given each of you a gift from His great variety of spiritual gifts. Use them well to serve one another.

~ 1 Peter 4:10 NLT

Matthew 25:19-29

GOOD AND FAITHFUL SERVANTS

In a parable that Jesus told, the master had gone away and left his servants with different amounts of money (talents). Two of the servants used the money to make more, while the third hid the money.

Jesus continued the parable by saying, "When their master returned from his trip, he called them to tell him how they had used his money.

The servant to whom he had given five talents came forward and showed him five more. The master praised him; 'Well done, my good and faithful servant. You have been faithful in handling this small amount, so now I will give you many more responsibilities.' The same happened with the servant who had received the two talents and had made two more.

Then the servant with the one talent came and said, 'Master, I was afraid I would lose your money, so I hid it. Look, here is your money back.' But the master was angry with him and called him a lazy, wicked servant. And the master took away the one talent he had."

The two servants who used their talents, pleased their master. They were given more important tasks and were allowed to keep their talents. But the lazy servant, who didn't want to risk using his talent, lost everything!

FIND OUT What two talents did David use? (1 Sam. 16:18, 17:50).

"Whoever has will be given more; whoever does not have, even what they have will be taken from them."

~ Mark 4:25

God told Moses to build a beautiful tabernacle for Him, and to let all those who were skilled (talented) help to make things for it (Exod. 35:10).

Matthew 25:31-34

THE SHEEP AND THE GOATS

Jesus said, "When I, the Son of Man come in My glory, with all the angels, I will sit upon My throne and all the nations will be gathered in My presence. I will separate the people as a shepherd separates the sheep from the goats. I will place the sheep on My right side and the goats on My left.

Then I will say to those on the right, '*Come*, you who are blessed by My Father, inherit the Kingdom prepared for you from the creation of the world.'

Then I will turn to those on the left and say, '*Away from Me*, you that are under God's curse!'"

God is righteous – He can only do what is right, and He has given Jesus the authority and the right to judge people (John 5:27). Yet, Jesus has also taken the blame and punishment for our sin so that we can be made pure.

Anyone who chooses to follow Jesus has eternal life and will enter His everlasting kingdom. But those who choose to carry on living a sinful life instead of doing what is good and right will be separated from Him.

Thank You, Lord, that I am one of Your precious sheep. Amen.

Know that the Lord is God. It is He who made us, and we are His; we are His people, the sheep of His pasture.

~ Psalm 100:3

Jesus knows His sheep; they listen to His voice and follow Him. He keeps them safe and gives them eternal life (John 10:27-28).

Matthew 25:34-40

DOING GOOD

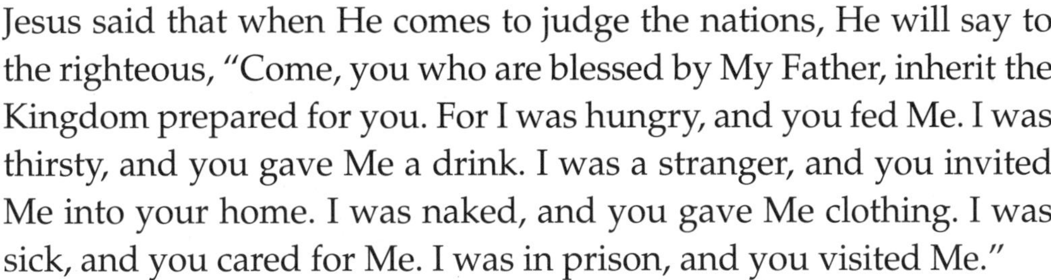

Jesus said that when He comes to judge the nations, He will say to the righteous, "Come, you who are blessed by My Father, inherit the Kingdom prepared for you. For I was hungry, and you fed Me. I was thirsty, and you gave Me a drink. I was a stranger, and you invited Me into your home. I was naked, and you gave Me clothing. I was sick, and you cared for Me. I was in prison, and you visited Me."

The righteous ones will reply, "Lord, when did we do all these things for You?"

Then Jesus will say, "I tell you the truth, whatever you did for one of the least of these brothers and sisters of Mine, you did for Me!"

Trying to be good doesn't get us to heaven – Jesus does! He makes us good by taking away our sin (when we ask Him to) and puts His goodness in us. But Jesus does expect us to show our changed hearts by the way we live.

We must become more and more like Him by being kind and caring. And remember, whatever you do for someone, you are actually doing for Jesus!

Lord, help me to see what I can do for others. Amen.

What good is it, my brothers and sisters, if someone claims to have faith but has no deeds? Can such faith save them?

~ James 2:14

When we do good, we must do it secretly (without making a show of it), then God is pleased with us and will reward us (Matt. 6:3-4).

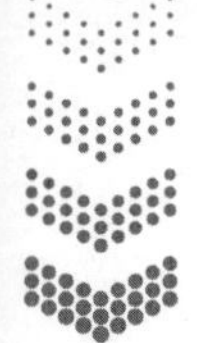

Matthew 26:1-2, 14-16

JUDAS SWITCHES SIDES

When Jesus had finished saying all these things, He said to His disciples, "As you know, the Passover begins in two days, and the Son of Man will be handed over to be crucified."

Then Judas Iscariot, one of the twelve disciples, went to the leading priests and asked, "How much will you pay me to betray Jesus to you?" And they gave him thirty pieces of silver. From then on Judas looked for the right time and place to hand Jesus over to them (when the crowds weren't around because the priests feared that people would become angry).

Judas had played his part as a disciple quite well until now. No one, except Jesus, knew what was going on in his mind and in his heart. Perhaps his comment, when Mary poured her perfume on Jesus, may have shown what was in his heart (John 12:4-6). His heart was drawn to money rather than remaining loyal to Jesus.

So Judas went to the priests, knowing that they were planning to have Him killed, and told them that he was willing to lead them to where Jesus would be. Thirty pieces of silver is what Judas got out of the deal – a bag of money for the King of kings.

Draw a bag of money in the block ⇨

Is anything worth more than your soul?

~ Mark 8:37, NLT

The betrayal of Jesus was prophesied in the Old Testament about 500 years before it happened (Zech. 11:12-13).

Luke 22:7-13; Matthew 26:17-19

PREPARING THE PASSOVER MEAL

The next day, Jesus said to Peter and John, "Go and make preparations for us to eat the Passover. As you enter the city (Jerusalem), a man carrying a jar of water will meet you. Follow him into the house he enters and say to the owner, 'The Teacher asks, Where is the room where I can eat the Passover meal with my disciples?'

He will take you upstairs to a large room that is already set up. That is where you should prepare our meal." So they went and found everything just as Jesus had said, and prepared the meal there.

Jesus sent Peter and John off, not mentioning the name of the man they'd meet. This meant that Judas couldn't find out where they'd be and go tell the priest the exact time and place they could arrest Jesus. Jesus wanted the meal to be undisturbed, and the exact timing of what was to happen was important.

In the same way, every detail of your life is important to the Lord because He cares about you. He has made you and He will carry you (Isa. 46:4).

REMEMBER No person can upset God's plan for your life.

My times are in Your hands; deliver me from the hands of my enemies, from those who pursue me.

~ Psalm 31:15

In Bible times, the women usually carried the water. So it was easy for the disciples to recognize the *man* carrying water.

Exodus 12:14; 25-27

THE PASSOVER

The Passover feast was celebrated every year to remind the Jewish people of how God had rescued them from slavery in Egypt.

At that time, God told the Israelites to kill a lamb on the evening of the fourteenth day of the month and spread some of the blood on the top and sides of the door frames (Exod. 12:3-7).

When the angel of death came that night, he passed over the houses with the blood on the door frames. Where there was no blood on the door frames, the oldest son died.

To prepare for the Passover meal, Jesus' disciples would have to sweep the room; arrange the furniture; top up the lamps with oil; fill up the water jars, and get the food for the meal (Exod. 12:8). The meal included:

- Roast lamb, which reminded them of the lamb that had to die so that its blood could save a life (Exod. 12:13). In the same way, Jesus the Lamb of God died so that we will not die, if by faith we believe that His blood saves us (1 Cor. 5:7; Eph. 1:7).
- Bitter herbs reminded them of the bitterness of their slavery in Egypt (Exod. 1:14).
- Unleavened bread (bread made without yeast) reminded them of the haste with which the Israelites left Egypt – they couldn't wait for their bread to rise (Exod. 12:33-34).

Although the Passover feast is still celebrated every year, the sacrifice of animals ended when the temple in Jerusalem was destroyed.

Lord, thank You for saving us. Help us to remember and celebrate all you have done. Amen.

But if we walk in the light, as He is in the light, we have fellowship with one another, and the blood of Jesus, His Son, purifies us from all sin.

~ 1 John 1:7

John 13:1-11

JESUS WASHES THE DISCIPLES' FEET

That evening, having gathered with His disciples in the upstairs room, Jesus knew that the time had come for Him to leave the world and return to His Father. He loved His disciples and wanted to show them just how much He loved them. So He got up, took off His robe and wrapped a towel around His waist. Then He began to wash the disciples' feet, drying them with the towel He had around Him.

When it came to Peter's turn, he didn't want Jesus to wash his feet.

But Jesus said, "Unless I wash you, you won't belong to Me."

Jesus had no parting gift to give His disciples because He owned nothing, so He gave them a very personal gift – *Himself*. He did for the disciples what a servant should have done: wash everyone's dirty feet!

But Peter was embarrassed to have the Lord kneel down and wash his feet – it should have been the other way around. Yet, not allowing Jesus to do this would have been like saying *no* to Jesus' gift; the priceless gift of Himself that makes us clean before God.

How would you feel if Jesus were to wash your feet?

Let us thank God for His priceless gift!

~ 2 Corinthians 9:15

If we follow Jesus, we are His disciples too, and He loves us the way He loved His twelve disciples. All who are saved are disciples (Acts 6:7).

John 13:12-17

"I HAVE SET YOU AN EXAMPLE"

After washing the disciples' feet, Jesus put on His robe again and sat down. He asked them, "Do you understand what I have done for you? You call Me 'Teacher' and 'Lord,' and you are right, because that's what I am. And since I, your Lord and Teacher, have washed your feet, you should also wash one another's feet."

"I have set you an example to follow. Do as I have done to you. Now that you know these things, God will bless you for doing them."

Love in action is a love that you can see and feel. It's more than just a few kind words or a smile. To love the way Jesus wants us to may not always be easy, yet it is possible; that's why it is a command.

- God is love (1 John 4:16).
- Real love can only come from God (1 John 4:7).
- The Holy Spirit pours God's love into our hearts (Rom. 5:5).
- Jesus shows us how to love (1 John 3:16).

Do something kind for someone, like Jesus did.

"This is My commandment: Love each other in the same way I have loved you."

~ John 15:12, NLT

Don't worry that you're still young; set an example by the way you speak; the way you live, and the way you love (1 Tim. 4:12).

Matthew 26:26-29

THE LORD'S SUPPER

While they were eating, Jesus took some bread and gave thanks for it. Then He broke pieces off and gave them to the disciples, saying, "Take this and eat it, for this is My body."

Then He took a cup of wine and gave thanks to God for it. He gave it to them and said, "Each of you drink from it, for this is My blood, which confirms the covenant between God and His people. It is poured out as a sacrifice to forgive the sins of many. I will not drink from this fruit of the vine from now on until I drink it new with you in My Father's kingdom."

This was the last meal that Jesus would have before He went to the cross to die. He used two symbols (touchable signs) to tell the disciples what would soon happen to Him, and also to remind us of His death for us.

By breaking the bread, Jesus was showing how His body would be broken on the cross; and the red wine was like His blood that would flow from His body. Jesus' death brought us eternal life, and that is what we remember when we think of the bread and the wine.

Thank You, Lord for this practical reminder of Your love. Amen.

Whenever you eat this bread and drink this cup, you proclaim the Lord's death until He comes.

~ 1 Corinthians 11:26

Before we eat the bread and drink the wine, we should make sure that our hearts are right – that there is no unforgiven sin (1 Cor. 11:28-29).

Matthew 26:17-30

WHAT IS COMMUNION?

Jesus told us to continue remembering His death by using the symbols of the bread and wine, as He did when He ate the Passover meal with His disciples. We call this special time

- *The Lord's Supper* because it was an evening meal (1 Cor. 11:23-25), or
- *Communion* because we do it when believers get together (in community) with others.

The "meal" is a sign of the New Covenant (agreement) between God and us (Luke 22:20):

- That He will *take away* our sin and *give* us eternal life.
- if we *believe* that Jesus' blood washes away our sin, and *ask* Him to forgive us and make us new.

The bread, which reminds us of His body, was broken into pieces and each person took a small part of the one 'loaf' of bread; and in that way, the bread was shared.

The red wine, which reminds us of Jesus' blood, was passed around (in a cup) from one person to the next and each one took a sip; and so, the wine was shared.

It is these two symbols that are important, and not so much how they are served in a particular church.

We take part in Communion because ...

- the Lord told us to do so (1 Cor. 11:24).
- we are reminded of what Christ has done for us through His life, death and resurrection (1 Cor. 11:25).
- it is an act of faith by which we tell of His death until He comes (1 Cor. 11:26).

Though we are many, we all eat from one loaf of bread, showing that we are one body.

~ 1 Corinthians 10:17, NLT

John 13:18-30; Matthew 26:20-25

JESUS' LAST WORDS TO JUDAS

While Jesus and the disciples were eating, He said to them, "I tell you the truth, one of you will betray Me."

Feeling deeply hurt, they asked Him one by one, "You don't mean me, do You, Lord?"

Jesus replied, "It is the one to whom I give the bread that I dipped in the bowl." And when He had dipped it, He gave it to Judas (prophesied in Ps. 41:9).

Judas, the one who would betray Him, also asked, "Rabbi, am I the one?"

Jesus answered him, "You have said it." Then Jesus said to him, "Hurry and do what you're going to do." So Judas went out. *And it was night!*

Jesus told Judas to hurry and do what he had planned to do – to go tell the priest where they could find Him. It was God's plan for Jesus to be betrayed that very night and die on the cross the following day – the day of Passover (and so become God's Passover Lamb).

Jesus came to earth to be our light (John 12:46), and His loyal disciples stayed close to that light; but for Judas, as he left Jesus and went out, it was night.

How did Jesus show His love for Judas? (John 13:1-5)

"Anyone who isn't with Me opposes Me, and anyone who isn't working with Me is actually working against Me."

~ Luke 11:23, NLT

Judas called Jesus *Rabbi*, which means teacher (John 1:38) for he could not call Him *Lord*, as the other disciples did.

John 13:31-35

A NEW COMMANDMENT

When Judas had left the room, Jesus said, "The Son of Man is now glorified, and because of Him, God is glorified. Dear children, I will be with you only a little longer. So now I am giving you a new command:

'Love one another. As I have loved you,
so you must love one another.'

By loving one another, everyone will know that you are My disciples."

The Old Covenant was an agreement between God and man that said: in order to be perfect, we have to keep the whole law (obey all the commands). But no one could do that, so Jesus came to earth to do what we couldn't do. He kept the whole law for us. Then He put in place the New Covenant, so that we would be *made perfect* by believing in Him.

So now, instead of trying to keep a whole list of commands, we only have one command: To love others. When we keep this command, we are keeping all the commands (because love wants what is best for others).

Love is not a command we can tick off as done: it never ends and has no limits, so we can never love enough.

For the whole law can be summed up in this one command: "Love your neighbor as yourself."

~ Galatians 5:14, NLT

Love is doing what God has commanded; and He commands us to love one another (2 John 1:6).

John 13:36-38; Matthew 26:31-35

JESUS PREDICTS PETER'S DENIAL

Jesus told the disciples that He would be with them only a little while longer (John 13:33). So Peter asked Jesus, "Lord, where are You going?"

Jesus replied, "Where I am going, you cannot follow now, but you will follow later."

"But why can't I come now, Lord?" Peter asked. "I am ready to die for You."

Then Jesus answered, "I tell you the truth, Peter – before the rooster crows tomorrow morning, you will deny three times that you even know Me. In fact, tonight all of you will desert Me. For the Scriptures say, 'God will strike the Shepherd, and the sheep of the flock will be scattered (Zech. 13:7).'"

Peter loved the Lord, but he needed to realize that in his own strength he would fail. The devil had decided to bring Peter down – one of Jesus' most loyal disciples (Luke 22:31-32).

Jesus wanted to prepare Peter, and He prayed for him so that his faith would not fail completely. What Jesus did for Peter, He also does for us when our faith is tested – Jesus *prays* for us (Rom. 8:34).

Thank You, Lord, that You help me when I am weak. Amen.

The Lord is faithful; He will strengthen you and guard you from the evil one.

~ 2 Thessalonians 3:3, NLT

God's loving help will be enough for us when our faith is tested. His power works best in our weakness (2 Cor. 12:9).

John 14:1-4

JESUS COMFORTS THE DISCIPLES

Jesus realized that the disciples were very worried about all that He had told them, so He said,

"Don't let your hearts be troubled.
Trust in God, and trust also in Me.

My Father's house has many rooms. If that were not true, would I have told you that I'm going to prepare a place for you? When everything is ready, I will come and get you, so that you will always be with Me where I am. You know the way to the place where I am going."

A while earlier, Jesus had told the disciples that He was going away and that they couldn't go with Him; but that they would follow later. Peter didn't realize that Jesus wasn't talking about an earthly place. He was talking about heaven.

Jesus wanted His disciples to know that victory lay ahead – that His *death* and *departure* laid the foundation of God's plan to save us from sin. His death would give us *eternal life*; and His going to heaven, the assurance of an *eternal place*.

REMEMBER Whenever you're feeling down, think of what lies ahead!

Why am I discouraged? Why is my heart so sad? I will put my hope in God! I will praise Him again – my Savior and my God!

~ Psalm 43:5, NLT

God blesses those who go through hard times of testing. When they have passed the test, they will receive the crown of life (James 1:12).

John 14:2

WHAT IS HEAVEN LIKE?

Jesus said that He was going away to get a place ready for us in heaven … and that was 2,000 years ago!

Heaven is God's home. God rules the whole universe from His throne in heaven (Ps. 103:19). It is an unimaginably beautiful place where the main street is made of gold so pure that it looks like glass.

Heaven is a real place where all believers go when they die. Believers, however, don't become angels; in fact, we will rule over angels (1 Cor. 6:3). Although we will be spirit-beings like the angels (Matt. 22:30), we will live in new and perfect bodies that will never feel pain or grow old.

What is *not* in heaven

- Sin Revelation 21:27
- Tears Revelation 21:4
- Pain Revelation 21:4
- Night Revelation 22:5
- Sun Revelation 21:23

Who and what *is* in heaven

- God Revelation 7:11
- Jesus Revelation 5:13
- Angels Revelation 5:11
- Singing Revelation 15:3
- Joy Revelation 19:7

Heaven is the place where you will go if you love and obey the Lord.

To the Lord your God belong the heavens, even the highest heavens, the earth and everything in it.

~ Deuteronomy 10:14

Heaven is a real place (Phil. 3:20).

John 14:8-11

THE FATHER REVEALED

While Jesus was talking to the disciples about heaven and about God, Philip said, "Lord, show us the Father and that will be enough for us."

Jesus replied, "I have been with you for a long time. Don't you know Me yet, Philip? Anyone who has seen Me has seen the Father. Don't you believe that I am in the Father and the Father is in Me?"

Peter, James and John had been on the mountain with Jesus when God appeared as a bright cloud (Matt. 17:5-6), but Philip had not been with them.

Although Philip had seen Jesus do mighty miracles, he wanted a peep into heaven (perhaps as proof of what Jesus had been telling them).

But instead of being shown God's awesome glory, Philip had been able to see His *love, mercy, patience and goodness* through Jesus (John 1:14). In this way, Philip saw what God is like without experiencing His frightening power and holiness.

Lord God, although I cannot see You, I know a little of what You are like from what I have learned about Jesus. Amen.

No one has ever seen God. God's only Son, the One who is closest to the Father's heart, has made Him known.

~ John 1:18

One day we will be able to look into the face of God the Father, when we are sinless and perfect in heaven (Matt. 5:8; Rev. 22:4).

John 14:12-14

IN JESUS' NAME

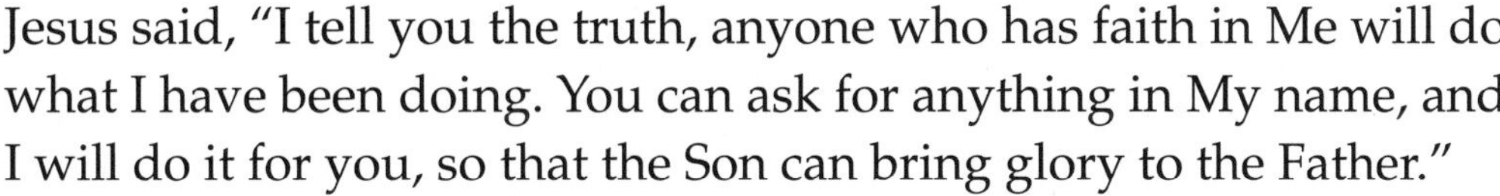

Jesus said, "I tell you the truth, anyone who has faith in Me will do what I have been doing. You can ask for anything in My name, and I will do it for you, so that the Son can bring glory to the Father."

When we pray, our prayers go straight to God! Our prayers don't need to go to any person first. God loves it when you, His child, talk to Him and tell Him what's going on in your heart (Heb. 4:15-16).

The Holy Spirit helps us to pray, and even when we don't know what to say, God knows what we're thinking.

When we ask for something in Jesus' name, we are asking God to hear our prayers because we know and love His Son. By praying the kind of prayer Jesus would have prayed on earth, we are praying for what *He* wants, and so we have His approval.

Then, as Jesus answers our prayers, He brings glory to His Father. But remember, even as Jesus did only what He knew His Father wanted Him to do, so we should pray for the kind of things that please God (1 John 5:14).

REMEMBER In Jesus' name means *as if Jesus had asked this.*

"You can pray for anything, and if you have faith, you will receive it."

~ Matthew 21:22, NLT

When we ask God for something, we must firmly believe that He is able to do what we have asked (James 1:6). That is faith!

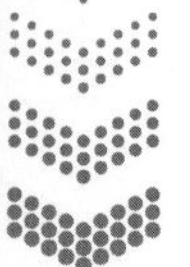

John 14:15-20

JESUS PROMISES THE HOLY SPIRIT

"If you love Me, obey My commands," Jesus said. "And I will ask the Father to give you another Helper, who will never leave you. He is the Holy Spirit, who leads you into all Truth. The world cannot receive Him, because it isn't looking for Him and doesn't recognize Him. But you know Him, because He lives *with* you now and later will be *in* you."

When we love Jesus and obey Him, we become His precious possession: "He chose to give birth to us by giving us His true Word. And we, out of all creation, became His prized possession" (James 1:18, NLT).

Until now Jesus had been the Helper, Encourager and Guide of the disciples. But now that He was going back to His Father, He would send someone in His place – someone who would *never* leave them.

Jesus had been teaching them Truths of the Kingdom; now the Holy Spirit would lead them into all Truth. For a while the Holy Spirit would *be with* them, but then He would come down and actually *live in* them, as He now does in us.

Thank You, Lord, that You live in me through the Holy Spirit. Amen.

"I am telling you the truth: it is better for you that I go away, because if I do not go, the Helper will not come to you. But if I do go away, then I will send Him to you."

~ John 16:7

The Holy Spirit comes to live in us the moment we ask for forgiveness; turn away from our sin, and let Jesus rule our lives (Acts 2:38; Rom. 8:11).

John 14:21-24

WHAT MAKES US SPECIAL?

Jesus went on to say, "Those who accept My commands and obey them are the ones who love Me. And because they love Me, My Father will love them. And I will love them and show Myself to each of them."

Then Judas (not Judas who was planning to betray Jesus) said to Him, "Lord, why are You going to show Yourself only to us and not to the world?"

Jesus replied, "All who love Me will do what I say and We will come and make Our home with each of them."

Judas wanted to know why Jesus would show Himself only to them and not to the world. The reason Jesus shows Himself to us is that we love and obey Him. And because we love Jesus, God loves us, and the Holy Spirit lives in us: that's why Jesus said that *We will make Our home with them!* And that is how we are able to see Him.

Although we can't see Jesus with our eyes, as we read about Him in the Bible, and the Holy Spirit helps our hearts to understand things about Him, we get to "see" things about Him that people of the world will never see.

May the eyes of my heart see You, Lord (Eph. 1:18). Amen.

You are a holy people, who belong to the LORD your God. Of all the people on earth, the LORD your God has chosen you to be His own special treasure.

~ Deuteronomy 7:6, NLT

If we love the Lord, then obeying His commands is not hard for us to do because our hearts want to please Him (1 John 5:3).

John 14:25-31; Mark 14:26

"PEACE I LEAVE WITH YOU"

While Jesus was having a meal with the disciples, He told them that He would die; rise again, and return to His Father. He also said that He would send the Holy Spirit to them. Then He said, "The Holy Spirit will remind you of all I have told you. I am leaving you with peace of mind and heart. The peace I give is a gift the world cannot give. So don't be troubled or afraid!"

Then He said, "I don't have much more time to talk to you for the evil ruler is coming, but he has no power over Me. Come; let us leave." And when they had sung a hymn, they went out to the Mount of Olives.

Jesus knew that He would be arrested that very night, yet He spoke to His disciples about peace to calm their troubled hearts. His reassuring words let them know that it's going to be okay – that His Father is in complete control of everything. And that is how we can have peace, even when things around us seem worrying and gloomy.

Yes, trouble lay ahead for the disciples, but God's love held them tight; for no one has the power to take God's precious ones away from His powerful love (Rom. 8:38-39).

Lord, I trust You to care for me, and that gives me peace. Amen.

God's peace, which goes beyond anything we can imagine, will guard your thoughts and emotions through Christ Jesus.

~ Philippians 4:7

The Lord did not save Daniel *from* trouble – getting thrown into the lions' den, but He did send an angel to protect him *in* the lions' den (Dan. 6:16-23).

John 15:9-12

COMPLETE JOY

Jesus continued talking to the eleven disciples, telling them what was on His heart. "I have loved you the same way the Father has loved Me," He said.

"Now remain in My love. If you keep My commands, you will remain in My love. I have told you these things so that you will be filled with My joy. Yes, your joy will overflow! My command is this: Love each other as I have loved you."

When we talk about being happy, we may think of things we *do* or things we *have* that make us happy. The joy that Jesus speaks about is not quite the same as happiness. Joy comes from having a loving relationship with someone.

However, the "joy-level" in our hearts will only be full when we remain in the love of Jesus (when we have a relationship with Him).

When we stay close to Jesus by doing what He wants us to do, we live in that love. And as we love others with the love of Jesus, His joy fills our hearts to overflowing.

The Lord fills you with His love and joy as you obey Him.

Satisfy us each morning with Your unfailing love, so we may sing for joy to the end of our lives.

~ Psalm 90:14, NLT

The Mount of Olives is a hill to the east of Jerusalem. Its name comes from the olive trees that grow on the slopes of the Mount (hill).

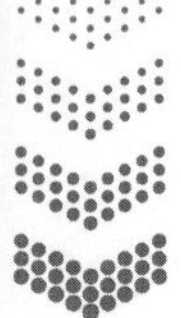

John 15:13-15

FRIENDS OF JESUS

Jesus said, "There is no greater love than to lay down one's life for one's friends. You are My friends if you do what I command. I no longer call you slaves, because a master doesn't confide in his slaves. Now you are My friends, since I have told you everything the Father told Me."

Jesus has no favorites. *Anyone* who obeys His commands is a friend of His.

We are not slaves of the Master, though we still call Him *Lord* because we honor Him; and we serve Him because we love Him. Yet we can call God *our Father*, and we can think of Jesus as our closest friend.

Have you ever told your best friend a secret you didn't want to share with anyone else? Well, Jesus said that because we are His friends, He has told us everything the Father has told Him.

A master doesn't share his personal plans with his slaves, yet he will talk to his best friend about what he is planning. Jesus has shared His plans for the future with us, and those plans are written for us in the Bible.

Lord, thank You for being my closest friend. Amen.

The Lord is a friend to those who fear Him. He teaches them His covenant.

~ Psalm 25:14, NLT

Jesus loved us so much that He died for us even before we became His friends (Rom. 5:7-8).

John 15:16-17

"I CHOSE YOU"

Jesus told the disciples, "You did not choose Me, but I chose you. I have appointed you to go and produce fruit that will last, so that the Father will give you whatever you ask for, using My name. This is My command: Love each other."

Do you remember how Jesus chose Peter, Andrew, James and John at the Sea of Galilee (Matt. 4:18-22)? Jesus came to them and said, "Follow Me!" It was Jesus who *chose* them. Yet each one had to decide whether or not they would *follow* Him.

In the same way, Jesus has chosen us. He has also given us a special work to do – to go and bear fruit. This fruit is not the same as the fruit of the Spirit, which is a sign of God's work in our lives (Gal. 5:22-23).

Jesus has chosen us to *go* and produce a harvest, as a farmer goes out into the field to plow, and sow, and reap. We are chosen firstly because God loves us. Yet Jesus has also chosen us to plant seeds of Truth and produce a harvest of goodness (fruit) that will last forever.

God has a special purpose for the way He made you!

We are God's masterpiece. He has created us anew in Christ Jesus, so we can do the good things He planned for us long ago.

~ Ephesians 2:10, NLT

God chose a shepherd boy with a sling to bring victory to the Israelite army (1 Sam. 17:48-52). God often chooses the weak to show *His* power.

John 15:18-19

"THE WORLD WILL HATE YOU"

Jesus prepared the disciples for the trouble that lay ahead: "If the world hates you, remember that it hated Me first," He said. "If you still belonged to the world, it would love you as one of its own, but you are no longer part of the world. I chose you to come out of the world, so it hates you."

When Jesus spoke of the world, He wasn't talking about the planet we live on; He was talking about unbelievers who love the sinful things of this world and hate what is good.

Jesus has also chosen us to come *out* of the world – to be separate and different from those *in* the world. Paul said, "Don't copy the behavior and customs of this world, but let God transform you into a new person by changing the way you think" (Rom. 12:2, NLT).

It is because we are different that the world hates us. People who do wrong want everyone else to be like them so that they don't feel guilty (they hate to be reminded of God). It takes courage to be different; but remember, you are one of Jesus' chosen ones!

Let your light shine brightly by doing what is right.

"Therefore, come out from among unbelievers, and separate yourselves from them," says the LORD. "Don't touch their filthy things, and I will welcome you."

~ 2 Corinthians 6:17, NLT

By doing what is good and right, God's light shines through us. But evil people hate that light because it shows up their evil ways (John 3:19-21).

John 16:5-11

THE WORK OF THE HOLY SPIRIT

Jesus told the disciples, "Now I am going back to My Father who sent Me. Although you are sad because of what I've told you, it is best for you that I go away. If I don't, the Helper (the Holy Spirit) won't come. If I do go away, I will send Him to you."

"When the Holy Spirit comes, He will prove unbelievers to be in the wrong about their idea of sin, because their sin is that they don't believe in Me. He will show people that true goodness is possible now that My work is done and I am going back to My Father. And the Holy Spirit will show people how wrong they are about the coming judgment, because the devil has already been judged."

The Holy Spirit, who is now here, is our helper, comforter, and guide. Because Jesus went back to heaven, the Holy Spirit now lives in the hearts of those who love Jesus. Yet He also works in the hearts of those who don't yet know Jesus. He works through the conscience of those who don't know Him, making them realize that their sinful ways are wrong; that God is Holy; and that they will stand before Him one day and be judged.

The Holy Spirit makes us sensitive about the things that please God, and the things that don't.

You heard and believed the message of Truth, the Good News that He has saved you. In Him you were sealed with the Holy Spirit whom He promised.

~ Ephesians 1:13

One's conscience is a built-in sense of what is right and what is wrong. Forgiveness and obedience to God keeps one's conscience clear (Acts 24:16).

John 16:16, 20

SORROW WILL TURN TO JOY

Jesus went on to say, "In a little while you will see Me no more. Then, after a little while, you will see Me again. You will have deep sorrow, but I will see you again; then you will rejoice, and no one can rob you of that joy."

Sadness is a longing that comes from being separated from someone we love. Jesus was about to die, and He knew the disciples would be very, very sad. They would feel as though it were the end – that they were defeated, with all their hopes and dreams shattered.

But Jesus said, "You will see Me again!"

Joy comes from being able to be with someone we love. How very happy the disciples would be a few days later when they would see Jesus alive again!

For us, life on earth brings many ups and downs. But our firm hope is this: that because we are faithful to the Lord and love Him, it will all be worth it!

Our faith in the One we cannot see will be rewarded when at last we will see Him; and no one can take away our joy!

Because of our faith in Jesus, our hope brings us joy.

You love Him even though you have never seen Him. Though you do not see Him now, you trust Him; and you rejoice with a glorious, inexpressible joy.

~ 1 Peter 1:8, NLT

We have a sure hope that even though we are sad when someone dies, our sadness will turn to joy one day (1 Thess. 4:13-18).

John 17:1-5

JESUS PRAYS FOR HIMSELF

After talking to the disciples, Jesus looked up to heaven and said, "Father, the hour has come. Glorify Your Son so He can give glory back to You. For You have given Him authority over everyone. He gives eternal life to all those You have given Him."

"And this is the way to have eternal life –
to know You, the only true God,
and Jesus Christ, the One You sent to earth."

"I brought glory to You here on earth by completing the work You gave Me to do. Now, Father, bring Me into the glory We shared before the world began."

Jesus' work of telling the people about the kingdom of God was done, and His main purpose for coming to earth would be completed within the next day; that of bringing about a New Covenant between God and man by dying in our place.

Because of this agreement of grace that can never be changed, those who know God (believe in Him) have eternal life.

We bring glory to Jesus by receiving His forgiveness and honoring God with our changed lives.

Through Christ you have come to trust in God. And you have placed your faith and hope in God because He raised Christ from the dead and gave Him great glory.

~ 1 Peter 1:21, NLT

To know God is more than just knowing *about* Him. To know God means to have a relationship with Him (through the Holy Spirit who lives in us).

John 17:6-10

JESUS PRAYS FOR HIS DISCIPLES

Jesus prayed for His disciples. He said to His Father, "I have told them about You so that they may know You. They live in this world and they belong to You, yet You gave them to Me. I have told them the message You gave Me and they understood it. They believe that I came from You, and that You sent Me."

"I pray for them. I am not praying for the world, but for those You have given Me, for they are Yours."

God gave the disciples to Jesus, as an owner would give his sheep to a shepherd to care for. Although the sheep belonged to God, they didn't know Him at first. Then Jesus made those sheep His own. He cared for those who followed Him and taught them about God.

Jesus' heart was for those He'd been given to look after by His Father. So His prayer was not for the whole world (because there were so many who wanted nothing to do with Him); He chose rather to pray a meaningful prayer for those who were His.

Thank You that I belong to You, Jesus; that You care for me, and that You pray for me. Amen.

"This is the will of Him who sent Me, that I shall lose none of all those He has given Me, but raise them up at the last day."

~ John 6:39

We have the assurance that, because Jesus is the Great Shepherd, no one can snatch us away from Him (John 10:28).

John 17:11-12

"FATHER, PROTECT THEM"

Jesus continued the prayer to His Father, saying, "I won't be in the world much longer, but they are still in the world, and I am coming back to You. Holy Father, protect them by the power of Your Name, the Name that You gave Me, so that they may be united in the same way We are. While I was with them, I kept them safe and watched over them so that none of them, except one person [Judas], became lost."

Jesus prayed that God would watch over His followers and protect them. Until now, Jesus had been there for them through thick and thin. He had calmed the storm when their boat almost sank (Mark 4:35-39), and He had prayed for their spiritual protection (Luke 22:32). Jesus was now asking His *Father* to protect them because *He* could no longer be with them the way He had been.

Even though Jesus has gone back to heaven, He is still interceding for us (Rom. 8:34). He is praying earnestly that we will stay in God's will, and is asking Him to keep us safe until we are together in heaven.

Thank You for keeping me safe and for watching over me. Amen.

He is able, now and always, to save those who come to God through Him, because He lives forever to plead with God for them.

~ Hebrews 7:25

The Lord will protect us from the wicked plans of the devil and bring us safely into His kingdom (2 Thess. 3:3; 2 Tim. 4:18).

John 17:13-19

"MAKE THEM HOLY"

Jesus said to His Father, "I am not asking You to take them out of the world, but to keep them safe from the evil one. They don't belong to the world any more than I do. Use the Truth to make them holy. Your words are Truth. I'm dedicating Myself to the work I am doing for them so that they can be sanctified (made holy) by Your Truth."

When we ask Jesus to forgive us and make us new inside, He puts a new spirit in us (Ezek. 36:26) – one that will live forever. From the moment we are born again (made new inside) we are holy in God's eyes.

"Christ made us right with God; He made us pure and holy, and He freed us from sin" (1 Cor. 1:30, NLT). That's why God by His Spirit can live in us.

But although our spirit is new, our minds and hearts are still sinful. That's why we still have wrong thoughts and bad attitudes.

Jesus wants us to become more and more like Him, and even though we might not get it right all the time, we should keep growing in our faith and love for the Lord. The way we become more like Jesus is by *reading* the Word of God and by *living* what it says.

Lord, help me to live my life the way You want me to. Amen.

By one sacrifice He has made *perfect* forever those who are *being made holy*.

~ Hebrews 10:14

The word *sanctify* means to use something for no other purpose than that for which it was made, and by no one else except its owner (like your toothbrush).

NOVEMBER

1 WAY
FOLLOW IT

1 TRUTH
BELIEVE IT

1 LIFE
LIVE IT

John 17:20-23

JESUS PRAYS FOR ALL BELIEVERS

Jesus finished His prayer by saying, "I am praying not only for these disciples but also for all those who will believe in Me through their message."

"I pray that they will all be united as one, just as You and I are one. I am in them and You are in Me. May they experience such perfect unity that the world will know that You sent Me and that You love them as much as You love me."

This last part of Jesus' prayer is for all those who, through the years, would believe in Him and form part of His body, the church (1 Cor. 12:25-27).

Just as all the different parts of your body are joined together and work together, so every believer is a different yet important part of the body of Christ (and that includes you).

Every part of the body depends on the other parts to do their bit in order for the body to work properly. That's why Jesus prays for unity – that we would love and serve each other and do whatever task God has given us to do, even if it doesn't seem like an important task.

We are all different – that's why we need each other.

The human body has many parts, but the many parts make up one whole body. So it is with the body of Christ.

~ 1 Corinthians 12:12, NLT

Jesus' prayer for unity was answered when thousands of new believers came together and started the first church in Jerusalem (Acts 4:32).

Matthew 26:36-39; Luke 22:39-43

JESUS PRAYS IN THE GARDEN

Jesus went with the disciples to a place called Gethsemane and said to them, "Sit here while I go over there to pray." He took Peter, James and John along with Him. Then He said to them, "The sorrow in My heart is so great that it feels as if I am dying. Stay here and keep watch with Me."

He went on a little farther and bowed with His face to the ground, praying, "My Father! If it is possible, let this cup of suffering be taken away from Me. Yet I want Your will to be done, not Mine." Then an angel from heaven appeared and strengthened Him.

Jesus prayed to His Father, that if it were possible – if there were any other way to save people from their sins – that God would not let Him die by laying the world's sin on Him.

God *heard* Jesus' prayer, but there was no one else who could take the punishment for our sin. Jesus was the only sinless man who could die in our place, so God answered His prayer differently by sending an angel to strengthen Him in His time of weakness.

Jesus didn't let His feelings get in the way of God's plan.

During His life on earth, Jesus prayed to God, who could save Him from death. He prayed and pleaded with loud crying and tears, and He was heard because of His devotion to God.

~ Hebrews 5:7

Although God allowed people to sacrifice an animal to show that they were sorry for their sin, the animal couldn't take away their sin (Heb. 10:4).

Matthew 26:40-44

KEEP WATCH AND PRAY

Jesus, who had gone to pray alone, came back to the small group of disciples and found them asleep. He said to Peter, "Couldn't you watch with Me even one hour?

Keep watch and pray,
so that you will not give in to temptation.
For the spirit is willing, but the body is weak!"

Then Jesus left them a second time and went to pray. When He returned to them, He found them sleeping again, for they couldn't keep their eyes open. So He went on His own to pray for a third time.

Do you struggle to pray at night? After a tiring day, praying in the dark isn't easy. It was late at night and the disciples were struggling to stay awake. Jesus hadn't ask them to pray for Him; He told them to pray for themselves because He knew what would soon happen.

Our enemy, the devil, knows when our bodies are weak. He will try to keep us from praying, or tempt us to skip our Bible reading because he knows how important it is to spend time with God.

Give the best part of your day to the Lord, every day!

Stay alert! Watch out for your great enemy, the devil. He prowls around like a roaring lion, looking for someone to devour.

~ 1 Peter 5:8, NLT

We should always be alert and ready for spiritual battle by putting on all the armor that God supplies (Eph. 6:11-18).

Matthew 26:46-50

THE KISS OF JUDAS

When Jesus returned to the disciples, He said, "Get up! Let's go! Here comes My betrayer."

Just then, Judas Iscariot, one of the twelve disciples arrived with a crowd carrying swords and clubs. The traitor, Judas, had said to them, "The One I greet with a kiss is the man you want. Arrest Him!"

So Judas came straight to Jesus. "Greetings, Rabbi!" he exclaimed and kissed Him. Then the others grabbed Jesus and arrested Him.

The Pharisees and priest wanted to make sure they got the right man, especially in the dark. They had offered Judas money to lead them to Jesus because he knew where Jesus was likely to be with His disciples (John 18:2).

It all seemed like an evil plan thought up by jealous people, which it was; yet it was also part of God's plan to save us. Even though the temple leaders thought that this was their clever scheme, and that they were in control, they didn't realize that they were only doing what God had planned, and that *He* was in control.

All of Your plans are perfect, Lord (Isa. 46:10). Amen.

People may plan all kinds of things, but the LORD's will is going to be done.

~ Proverbs 19:21

In Bible times, and still in some countries today, the kiss (usually on the cheek) is a form of greeting, much like a handshake (2 Cor. 13:12).

Luke 22:49-51; John 18:10-11

PETER IS READY TO FIGHT

When the disciples saw that Jesus was about to be arrested, they exclaimed, "Lord, should we fight with the swords we brought?" (Luke 22:38). But before Jesus could answer, Peter drew a sword and slashed off the right ear of Malchus, the high priest's servant.

Jesus said to Peter, "Put your sword back into its sheath. Shall I not drink from the cup of suffering the Father has given Me?" And He touched the man's ear and healed him.

Peter was ready to defend Jesus and prove that what he had said, he would do. He had said to Jesus earlier that evening, "Even if everyone else deserts You, I will never desert You" (Matt. 26:33). Peter was willing to take on a mob that was armed with swords and clubs.

But Jesus didn't need to be defended. He knew that what was happening was in His Father's hands because He'd been praying that His Father's will be done.

Instead of fighting, Jesus showed kindness to His enemy: He healed one last person before dying on the cross – one of those who had come to arrest Him.

Lord, help me to forgive my enemies and be kind to them. Amen.

"I tell you, love your enemies and pray for those who persecute you."

~ Matthew 5:44

A relative of Malchus challenged Peter a few hours later about being one of Jesus' disciples (John 18:26).

Matthew 26:55-56; Luke 22:52-54

JESUS IS ARRESTED

Jesus said to the crowd, "Have you come out with swords and clubs to arrest Me as if I were a criminal? I used to sit teaching in the temple courtyard every day, and you didn't arrest Me then. But this is happening to fulfill the words of the prophets in the Scriptures."

At that point, all the disciples deserted Him and fled.

Jesus pointed out to the mob that He had been among them in the temple courts but they had done nothing to Him there. Yet now a whole crowd, including soldiers, had come to arrest Jesus (one man) in the middle of the night.

They were cowards! They didn't dare arrest Jesus in public because they were afraid that the people would turn on them (Matt. 21:46).

A short while before, Jesus had prepared the disciples by telling them that He (the Shepherd) would be killed and that they (the sheep) would be scattered – they would run for their lives (Matt. 26:31). And they did, because they were afraid that the mob would turn on them.

May my confidence never be in myself, Lord, but in You. Amen.

I do not trust in my bow or in my sword to save me.

~ Psalm 44:6

When the mob caught one of the men following Jesus, the man slipped out of the robe he was wearing and ran away naked (Mark 14:52).

Mark 14:53-62; Matthew 26:57-64

JESUS IS TAKEN TO THE HIGH PRIEST

The crowd that had arrested Jesus took Him to the high priest's home where the priests, the elders and the teachers of the law had gathered. Meanwhile, Peter followed Jesus at a distance and went right into the courtyard.

Inside, the priests were trying to find some crime for which they could put Jesus to death. But they couldn't find any. Instead they told lies about Him. Then the high priest asked Jesus, "Are You the Messiah, the Son of the Blessed One?"

Jesus said, "I Am. And you will see the Son of Man seated in the place of power at God's right hand and coming on the clouds of heaven."

Because Jesus had never done any wrong, the people started lying about Him and tried to make up something for which they could punish Him. Rather than looking for the truth, this 'court' was looking for false evidence. Yet in the end, the only thing they could accuse Jesus of was an actual fact – that He is the Son of God.

Jesus told them that they would see Him again as Judge (Matt. 25:31). Jesus was being judged *unfairly* by the people; but when He comes to judge, He will judge everyone *fairly* because His judgment is true.

Jesus, who was sinless, was judged by sinful people.

Jesus said, "If I do judge, My decisions are true, because I am not alone. I stand with the Father, who sent Me."

~ John 8:16

This trial of Jesus was held at night (and in a private home) even though the Jewish law stated that a trial might not be held at night (in the dark).

Matthew 26:69-75; Luke 22:55-62

PETER DENIES JESUS

It was cold, and Peter who was in the courtyard outside the house was warming himself with the others who were there. A servant girl came over and said to him, "You were one of those with Jesus of Galilee."

But Peter denied it in front of everyone. "I don't know what you're talking about," he said.

Then he went out to the gateway, where another servant girl saw him and said to the people there, "This fellow was with Jesus of Nazareth."

Again Peter denied it, this time with an oath. "I don't even know the man," he said.

After a little while the men standing there came to Peter and said, "It's obvious you're also one of them. Your accent gives you away!"

Peter swore, "A curse on me if I'm lying – I don't know the man!" And immediately the rooster crowed. Peter remembered what Jesus had said: "Before a rooster crows, you will say three times that you don't know Me." Then Peter went outside and cried bitterly.

Peter, the one who bravely tried to defend Jesus earlier on, suddenly became afraid of a servant girl.

Lord, I pray that You will make me bold (Ps. 27:14). Amen.

If you think you are standing strong, be careful not to fall.
~ 1 Corinthians 10:12, NLT

If you've ever let Jesus down in front of others, ask Him to forgive you, and He will (1 John 1:9; Rom. 8:1).

Matthew 27:1-10

A SAD WAY TO END

Early in the morning all the chief priests and the elders made their plans to have Jesus put to death. They tied Him up, led Him away, and handed Him over to Pilate, the governor.

When Judas, who had betrayed Him, realized that Jesus had been condemned to die, he felt terribly guilty. So he took the thirty pieces of silver back to the priests and elders. "I have sinned," he said, "for I have betrayed an innocent man."

"What do we care?" they replied. "That's your problem." So Judas threw the silver coins down in the temple and went out and hanged himself. Then the chief priests said, "It wouldn't really be right to add this money to the temple treasury, since it was payment for someone's life." So they decided to use it to buy a potter's field for the burial of strangers.

Judas would always be remembered as *the traitor* – the one who betrayed his Friend. Judas had the privilege of walking alongside Jesus; learning from Him; seeing His power in action, and experiencing His love.

Yet he sold the King of kings for thirty silver coins, and traded his eternal life for a handful of coins he didn't even use.

Regret (feeling sorry) is not repentance (saying sorry).

Godly sorrow brings repentance that leads to salvation and leaves no regret, but worldly sorrow brings death.

~ 2 Corinthians 7:10

Zechariah prophesied that the thirty pieces of silver would be thrown down in the temple and used to buy the potter's field (Zech. 11:13).

Luke 23:1-7

JESUS BEFORE PILATE

It was Friday and also the day of the Passover. The Jewish leaders led Jesus from the home of Caiaphas to the palace of Pilate, the Roman governor. They said to Pilate, "This man has been leading our people astray by telling them not to pay taxes to the Roman government and by claiming that He is the Messiah, a King."

So Pilate questioned Jesus. Then he said to the priests, "I find nothing wrong with this man!" But the Jews carried on accusing Jesus of causing trouble. Eventually, when Pilate found out that Jesus was from Galilee, he sent Him off to Herod, the ruler of Galilee.

Pilate realized that the Jewish leaders had brought Jesus to him as a criminal because they were jealous of Him (Matt. 27:18). He also knew that Jesus was innocent. Being a governor, Pilate had the power to declare Jesus *not guilty* and order that the Jews release Him.

But Pilate didn't want to argue with the Jewish leaders because he knew that they could cause trouble in the city, which meant that he could lose his job as governor. And so he tried to pass his problem on to Herod.

Like Pilate, we have to choose between the Truth and lies.

Whoever knows the right thing to do and fails to do it, for him it is sin.

~ James 4:17

Pilate was replaced as a Roman governor a few years after the trial of Jesus, and he died soon afterwards.

Luke 23:7-12

JESUS SENT TO HEROD

When Pilate found out that Jesus was from Galilee, he sent Him to Herod, who happened to be in Jerusalem at that time.

Herod, the ruler of Galilee, was pleased to see Jesus because he had heard about Him and hoped to see Jesus perform some kind of miracle. He asked Jesus question after question, but Jesus refused to answer.

Then Herod and his soldiers began to mock Jesus and made fun of Him. They put a colorful robe on Him and sent Him back to Pilate.

The problem people, like Herod, have with following Jesus is that they want to know what Jesus can do for them. They expect Jesus to do a miracle just for them, as if they are so important.

They *first* want Jesus to prove Himself in some way before they'll decide whether or not to believe in Him. And when Jesus is silent, and nothing happens, they mock those who believe and make fun of those who put their faith in Him.

Faith only comes once we are *willing* to believe.

He was oppressed and treated harshly, yet He never said a word. He was led like a lamb to the slaughter. And as a sheep is silent before the shearers, He did not open His mouth.

~ Isaiah 53:7, NLT

Anyone who believes in Jesus crosses over from death to eternal life (John 5:24). That miracle happens by believing.

Luke 23:13-25; Matthew 27:19

JESUS IS SENT BACK TO PILATE

Pilate announced to the chief priest and the crowd that Jesus is *not guilty* of any crimes and that He has done *nothing* to deserve death.

The governor had a custom to release one prisoner at the Passover. So he said to the crowd, do you want me to release Jesus, or Barabbas? (Barabbas was a murderer.) Then the crowd shouted, "Take this man Jesus away and kill Him; and let Barabbas go!"

As Pilate was sitting on the judgment seat, his wife sent him this message: "Leave that innocent man alone. I've had a terrible dream about Him."

So Pilate spoke to the crowd again because he wanted to release Jesus. But the crowd shouted, "Crucify Him!" So Pilate did what they wanted and handed Jesus over to be crucified.

Fear of what people might say, or wanting to please the crowd in order to stay popular, is one way in which the devil gets us off track.

So, when your friends want you to do something that you know is not right, be bold and say 'No!' You may find that by doing what is right, others will be encouraged to follow your good example.

Lord, please give me the courage to do what is right. Amen.

Never follow a crowd in doing wrong. When you testify in court, don't side with the majority to pervert justice.

~ Exodus 23:2

Spending a lot of time with those who do wrong will spoil one's good character (1 Cor. 15:33).

Matthew 27:27-31

SOLDIERS MOCK JESUS

The soldiers of the governor took Jesus into their quarters and gathered the whole troop around Him. They stripped Him and put a red robe on Him. They twisted some thorns into a crown, placed it on His head, and put a stick in His right hand. They knelt in front of Him and made fun of Him by saying, "Long live the King of the Jews!"

After the soldiers had finished making fun of Jesus, they took off the robe and put His own clothes on Him again. Then they led Him away to be crucified.

Jesus hadn't suddenly become helpless. At any time, He could have called on His Father to send thousands of angels to rescue Him (Matt. 26:53). Instead, He allowed the soldiers to slap Him and spit on Him so that He could save us: that is *love*.

God, who created the universe, watched His much-loved Son being beaten and mocked by wicked sinners so that He could make a way for us to spend eternity with Him: that is *mercy*.

Jesus suffered for the joy of saving us (Heb. 12:2).

He was handed over to die because of our sins, and He was raised to life to make us right with God.

~ Romans 4:25, NLT

The crown of thorns reminds us of two things: Thorns are a curse of sin (Gen. 3:17-18), and the crown is the symbol of a king (Rev. 19:16).

Mark 15:21; Luke 23:26-28

SIMON CARRIES THE CROSS FOR JESUS

At first, the soldiers made Jesus carry His own cross. But along the way, a man named Simon was coming in from the countryside just then, and the soldiers forced him to carry Jesus' cross.

A large crowd followed Jesus; among them were some women who were weeping for Him. But Jesus turned and said to them, "Daughters of Jerusalem, do not weep for Me, but weep for yourselves and for your children" [because Jerusalem would be destroyed].

A few years earlier, Jesus had said to the crowds, "Come to Me, all of you who are weary and carry heavy burdens, and I will give you rest" (Matt. 11:28). Jesus was talking about the load of worries, guilt, and other bad feelings we carry around inside.

But in order to give us the hope that comes from a relationship with Him, He had to carry all those burdens. The cross is where God took the sin-burden of each one of us and put it on His Son (Isa. 53:6). In exchange for our burdens, Jesus gives us rest – the peace and assurance of being right with God.

Help carry someone's load by being kind and helpful.

Help carry each other's burdens. In this way you will follow Christ's teachings.

~ Galatians 6:2

A Roman soldier had the right to order anyone to carry his equipment or something else for the distance of one mile (Matt. 5:41).

Luke 23:32-33; Mark 15:22

JESUS IS CRUCIFIED

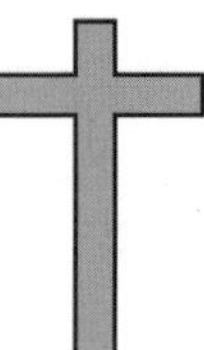

It was Friday, about nine o'clock in the morning. They came to a place on a hill, which is called Golgotha. There they nailed Jesus to a cross, along with two criminals – one on His right, the other on His left. This was the day …

- The day that Jesus had been telling the disciples about (Matt. 16:21).
- The day on which Old Testament prophecies came true (Ps. 22:1; 22:18).
- The day on which the Creator of the universe died (Col. 1:16-20).
- The day that Jesus would break the power that the devil had over death (Heb. 2:14).
- The day that made it possible for us to be forgiven and have eternal life (Eph. 1:7).
- The day on which we were set free from having to keep the Old Testament law (Rom. 8:2).
- The day on which ordinary people could draw near to God for the first time (Heb. 10:19-22).

Thank Jesus in your own words for what He did for you.

Jesus gave His life for our sins, just as God our Father planned, in order to rescue us from this evil world in which we live.

~ Galatians 1:4, NLT

The word *crucify* comes from an old Latin word meaning *cross* – the shape of the wooden beams to which a person was nailed.

Luke 23:34-38; John 19:19-22

KING OF THE JEWS

As Jesus was being crucified, He said, "Father, forgive them, for they do not know what they are doing."

The crowd watched and the leaders scoffed. "He saved others," they said, "let Him save Himself if He is really God's Messiah, the Chosen One."

The soldiers mocked Him, too, and said, "If You are the King of the Jews, save Yourself."

Pilate wrote a notice and put it on the cross. It read,

"Jesus from Nazareth, the King of the Jews."

The sign was written in Aramaic, Latin, and Greek, so that many people could read it.

Jesus prayed for the soldiers who crucified Him, asking His Father to forgive them because they didn't realize who He was – God's Son. But the Jewish leaders knew.

They had heard Jesus say that He is the Son of God (John 19:7). He was also their King (John 19:14-15). However, the Jews didn't want Him as their King. Yet that didn't change the fact that Jesus *is* King – not only of the Jews – but of all creation, and *every* knee will bow before Him (Phil. 2:10).

You are my King, O Lord; and I gladly bow to You! Amen.

On His robe and on His thigh He has this name written: KING OF KINGS AND LORD OF LORDS.

~ Revelation 19:16

When you ask Jesus to rule in your life, you become a child of the King (John 1:12-13).

Matthew 27:35-36; John 19:23-24

SOLDIERS DIVIDE UP JESUS' CLOTHES

After they had nailed Jesus to the cross, the soldiers gambled for His clothes by throwing dice. They took His outer garments and made four parts, a part for each soldier. They also took His robe, which was woven in one piece from top to bottom, so the soldiers said to each other, "Let's not rip it apart.

Let's throw dice to see who will get it." In this way the Scripture came true: "They divided My clothes among themselves. They threw dice for My clothing" (Ps. 22:18).

Though Jesus created the universe, He had no earthly possessions except for His clothes. Here at the cross, soldiers took even the little He had. Jesus wore a robe that had not been sewn – the robe of a priest (Exod. 28:31-32).

The robe tells us that Jesus is our High Priest. The High Priest wore such a robe at Passover, and Jesus took over that role by becoming our Great High Priest and going into God's presence to offer Himself for our sins, and so make us holy in God's eyes.

REMEMBER Satan accuses us, but Jesus defends us (Rom. 8:33-34).

Since we have a Great High Priest who has entered heaven, Jesus the Son of God, let us hold firmly to what we believe.

~ Hebrews 4:14, NLT

There is only one Priest that can make us right with God – Jesus Christ. He stands in our place before God (Heb. 7:23-27; 1 John 2:1).

John 19:25-27; Matthew 27:55

THOSE AT THE CROSS

Standing near the cross were women who had followed Jesus, His mother, and John. When Jesus saw His mother standing next to the disciple He loved (John), He said to her, "Dear woman, here is your son." And He said to John, "Here is your mother." And from then on John took her into his home.

Years before, Mary the mother of Jesus was thrilled when an angel told her that she would have a baby – Jesus the Son of God (Luke 1:26-38).

When Jesus was taken to the temple as a baby, an old man named Simeon told Mary and Joseph that because of Jesus, many would be condemned while others would be saved; and he also said to Mary that a sword would pierce her soul (Luke 2:35). And now, here she was, watching her son die a cruel, painful death.

Jesus, from the cross, tells John to care for Mary as though she were his mother. And for His grieving mother, Jesus makes sure she has a son who will see to her needs; as He – the oldest son in the family – would not be there to comfort her and care for her.

FIND OUT How many Marys were at the cross? (John 19:25).

Therefore, as we have opportunity, let us do good to all people, especially to those who belong to the family of believers.

~ Galatians 6:10

Just as Jesus cared about His mother, God cares for the widows and orphans of this world; and He expects us to help them (Ps. 146:9; James 1:27)

Luke 23:39-43

ETERNITY IN HEAVEN

One of the criminals hanging on a cross beside Jesus mocked Him, "So You're the Messiah? Prove it by saving Yourself and us!"

But the other criminal said to him, "Don't you fear God even when you are going to die? We *deserve to die* for what we did, but He has done nothing wrong."

Then he said to Jesus, "Remember me when You come into Your kingdom."

Jesus answered him, "Believe Me when I say to you, today you will be with Me in paradise."

The grace of Jesus is the fact that He took our punishment and made us pure in God's sight even though we've done nothing to deserve His kindness. Did the criminal *do* anything to deserve forgiveness and go to paradise? No!

He *believed* that Jesus could save him and take him to heaven. We may not be as bad as the criminal, but we have sinned just as he did; and so, like the criminal, we don't deserve to go to heaven. But we can believe in Jesus and ask Him to forgive us and save us.

Thank You, Lord, for Your amazing grace! Amen.

Therefore, since we have been made right in God's sight by faith, we have peace with God because of what Jesus Christ our Lord has done for us.

~ Romans 5:1, NLT

Jesus said that if He is lifted up [on a cross], He will draw all people to Himself (John 12:32-33). Yet, like the criminals, everyone has to make a choice.

Matthew 27:45; Luke 23:44

DARKNESS COVERS THE EARTH

Jesus was hanging on the cross. By this time it was about midday, and it became dark across the whole land until three in the afternoon.

We read in Genesis 1:3-4 that, in the beginning, God created light. God was pleased with the light because God *is* Light and in Him there is no darkness (sin).

Through Jesus, all of creation came into being. He formed man and placed the sun in the sky. In Jesus was Life and that Life was the Light of men (John 1:1-4).

The Life that is in Jesus is our Light (Ps. 36:9). But for three hours, as Jesus' physical life drained away, the sun stopped shining – absolute darkness. Perhaps it was creation's way of showing people what it would be like without His light.

Jesus came into the world as a spiritual light for us, but people loved the dark rather than the light because their actions were evil (John 3:19). They wanted to put out the *Light of Truth*, and the only way they could do that was to take the *life of Jesus*.

Thank You, Lord, for rescuing me from darkness (Col. 1:13). Amen.

"Arise, shine, for your light has come, and the glory of the LORD rises upon you. See, darkness covers the earth and thick darkness is over the peoples, but the LORD rises upon you and His glory appears over you."

~ Isaiah 60:1-2

God also brought darkness on the Egyptians for three days when Pharaoh would not let His people go free (Exod. 10:22-23).

Matthew 27:46-49

"WHY HAVE YOU ABANDONED ME?"

At about three in the afternoon Jesus called out with a loud voice from the cross, *"Eli, Eli, lema sabachthani?"* which means

"My God, My God, why have You forsaken Me?"

Some of the bystanders misunderstood and thought He was calling for the prophet Elijah. Others said, "Let's see whether Elijah comes to save Him."

The words that Jesus called out are words from Psalm 22:1. Jesus was abandoned, not only by His disciples, but by His Father. He was separated from His heavenly Father for the first time and the only time in all of eternity. This was also the only time that Jesus did not address God as Father.

Jesus had taken the world's filthy sin upon Himself, and because God cannot look at sin (Hab. 1:13), He could not look at Jesus on the cross; especially, being the sinless Son that He loved so much.

We cannot understand how Jesus being God, could for that moment not be God. Jesus did more than just take the punishment for our sin, He *became sin* so that we can become as pure and good as He is.

Your sin (every single one) was also put on Jesus.

God made Him who had no sin to be sin for us, so that in Him we might become the righteousness of God.

~ 2 Corinthians 5:21

God has promised never to leave us nor abandon us (Deut. 31:8).

John 19:28-29

"I AM THIRSTY"

Jesus knew that His task on earth was now finished, and to fulfill Scripture He said, "I am thirsty." A jar of sour wine was there, so they soaked a sponge in it, put it on a hyssop branch, and held it up to His lips.

Many years later, as John – the only disciple at the cross – remembered what happened on this day, he wrote exactly what Jesus said on the cross, and stated that His words, *I am thirsty*, were prophetic.

Perhaps John was thinking of these verses: "My strength has dried up like sunbaked clay. My tongue sticks to the roof of my mouth" (Ps. 22:15); and, "They offer me sour wine for my thirst" (Ps. 69:21).

Jesus had given His life to serving and saving people in need. He had turned water into wine at the wedding in Cana; He had offered the woman at the well water that would become a spring of eternal life inside her.

In fact, Jesus invited *all* those who are spiritually thirsty to come to Him and drink living water – have eternal life (John 7:37-38).

Yet, on the cross, Jesus became terribly thirsty so that we, like the woman at the well, can drink from the fountain of Salvation.

Thank You, Lord, for being the Fountain of Eternal Life. Amen.

With joy you will drink deeply from the fountain of salvation!

~ Isaiah 12:3, NLT

The hyssop branch used at the cross reminds us that the Israelites used a hyssop branch to spread the blood of the Passover lamb (Exod. 12:22-23).

John 19:30; Luke 23:46

"IT IS FINISHED!"

Jesus had been on the cross for six hours. Someone gave Him sour wine to drink, and when He had tasted it, He said,

"It is finished!"

Then Jesus called out with a loud voice, "Father, into Your hands I commit My spirit." After this, Jesus bowed His head and died.

This was the greatest victory in all of history – the day Jesus declared, "It is finished!"

- Jesus had finished the work His Father sent Him to do (John 4:34).
- Jesus had paid the debt owed for the sin of mankind in full (Rom. 6:23).
- Jesus' death ended the sacrifice of animals for the forgiveness of sin (Heb. 10:11-12).
- Jesus took away the devil's power over sin and eternal death (Heb. 2:14).

Jesus died on the day of Passover when the Jews killed a lamb in the temple. From this day on, Jesus would be the *perfect* Passover Lamb, given by God, to forgive the sins of all who come to Him (John 1:29).

Lord, Your darkest day in history brought us Light and Hope. Amen.

In this way, He disarmed the spiritual rulers and authorities. He shamed them publicly by His victory over them on the cross.

~ Colossians 2:15, NLT

On the cross, Jesus wore a crown of thorns. Yet like a king who conquers his enemy, Jesus now wears the crown of a reigning King (Rev. 14:14).

Matthew 27:51-52

THE TEMPLE CURTAIN IS TORN

When Jesus died, the curtain in the temple that closed off the very holy place was torn in two from top to bottom. The earth shook and rocks split apart. Some tombs broke open and the bodies of many godly men and women who had died were raised from the dead.

At the exact moment that Jesus died, the temple veil that had closed off the Holy of Holies was torn in two. The Holy of Holies, was the most sacred place in the temple where God lived on earth among His people.

The veil was not a thin curtain like they have in theatres. It was very thick and heavy. It would have taken a lot more than human strength to tear it. This was a miracle!

The curtain was torn from top to bottom to show that God had opened the way for us to come in and have a relationship with Him. Jesus gave His life so that the curtain – that separated us from God because of our sin – was no longer needed.

Jesus took the place of the curtain, not to keep us away from God because of our sin, but to make us sinless as we go *through* Him into the presence of God.

Thank You, God, that I can be close to You! Amen.

Therefore, since we have confidence to enter the Most Holy Place by the blood of Jesus, by a new and living way opened for us through the curtain, that is, His body.

~ Hebrews 10:19-20

The veil was about 20 meters high, 10 meters wide, and as thick as a few fingers. It was woven with blue, purple and scarlet linen (Exod. 26:31).

Matthew 27:54; Luke 23:47-48

SURELY HE WAS THE SON OF GOD

A Roman officer and the soldiers who were at the cross, became terrified when they saw how Jesus died, for there was an earthquake and it became dark over the land.

The officer worshiped God and said, "Surely this man was the Son of God!" When the crowd that had gathered saw what happened, they went home sad and upset.

The Roman officer and the soldiers were accustomed to crucifying criminals. It was their job. But they realized there was something different about Jesus. They had heard enough about Jesus to know that He was innocent.

They also heard Him ask God to forgive them for what they were doing to Him. And while the criminals on each side of Jesus were cursing, Jesus made sure His mother would be cared for by John.

That morning, the officer and the soldiers had mocked Jesus – but here at the cross, they realized that Jesus truly was the Son of God. They saw and believed.

The love of Jesus can make the hardest people believe.

"Whoever believes in the Son has eternal life, but whoever rejects the Son will not see life, for God's wrath remains on them."

~ John 3:36

Once we know about Jesus, our lives will never be the same. Either we believe that Jesus is the Son of God, or we reject Him (John 1:11-12).

Mark 15:42-46; John 19:38

THE "SECRET" DISCIPLE

The crucifixion of Jesus happened on Friday, the day before the Sabbath. Joseph of Arimathea took a risk and went to Pilate to ask for the body of Jesus. (Joseph was a member of the Jewish high council, but had also been a secret disciple of Jesus, yet he had not told the Jews because he was afraid of them.)

Pilate let Joseph have the body, so Joseph went and bought a long sheet of fine linen cloth. Then he took the body of Jesus down from the cross and wrapped it in the cloth.

Joseph had started off as a cowardly disciple of Jesus. He feared what others in the Jewish council would say (and perhaps do) if they found out that he was a traitor who believed in Jesus.

But then, even as Jesus' true disciples were nowhere to be found because they were afraid of the leaders, Joseph appeared out of nowhere and boldly asked for permission to bury Jesus.

Don't be afraid to be bold for Jesus; because what Jesus did for you on the cross is more than just a Bible story – it really happened!

Lord, help me to let others know and see that I love You. Amen.

"Everyone who acknowledges Me publicly here on earth, I will also acknowledge before My Father in heaven."

~ Matthew 10:32, NLT

Other Jewish leaders also believed in Jesus, but because they were afraid of being kicked out of the synagogue, they didn't admit it openly (John 12:42).

John 19:39-42; Matthew 27:59-60

JESUS IS BURIED IN A TOMB

After Jesus had died, Nicodemus – the man who had come to Jesus at night (John 3:1-2) – brought about seventy-five pounds of perfumed ointment made from myrrh and aloes. He helped Joseph wrap Jesus' body with the spices.

Nearby was a garden with an empty tomb that belonged to Joseph. So they laid the body of Jesus there and rolled a large stone across the entrance of the tomb to close it off.

Jesus did not have His own grave, but God provided someone whose grave He could use for three days. It was outside the city, near where Jesus was crucified; and it was a cave (carved out of a large rock) that could be secured with a big stone.

This tomb fulfilled a prophecy in Isaiah 53:9, "He had done no wrong and had never deceived anyone. But He was buried like a criminal; He was put in a rich man's grave." Joseph, whose tomb it was, was a rich man (Matt. 27:57); and Jesus had died as if He had been a criminal or a sinner; yet He didn't die for His own sin, but for ours.

Thank You, Jesus, for taking the punishment for my sin. Amen.

He was wounded for our rebellious acts. He was crushed for our sins. He was punished so that we could have peace, and we received healing from His wounds.

~ Isaiah 53:5

A prophecy is a message from God. It is often about a future event to show us God's plan (Amos 3:7).

Matthew 27:61-66

SOLDIERS GUARD THE TOMB

Both Mary Magdalene and the other Mary were sitting across from the tomb where Jesus was buried.

The next day, on the Sabbath, the priests and Pharisees went to see Pilate. They said, "Sir, we remember that the deceiver [Jesus] said, 'After three days I will be brought back to life.' So we ask that you seal the tomb so that His disciples cannot steal His body and then tell everyone that He was raised from the dead!"

Pilate replied, "Take guards and secure it the best you can." So they put a seal on the stone that closed off the tomb, and had Pilate's guards protect it.

The Pharisees wanted to stop people believing in Jesus. They thought that Jesus' disciples may take away His body and tell everyone that He had risen. However, the disciples had run away even before Jesus was crucified and were hiding in a room (John 20:19). Why would they risk their lives now that Jesus was dead?

Yet, it was part of God's plan to secure the tomb, so that years later, people wouldn't be able to say, "Jesus didn't rise from the dead; His disciples took His body."

Jesus' body was dead but His spirit was ______ (1 Pet. 3:18).

You will not abandon Me [Jesus] in the world of the dead; You will not allow Your Faithful Servant to rot in the grave.
~ Acts 2:27

When Daniel was thrown into a den of lions, a stone was also placed across the entrance, and sealed with the king's own ring (Dan. 6:17).

Matthew 28:1-4; Luke 24:1-11

EARTHQUAKES AND ANGELS

Early on Sunday morning, as the new day was dawning, Mary Magdalene and the other Mary took the spices they had prepared and headed out to the tomb. They wondered who would roll the stone away for them (Mark 16:3).

Meanwhile, there was a great earthquake, for an angel came down from heaven and rolled back the stone. Then he sat on it. His face shone like lightning, and his clothes were white as snow. The guards were so afraid of him that they collapsed like dead men.

When the women arrived at the tomb, they saw that the stone had been rolled away from the entrance. So they went in, but they didn't find the body of the Lord Jesus.

Death, the heavy stone, the seal, and the guards could not keep Jesus in the grave!

Yet, at this point, no one knew what had happened. The women saw an empty tomb, and the guards had fainted … but soon the world would know that Jesus had conquered death!

Draw the tomb (cave) and the stone.

God raised Him from the dead, freeing Him from the agony of death, because it was impossible for death to keep its hold on Him.

~ Acts 2:24

A stone that was used to seal a tomb could weigh up to two tons. It had the shape of a wide disc that was rolled into place using poles as levers.

Matthew 28:5-8

JESUS HAS RISEN!

The angel said to the women, "Do not be afraid. I know that you are looking for Jesus, who was crucified. He is not here; He has been brought back to life just as He said would happen. Come and see the place where His body lay. And now, go quickly and tell His disciples that He has risen from the dead!"

The women ran quickly from the tomb. They were very frightened but also filled with great joy, and they ran to tell His disciples.

On their way to the tomb, the women had wondered who would roll the stone away so that they could finish putting spices on Jesus' body.

Now, they didn't need to worry about the stone because an angel had rolled it away; but they also didn't need the spices anymore because Jesus had come back to life. Their darkness and sadness was suddenly filled with light and joy as the angel told them: "Jesus has risen!"

When God raised Jesus from the dead it showed that His death was enough to pay for *every* sin and make us absolutely pure, as though we had never sinned.

He was handed over to die because of our sins, and He was raised to life to make us right with God.

~Romans 4:25, NLT

Jesus Christ was not the first person to be raised from the dead, but He was the first to rise and not die again (1 Cor. 15:20; Acts 26:23).

DECEMBER

1 WAY
FOLLOW IT

1 TRUTH
BELIEVE IT

1 LIFE
LIVE IT

John 20:2-9

EXCITEMENT, CONFUSION AND BELIEF

Mary went running to Peter and John, and said, "They have taken the Lord's body out of the tomb, and we don't know where they have put Him!"

So Peter and John ran to the tomb. John reached the tomb first and stooped to look in. He saw the linen wrappings lying there, but he didn't go in.

Then Peter arrived and went inside. He also noticed the linen wrappings lying there, while the cloth that had covered Jesus' head was folded up and lying apart from the other wrappings.

Then John also went in, and he saw and believed (for until then they hadn't understood that Jesus *must* rise from the dead).

There was confusion at the tomb on Sunday morning: Where is Jesus? What has happened to His body? Yet the disciples, of all people, should have expected Him to rise, for Jesus had told them three times that He would die and rise after three days (Mark 8:31, 9:31, 10:33-34). But when John went into the tomb and saw that it was empty, he believed.

Did Mary believe that Jesus had risen? ________

After a life of suffering, He will again have joy; He will know that He did not suffer in vain. My devoted Servant, with whom I am pleased, will bear the punishment of many and for His sake I will forgive them.

~ Isaiah 53:11

Just as Jesus' physical body was transformed into a glorious body (Phil. 3:21), so will our bodies, when Jesus comes back for us.

John 20:10-16

JESUS APPEARS TO MARY MAGDALENE

The two disciples then went back home. Meanwhile, when Mary Magdalene arrived back at the tomb, she stood outside, crying. Then she went to look inside the tomb and saw two angels sitting where Jesus' body had been. They asked her, "Why are you crying?"

"They have taken away my Lord," she replied, "and I don't know where they have put Him." As she turned to leave, she saw someone standing there. It was Jesus, but she didn't recognize Him and thought He was the gardener. "Sir," she said, "if you have taken Him away, tell me where you have put Him."

Jesus said to her, "Mary."

She stared at Jesus and cried out, "Teacher!"

Unlike the disciples, Mary was at the tomb looking for Jesus. Through her tears, she saw Jesus in His glorified body; and although she didn't recognize Him at first, something in the way He said her name helped her to realize that it was her Lord.

Sometimes, when in your sadness and tears, it feels like you don't know where Jesus is; you should close your eyes, listen with your heart, and know that He is saying your name.

Lord, when You say my name I know that all will be well. Amen.

"Do not be afraid, for I have ransomed you. I have called you by name; you are Mine."

Isaiah 43:1, NLT

Mary Magdalene (or Mary of Magdala – her hometown) was part of a group of women who followed Jesus (Luke 8:1-2).

John 20:17-18; Matthew 28:9-10

"I HAVE SEEN THE LORD!"

Jesus said to Mary, "Do not hold on to Me, for I have not yet gone back to the Father. But go find My brothers and tell them, 'I am returning to My Father and your Father, to My God and your God.'"

So Mary went to the disciples with the news: "I have seen the Lord!" Then she told them what Jesus had said.

Mary was the first to see Jesus – and even touch Him – because she was there, looking for Him. She was also the first to tell others the good news that Jesus is alive; a message which has spread around the world.

Mary clung to Jesus, not wanting to be separated from Him again. But Jesus would not be on earth much longer, and He didn't want her to become fixed on the idea that things would continue as before.

Jesus would spend the next 40 days 'wrapping things up' before going back to His Father. Then He would send the Holy Spirit into the hearts of those who love Him. And so, fellowship with Jesus would continue, but it would be a spiritual closeness, not His physical presence.

When we long for a close friendship with the Lord, He draws near to us through His Spirit (Jer. 29:13).

Come near to God and He will come near to you.

~ James 4:8

It was important for Jesus to let Peter know that He was alive (Mark 16:7), so He appeared first to Peter, who had denied Him (1 Cor. 15:5).

Matthew 28:11-15

THE PHARISEES' PLAN

As Mary and the other women were on their way, the guards went into the city and told the leading priests what had happened at the tomb.

The chief priests gathered together with the leaders and agreed on a plan. They gave the soldiers a large amount of money and told them to say that Jesus' disciples had come during the night and had stolen His body while they were sleeping.

"If Pilate hears about it," they said, "we will stand up for you and keep you out of trouble." So the soldiers took the money and did as they were told. (Their story has been spread among the Jewish people to this day.)

The Pharisees were powerless to change God's plan. They probably thought that they had finally got their way by crucifying Jesus … but they couldn't keep Him in the grave (although they had tried). So all they could do now was to twist the truth.

The "religious" chief priests bribed and lied in order to make people believe that Jesus was still dead. But instead, their made-up story of what happened got out and spread among the Jews.

Lies, however convincing they are, cannot change facts.

Kings take their stands. Rulers make plans together against the Lord and against His Messiah.

~ Psalm 2:2

Jesus could see the hearts of the Jewish leaders, who managed to bluff others about how religious they were, but their hearts didn't belong to God (John 8:44).

Luke 24:13-21

TWO ON THE ROAD TO EMMAUS

That same day (on Sunday) two of Jesus' followers were walking from Jerusalem to their village Emmaus. As they walked along, they were talking about Jesus' crucifixion. Then Jesus Himself came up and walked along with them, but they didn't recognize Him. He asked them, "What are you two talking about?"

One of them, Cleopas, replied, "You must be the only person in Jerusalem who hasn't heard about all the things that have happened there the last few days."

"What things?" Jesus asked.

"The things that happened to Jesus," they said. "He was a Prophet who did many miracles; and a great Teacher. We had hoped He was the Messiah who had come to rescue Israel. This all happened three days ago."

All hope seemed lost. The two followers were on their way home – defeated. Jesus was about to change that! He knew what they were thinking, and although He knew how sad they were, He wanted them to tell Him what was troubling them. In the same way, Jesus is with *us* and He wants us to share our hearts with Him.

Thank You, Lord, that You are always close to me. Amen.

Jesus said, "Be sure of this: I am with you always, even to the end of the age."

~ Matthew 28:20, NLT

Jesus said that wherever two or three of His followers are together, there He will be with them (Matthew 18:20). A good reason to be among believers!

Psalm 121:1-2

DEALING WITH DISAPPOINTMENTS

The two on the road to Emmaus were very sad and discouraged. All they could think of and talk about was that Jesus had been crucified; and for them, all hope was gone. Yet the very thing that caused their deep sadness, was God's plan to bring us hope, and joy, and eternal life.

Sometimes, something bad happens, or we are disappointed when things don't work out the way we had expected. However, we know that God, who knows all things, is in control.

Disappointment comes from expectations that have not worked out the way we had hoped they would. The two that met Jesus said to Him, "We had hoped …"

When something bad happens:

- **Talk** to someone about your disappointment, like the two who told Jesus why they were feeling so sad.
- **Write** a note to yourself about what happened.
- **Pray** and tell the Lord what you are feeling. He knows what it is like to be disappointed (Gen. 6:6; Luke 19:41-42).
- **Think** about what hasn't changed – things that are good and give you renewed hope (Ps. 42:11).

Disappointments

- draw us near to God (Ps. 34:17-18).
- help us to become strong and keep going (Rom. 5:3-4).
- help us to comfort others (2 Cor. 1:3-4).
- have a purpose (Rom. 8:28; Jer. 29:11).
- help us to focus on what is important and lasting (2 Cor. 4:16-18).

Jesus said, "Here on earth you will have many trials and sorrows. But take heart, because I have overcome the world."

~ Luke 24:22-31

Luke 24:22-31

THEIR EYES ARE OPENED

On Sunday afternoon, two of Jesus' followers were walking home, very sad that Jesus had died. But suddenly, Jesus was walking alongside them.

Not knowing that it was Jesus they were talking to, they told Him that the One they had hoped would be the Messiah had been crucified. "And that's not all," they said. "Some women, who are also followers, were at His tomb, but they didn't find His body."

Then Jesus said to them, "How foolish you are not to believe what the prophets wrote." Then Jesus told them that it was God's plan that the Messiah would have to suffer and then enter His glory.

When they arrived at the town of Emmaus, the two invited Jesus to stay with them for the night. As they sat down to eat, Jesus took the bread and blessed it. Then He broke it and gave the pieces to them. Suddenly, their eyes were opened, and they recognized Him.

It would seem that God kept the two from recognizing Jesus until He had explained that He (the Messiah) had to suffer and rise so that we could be forgiven and have eternal life. Only once their spiritual eyes were opened to the Truth, their physical eyes saw that it was Jesus.

Open the eyes of my heart, Lord. Help me to know You. Amen.

Open my eyes to see the wonderful truths in Your instructions.

~ Psalm 119:18, NLT

Jesus could have used many Scriptures that tell about His death and rising again. This one is about His crucifixion: Psalm 22:16-18 and Amos 8:9.

Luke 24:31-36; John 20:19

JESUS APPEARS TO THE DISCIPLES

Two travelers had invited a "stranger" to their home. The moment they realized that it was Jesus, He disappeared from their sight. So they got up straight away and headed back to Jerusalem. There they found the disciples and others gathered behind locked doors.

The two from Emmaus told them what had happened and how Jesus had appeared to them. While they were still telling them about this, Jesus stood among them and said to them, "Peace be with you."

That morning, the disciples had heard Mary tell them that Jesus had spoken to her at the tomb. Peter and John had also gone to the tomb and found it empty. Now, these two followers were saying that they had seen Jesus too.

We don't know what was going through the minds of the disciples. We can only imagine that together with their fear of being arrested, they were anxiously trying to figure out what was going on. Then Jesus appeared among them and calmed their troubled hearts by saying the words, *peace be with you.*

Thank You, Jesus, for the peace You bring to my heart. Amen.

"Peace I leave with you; My peace I give you. I do not give to you as the world gives. Do not let your hearts be troubled and do not be afraid."

~ John 14:27

Jesus simply appeared inside a locked room, which means that the tomb stone was rolled away not that He could get out, but that people could see in.

Luke 24:37-45

"SEE MY HANDS AND MY FEET"

The disciples had gathered in a room behind locked doors for fear of the Jewish leaders. Suddenly Jesus stood there among them.

All those in the room were frightened, thinking they were seeing a ghost! "Why are you frightened?" Jesus asked. "Look at My hands and feet, and see that it is really Me. Touch Me, and see for yourselves."

They stood there in disbelief, yet filled with joy and wonder. Then Jesus asked, "Do you have anything to eat?" So they gave Him some fish, and He ate it as they watched.

Afterwards, Jesus said to them, "Remember how I told you exactly what would happen?" Then He opened the eyes of their hearts and used the Scriptures to help them understand what God had said.

What had happened to Jesus made no sense to the disciples. Although they were relieved and very happy to see Him again, they were still confused. So Jesus used Old Testament Scriptures to help them understand why He had to die and rise again. It was all there – but they hadn't understood God's plan.

Today, we have the full Bible (the Old *and* the New Testament), and we also have the Holy Spirit to help us see the big picture of God's amazing plan to make us His children.

REMEMBER Even children can understand the Bible (2 Tim. 3:14-15).

We know also that the Son of God has come and has given us understanding, so that we may know Him who is true.

~ 1 John 5:20

The Holy Spirit helps us to understand the spiritual Truths of God's Word (1 Cor. 2:12-13).

John 20:24-29

JESUS SPEAKS TO THOMAS

One of the disciples, Thomas, was not with the others when Jesus appeared to them. When the other disciples told him, that they had seen Jesus, Thomas said, "I refuse to believe this unless I put my fingers where the nails were, and feel the wound in His side."

Eight days later the disciples were together again. This time, Thomas was with them. The doors were locked; but suddenly, as before, Jesus came and stood among them. He said to Thomas, "Put your finger here; see My hands. Reach out your hand and put it into My side. Stop doubting and believe."

Thomas said, "My Lord and My God!"

We always find it easier to believe the things we can see and feel. However, there are many things we cannot see with our eyes, like distant planets and atoms; yet we choose to believe that they exist because they are known to be facts.

Thomas, like the other disciples, didn't believe that Jesus was alive until he saw Him. Unlike those disciples in the room, we cannot see Jesus. Yet our faith grows when we believe even though we cannot see. Jesus said, "Blessed are those who have not seen, yet believe."

REMEMBER Jesus is alive, and that's a fact!

For we live by believing and not by seeing.

~ 2 Corinthians 5:7, NLT

Encouragement: Sometimes, you may not want to believe or hope in something for fear of being disappointed. But remember, you can *always* trust God (Rom. 10:11).

Galatians 3:11

UNBELIEF, DOUBT AND FAITH

Our reason for hope, as Christians, is that Jesus has risen. Because Jesus is alive, we are forgiven and will live forever with Him. Thomas had lost all hope because he didn't believe that Jesus had come back to life.

But then Thomas started meeting with the other believers … and that's when He met Jesus! When you start doubting, then keep on praying, reading the Bible and meeting with other believers.

Unbelief is choosing not to believe in God and deciding to live one's life as if there is no God (Ps. 14:1).

Doubt is being unsure of things. Yet, uncertainty is not wrong: in fact, it is the ground in which our faith has a chance to grow. It is normal to have doubts about things we cannot see.

However, doubt can also be one of the ways the devil tries to weaken our faith, like when he tempted Eve (Gen. 3:1). But remember, faith conquers doubt!

Faith is simply believing that God exists and that He will do all He has promised for those who trust Him (Heb. 11:6).

- Faith comes by hearing the Word of God (Rom. 10:17).
- Faith is also a gift (Eph. 2:8). God gives us faith as we obey Him and put our trust in Him, like the father who asked Jesus to help his weak faith (Mark 9:24).
- We are encouraged in our faith when we meet with other believers (Heb. 10:24-25).
- We grow in faith when we pray, believing that God hears our prayers (1 John 5:14-15).
- When you start doubting, hold on to the fact that God is faithful and that He loves you.

For every child of God defeats this evil world, and we achieve this victory through our faith.

~ 1 John 5:4, NLT

John 21:1-14

THE GREAT CATCH OF FISH

Jesus had told the disciples to go to Galilee (Matt. 28:16). While they were waiting for Jesus at the Sea of Galilee, Peter said to the other disciples, "I'm going fishing." The others joined Peter in the boat, and they headed out. But they caught nothing all night.

Early in the morning, Jesus was standing on the beach, but the disciples couldn't see who He was. He called out to them, "Friends, have you caught any fish?"

"No," they answered.

Then He said, "Throw out your net on the right-hand side of the boat, and you will get some!" So they did, and they caught so many fish that they struggled to drag the net ashore. Then Jesus said, "Bring some of those fish and come and have breakfast."

This may have been a lesson for the disciples: without Jesus, one can work hard all day (or all night) and catch nothing.

One may even have the right skills and lots of experience; be in the right place and have the right gear; but it is only Jesus that makes the work of bringing people into the kingdom worthwhile.

Fish for people by sharing the Good News of Jesus.

"Come, follow Me," Jesus said, "and I will send you out to fish for people."

~ Mark 1:17

John, who wrote the Gospel of John (John 21:24), calls himself *the disciple whom Jesus loved* (John 21:7).

John 21:15-17

JESUS TALKS WITH PETER

After breakfast Jesus asked Simon Peter, "Simon, son of John, do you love Me more than these?"

"Yes, Lord," Peter replied, "You know I love You."

"Then feed My lambs," Jesus told him. Jesus asked Peter a second time; "Do you truly love Me?" Again, Peter told Jesus that he loves Him.

Then Jesus asked a third time, "Simon, do you love Me?"

Peter was sad because Jesus asked again. He said, "Lord, You know all things. You know that I love You!"

Three times, Peter had denied that he knew Jesus (Luke 22:55-62). Now, Jesus was giving Peter the opportunity to say what he'd been wanting to say since that dreadful night.

Simply saying sorry may have seemed like empty words to Peter, so Jesus let Peter say what he really longed to say – the words, **I love You**. Jesus helped Peter put that failure behind him and prepared him for the task ahead – to lead His sheep (followers).

Tell Jesus, every day, in your prayers that you love Him.

O Lord, You are so good, so ready to forgive, so full of unfailing love for all who ask for Your help.

~ Psalm 86:5, NLT

Not long after this conversation between Jesus and Peter (Simon), Peter boldly preached to a large crowd (Acts 2:14-36).

JESUS APPEARS TO 500 OTHERS

The disciples weren't the only ones to see Jesus alive. Jesus appeared to 500 others too. Most of these people were still alive when Paul wrote his first letter to the Corinthians about 20 years later.

John and others who wrote the New Testament told us what they had seen and heard so that we, too, can have a relationship with Jesus (1 John 1:3).

You may know some people who don't believe that Jesus came to earth, or some who say that Jesus didn't rise from the dead. Yet there is so much proof in history (His-story) that Jesus actually lived on earth and that He did come back to life.

His closest friends, the disciples, who knew Jesus better than most, recognized the risen Jesus and continued to serve Him even after He went back to heaven. They suffered persecution and were killed for their loyalty to Jesus.

They were so sure that Jesus had risen from the dead that they were willing to die rather than give up their faith in Him.

How many years ago was Jesus born? ________

If Christ has not been raised, then all our preaching is useless, and your faith is useless. But in fact, Christ has been raised from the dead. He is the first of a great harvest of all who have died.

~ 1 Corinthians 15:14, 20, NLT

Our calendar years run according to the birth of Jesus (BC and AD). BC refers to the years Before Christ. AD is the year in which Jesus was born.

Matthew 28:18-20; Luke 24:44-49

JESUS' INSTRUCTION TO THE DISCIPLES

While the disciples were in Galilee, Jesus came to them and said, "I have been given all authority [the right and power to rule] in heaven and on earth. Therefore, go out and make disciples of all nations and teach these new disciples to obey My commands. Remember that I am with you always, until the end of time."

The disciples weren't meant to keep the Good News to themselves – they were to share it with others so that the Gospel would spread around the world to every nation.

The reason that you have heard about Jesus is that those few disciples were obedient and did what Jesus told them. They were no longer afraid of what people would think of them or do to them. They went out and boldly spread the news that Jesus gives us eternal life. "The disciples went and preached everywhere, and the Lord worked with them and proved that their preaching was true by the miracles that were performed" (Mark 16:20).

Help me, Lord, to tell others about Your love and forgiveness. Amen.

The gospel is bearing fruit and growing throughout the whole world – just as it has been doing among you since the day you heard it and truly understood God's grace.

~ Colossians 1:6

The Bible (or a part of it) has been translated into more languages than any other book in the world (well over 2,000).

Mark 16:15

SHARING THE GOOD NEWS

Just as the disciples told others about Jesus, so we who know Him should pass on that which we have heard. Even though you may not know the Bible well and there are things you don't understand, you can simply tell others what Jesus has done for you.

Perhaps you could write down some verses to remind you of what to say when someone wants to know why you believe (1 Pet. 3:15).

For there to be good news, there is usually bad news first.

The bad news is that ...

- Everyone has sinned.
  Romans 3:23
- Sin separates us from God and brings eternal death.
  Isaiah 59:2; Romans 5:12

The Good News is that ...

- God loves us.
  John 3:16
- Jesus died for our sins (and rose again).
  Romans 4:25; 1 Corinthians 15:3-4
- God forgives all our sins if we ask Him to.
  1 John 1:9
- God gives eternal life to those who are His.
  Romans 6:23

There is a lot more good news wrapped up in God's promises and plan for us (Eph. 2:10).

Let your faith, hope and joy be like a shining light for all to see.

"In the same way, let your light shine before others, that they may see your good deeds and glorify your Father in heaven."

~ Matthew 5:16

Luke 24:50-53; Acts 1:4-12

JESUS GOES BACK TO HEAVEN

It was 40 days since Jesus had risen from the dead. Having left Galilee, He and the disciples were now back in Jerusalem. Jesus told them not to leave Jerusalem, but to wait for the gift that His Father had promised – the gift of the Holy Spirit.

Jesus then led the disciples to a place near Bethany. There He blessed them. Then He was lifted up into the sky, and a cloud hid Him from their sight.

While the disciples were looking up, two men in white clothes stood beside them. "Why are you staring into heaven?" they said. "Jesus has been taken to heaven, but someday He will return in the same way you have seen Him go!"

And so the apostles went back down the Mount of Olives, and they returned to Jerusalem with great joy.

Jesus is now in heaven seated next to God the Father. He is watching over us, hearing our prayers and guiding us through the Holy Spirit. The exciting thing is that Jesus isn't just in one place, as He was when He was on earth; He now lives in everyone who believes in Him!

Jesus lives in heaven, but He also lives in our hearts!

Christ will make His home in your hearts as you trust in Him. Your roots will grow down into God's love and keep you strong.

~ Ephesians 3:17, NLT

The word *heaven* is used in different ways. One heaven is the sky above us (Isa. 55:10); the other is the place where God dwells (Ps. 103:19).

Acts 2:1-4, 8-12, 7:54-58

STEPHEN SEES JESUS

From heaven, Jesus sent the Holy Spirit to live in every one of His followers (Luke 24:49). Now, the Apostles weren't afraid anymore but preached the Truth of Jesus with power. Many people became believers and joined the Apostles. This is how the church started!

One of Jesus' followers, Stephen, did great miracles among the people. But some Jews, wanting to stop him, began to argue with him. Yet Stephen replied with words of wisdom and power. Even so, the men arrested Stephen and took him to the Jewish leaders.

Stephen spoke fearlessly to the leaders, telling them about Jesus and pointing out their stubborn unbelief. As he was speaking, he looked up and saw Jesus standing at the right hand of God in heaven. Then the angry Jews took Stephen out of the city and killed him.

The "right hand" of God is the place of honor, where Jesus is seated (Matt. 26:64). From earth, Stephen saw Jesus – not sitting, but standing to welcome him into heaven. When it is our turn to leave earth, Jesus will be there to welcome us too (2 Pet. 1:11).

Jesus, You are the One who gives us hope on earth. Amen.

After the Lord Jesus had spoken to them, He was taken up into heaven and He sat at the right hand of God.

~ Mark 16:19

Stephen was the first Christian martyr. A martyr is a person who is killed, or suffers greatly, for his faith (see what Jesus said in Matt. 16:24-25).

Acts 9:1-8

JESUS SPEAKS TO SAUL FROM HEAVEN

One of the Jewish leaders who was there when Stephen was put to death, was Saul. He threatened all those who believed in Jesus, and had permission to arrest and jail Christians in the city of Damascus.

On his way to Damascus, a bright light from heaven shone around him. He fell to the ground and heard a voice: "Saul! Saul! Why are you persecuting Me?"

"Who are You, Lord?" Saul asked.

The voice replied, "I am Jesus, the One you are persecuting! Get up and go into the city, and you will be told what you must do."

The men traveling with Saul heard the sound but did not see anyone. When Saul got up from the ground he was blind. So his companions took him by the hand and led him to Damascus.

Saul was a powerful leader who thought he was doing God a favor by getting rid of this new belief called Christianity. He didn't realize that he was actually fighting against Jesus the Son of God. There is only one way to please God, and that is by believing in Jesus!

Not all religions believe that Jesus is the only way to God.

There is salvation in no one else! God has given no other name under heaven by which we must be saved.

~ Acts 4:12, NLT

Saul was actually a very religious man (Phil. 3:5-6). His name was later changed to Paul (Acts 13:9).

Acts 9:9-19

JESUS APPEARS TO ANANIAS

Saul was on his way to Damascus to arrest Christians. Suddenly, a bright light appeared and Jesus spoke to him. Saul became blind and was led to Damascus.

There was a disciple in Damascus named Ananias. The Lord spoke to him in a vision, telling him to go to the house where Saul was staying.

Ananias feared Saul because he had heard about the terrible things Saul had done to the believers in Jerusalem.

But the Lord said to Ananias, "Go, for Saul is My chosen instrument to take My message to the Gentiles and to kings, as well as to the people of Israel."

So Ananias went to the house and said to Saul, "Jesus has sent me here so that you may see again." And immediately, Saul was able to see again.

God had a plan for Saul – later known as the Apostle Paul – who wrote most of the New Testament. Saul was passionate and determined, but he was on the wrong road.

He believed that there is only one God. He was right in believing that there is only one God, but he didn't realize that Jesus is God! Jesus came to earth in a body so that we could see what God is like.

Jesus, thank You for showing us the love of the Father. Amen.

Jesus said, "The Father and I are one."

~ John 10:30, NLT

Saul (Paul) was a tentmaker – a person who either weaved cloth for tents or actually made tents for a living (Acts 18:1-3).

Revelation 2:1-7

TO THE CHURCH IN EPHESUS

After many years, when John the disciple was old and living on the island of Patmos, he had a vision. Jesus appeared to him and told him to write letters to the seven churches (Rev. 1:1, 9-11).

The first letter was to the church in the city of Ephesus, and this is what Jesus told him to write:

> "I know all the things you are doing. I have seen your hard work.
> You have patiently suffered for Me and have not given up …
> Yet, you don't love Me as you did at first!"

When we get involved in something for the first time, like a new sport, we are usually enthusiastic and determined to do our best. But when the going gets tough, or we mess up, we may become discouraged and give up or simply plod along.

The church at Ephesus was still doing all the right things, but the heart of the people wasn't the way it used to be when they first believed. They carried on with all the usual church activities but they forgot to focus on the reason for all their hard work – the joy of serving the Lord because of their love for Him.

Lord, I want my love for You to grow stronger and deeper. Amen.

We love each other because He loved us first.

~ 1 John 4:19, NLT

Ephesus was the largest city in the province of Asia. It was a busy coastal city and the place where three main trade routes came together.

Revelation 2:8-11

TO THE CHURCH IN SMYRNA

Jesus said to John, "Write this letter to the church in Smyrna: These are the words of Him who is the First and the Last, who died and came to life again.

"I know about all the hardships you are going through …
Be faithful, even to the point of death,
and I will give you the crown of Life."

There is a crown of victory that the Lord will give to all those who keep going to the end – like an athlete who finishes a long marathon, or a soldier who carries on fighting until the battle is over.

Paul, who faced many hardships for the Gospel, said; "I have fought the good fight, I have finished the race, I have kept the faith. Now there is a crown waiting for me, and to all those who long for Jesus to come back" (2 Tim. 4:7-8).

A crown, like the one waiting for those in the church of Smyrna, will be given to each one who loves Jesus and keeps on serving Him faithfully.

Lord, help me to be courageous and faithful to the end. Amen.

God blesses those who patiently endure testing and temptation. Afterward they will receive the crown of Life that God has promised to those who love Him.

~ James 1:12, NLT

Smyrna was an ancient Greek city famous for its athletic games. It still exists (as Izmir) today and is a beautiful port city surrounded by mountains.

Revelation 2:12-17

TO THE CHURCH IN PERGAMUM

This is what Jesus said to the church in Pergamum; "These are the words of Him who has the sharp, double-edged sword. Although you have stayed true to My Name, you have allowed some among you to teach that it doesn't matter how you live once you are saved. These people say and do things that are wrong and speak against what is good.

> "Repent of your sin, or I will come and fight against them with the sword of My mouth."

When the church allows teaching that goes against God's Word, those who don't really know the Bible could easily be led to believe that they are following the Truth and so start doing certain things that displease God.

For this church it was important to stop those who were saying that doing certain wrong things was okay. For us it is important to *know* and *obey* the Bible, which is like a sharp sword that cuts through the many things we hear, and shows us right from wrong.

Thank You, Lord, that I can trust Your Word to lead me in the path of Truth. Amen.

The Word of God is alive and powerful. It is sharper than the sharpest two-edged sword.

~ Hebrews 4:12, NLT

Pergamum was a city with many idols. The people there worshiped pagan gods. It was the first city in Asia Minor to build a temple to Caesar.

Revelation 2:18-19

TO THE CHURCH IN THYATIRA

Jesus said to John, "Write this letter to the church in Thyatira. This is the message from the Son of God, whose eyes are like flames of fire and whose feet are like bronze:

I know all the things you do.
I have seen your love, your faith, your service,
and your patient endurance.
I also know that you are doing more
now than you did at first."

This church was by no means perfect. They had allowed someone in the church to mislead the people by teaching them wrong things. Jesus will never ignore sin in our lives, but He also takes note of the things we do right.

Jesus is watching us all the time. He sees the things we do and will reward us for all the good we have done – even the things no one knows about (Matt. 6:3-4).

He notices the things that are really important – like our love, faith, service, and loyalty. Like this church, we should keep growing spiritually (in our hearts) by doing more than when we first believed.

Lord, help me to please You in *everything* I do. Amen.

God is working in you, giving you the desire and the power to do what pleases Him.

~ Philippians 2:13, NLT

Thyatira was the smallest of the seven cities mentioned in the letters. It was an ancient Greek city famous for its dyeing of purple cloth (Acts 16:14).

Revelation 3:1-6

TO THE CHURCH IN SARDIS

Jesus said to the church in Sardis; "I know all the things you do. You have a reputation for being alive – but you are dead. Wake up! Strengthen the little that is left, for even what is left is almost dead. I find that your actions do not meet God's standard. If you don't wake up, I will come to you as unexpected as a thief.

> "Yet there are some who have not stained their clothes with evil.
> They will walk with Me in white, for they are worthy."

This church seemed to be spiritually alive, yet they were actually lifeless! The Holy Spirit – who brings life – was not active in their church because the people there didn't allow Him to keep working in their hearts.

Although they acted as though they were Christians, their disobedience stopped the flow of God's power to their lives (as described by Paul in 2 Tim. 3:5).

Yet there were some who had not dirtied themselves with the sin of the world. They had kept themselves clean and pure, and so *they* will walk with Jesus as His bride.

Thank You, Lord, for Your life and power that flows into me. Amen.

"Look, I will come as unexpectedly as a thief! Blessed are all who are watching for Me, who keep their clothing ready so they will not have to walk around naked and ashamed."

~ Revelation 16:15, NLT

The people living in the city of Sardis were famous for their abilities in arts and crafts. The art of dyeing wool is said to have been invented there.

Revelation 3:7-8, 11

TO THE CHURCH IN PHILADELPHIA

To the church in Philadelphia, Jesus said, "These are the words of Him who is holy and true: the One who has the key of David. What He opens, no one can close; and what He closes, no one can open."

"See, I have placed before you an open door that no one can shut.
I know that you have little strength, yet you have obeyed
My Word and you have not denied Me …

I am coming soon. Hold on to what you have,
so that no one will take away your crown."

The church in Philadelphia showed no signs of weakness, and so Jesus only had words of encouragement for this church. It's almost as if Jesus were saying, "Don't give up now … you're almost at the finish line."

The church may have been small or poor, yet their faith was strong. Often when we are weak, we depend more on the Lord and our faith grows stronger. So when things get tough, hold on to the Truths you have learned from the Bible – and don't ever give up!

Obedience, faith and love are the strong pillars of life.

Let us hold tightly without wavering to the hope we affirm, for God can be trusted to keep His promise.

~ Hebrews 10:23, NLT

The name of the city Philadelphia means "brotherly love" in Greek. This city suffered from many earthquakes.

Revelation 3:14-19

TO THE CHURCH IN LAODICEA

The last of the letters Jesus told John to write was the letter to the church in Laodicea. He said to the church in that city, "This is the message of the One who is the faithful and true witness: I know all the things you have done, that you are neither hot nor cold.

You say, 'I am rich. I have everything I want. I don't need a thing!' But you don't realize how miserable and pitiful you are. You are poor, blind and naked.

"I advise you to buy gold from Me – gold that has been purified by fire. Then you will be rich."

The church in Laodicea had everything. Life was easy. However, they blended in so well with the sinful lifestyle of unbelievers that one would hardly recognize them as being Christians. Jesus advised them to buy 'gold' from Him, gold which comes from a faith that has been tested by hardship and discipline.

An easy life requires no commitment and no effort. Yet an easy life that doesn't need faith, doesn't count for much in eternity.

May my faith be like pure gold to You, Lord. Amen.

These trials will show that your faith is genuine. It is being tested as fire tests and purifies gold – though your faith is far more precious than mere gold.

~ 1 Peter 1:7, NLT

Laodicea was a wealthy city on an important trade route. Paul prayed that this church may know the richness of God's plan (Col. 2:1-2).

Revelation 22:13-14

I AM THE BEGINNING AND THE END

In Revelation 4:1-2, John tells of how he, through the Spirit, was allowed to see heaven and things that would happen in the future. Now, in the last chapter of the Bible, Jesus says:

"I am the Alpha and the Omega, the First and the Last,
the Beginning and the End.

"Blessed are those who wash their robes (obey God) so that they may have the right to the Tree of Life and may go through the gates into the city."

The *Alpha* and *Omega* are the first and last letters of the Greek alphabet (like the A and the Z). Jesus is the First and the Last. However, because He is eternal and not bound by time, He has no beginning and no end.

Although *you* had a beginning when you were born, if your sin is forgiven, you will also live forever! When we ask Jesus to forgive us and make us new, He takes off our filthy clothes of sin (Zech. 3:4) and puts a clean robe of goodness on us (Isa. 61:10).

Thank You, Lord, that You have made me clean (Ps. 51:10). Amen.

This world is fading away, along with everything that people crave. But anyone who does what pleases God will live forever.

~ 1 John 2:17, NLT

The Tree of Life, which gives eternal life to those who eat of it, was in the Garden of Eden (Gen. 3:22-24). It is mentioned again in Revelation 22:2.

Revelation 22:16-17

I AM THE BRIGHT MORNING STAR

Jesus said, "I, Jesus, have sent My angel to give you this message for the churches. I am both the origin of David and heir to his throne.

"I am the Bright Morning Star."

"The Spirit and the bride say, 'Come!' Let those who hear these words say, 'Come!' Let those who are thirsty come and drink freely from the Water of Life."

One notices the morning star easily because it shines so brightly. But Jesus' light is different and far brighter. Jesus is our *eternal* Light – our *guide* and our *hope*.

Just as the morning star is a sign that the night is almost over and a new day is dawning, Jesus is the hope of our eternal daybreak – the dawn of our new life in heaven. We must pay attention to God's Word – our light in a dark (sinful) place – until the Day dawns, and Christ the Morning Star shines in our hearts (2 Pet. 1:19).

Jesus invites anyone and everyone to come to Him and accept His offer of eternal life.

Jesus, I look forward to that day when I will see You. Amen.

May the LORD bless you and protect you. May the LORD smile on you and be gracious to you. May the LORD show you His favor and give you His peace.

~ Numbers 6:24-26, NLT

The Bride, mentioned in the book of Revelation, is the church of Jesus Christ – those who have been saved (Rev. 19:7-8).

Revelation 22:7, 12, 20

I AM COMING SOON!

Jesus' final message is urgent and important: "I am coming soon!" Three times in the last chapter of the Bible, Jesus tells us that He is coming back for us.

- "Look, I am coming soon! Blessed are those who obey the words of prophecy written in this book."
- "Look, I am coming soon. I will bring my rewards with Me, to give to each one according to what he has done."
- He who is the faithful witness to all these things says, "Yes, I am coming soon!"

Jesus wants us to know what will happen in the future so that we won't be confused, but have the certainty and hope that encourages us to keep going to the end.

He is coming back to reward us and take us to heaven to be with Him. We will rise to meet Jesus in the air when He appears in the clouds (1 Thess. 4:13-18).

REMEMBER Jesus could come back at any time (Luke 12:40).

Now the prize awaits me – the crown of righteousness, which the Lord, the righteous Judge, will give me on the day of His return. And the prize is not just for me [Paul] but for all who eagerly look forward to His appearing.

~ 2 Timothy 4:8, NLT

When Jesus comes back, He will change our earthly bodies into new heavenly bodies so that we will be like Him (1 John 3:2).

Revelation 1:7

JESUS IS COMING BACK!

Much is written in the Bible about what will happen in the last days – when Jesus comes back. You may not understand everything (most people don't), but the important thing is that you keep on reading the Bible in order to discover new things, and that you grow to love Jesus more and more.

What are the signs that Jesus is coming soon?

One of the signs is that the hearts of people will become more sinful (2 Tim. 3:1-5); and because of the spread of evil, the love of many will grow cold (Matt. 24:12). Other signs are described in Matthew chapter 24.

Do we know when Jesus will come?

No one knows when Jesus will come – not even the angels. It will be a complete surprise! (Mark 13:32).

Why has Jesus not come already?

The Lord is not slow about keeping His promise: He is merciful and patient. He wants everyone to come to Him so that no one should die and be separated from Him (2 Pet. 3:9).

What should we be doing until Jesus comes back?

- Be a loyal servant of Jesus: use your time, your abilities and your gifts for Him (Heb. 10:24-25).
- Be an example to others (1 Tim. 4:12).
- Tell others about Jesus (2 Tim. 4:2).
- Stay pure – keep yourself from sin (2 Cor. 7:1).
- Live expectantly, eagerly waiting for Jesus to come back (Phil. 3:20).

Jesus said, "Yes, I am coming soon."

~ Revelation 22:20

Amen. Come, Lord Jesus!